George Puscas

✦ ✦ ✦ ✦ ✦

DANDIES, EH?

50 years of sports history
through his columns
in the Detroit Free Press

𝔇𝔢𝔱𝔯𝔬𝔦𝔱 𝔉𝔯𝔢𝔢 𝔓𝔯𝔢𝔰𝔰

Editor: Owen Davis

Assistant editor: Tom Panzenhagen

Art direction and production: Wayne Kamidoi

Copy editing: Gene Myers, Steve Schrader and the Free Press sports copy desk

Research: Holly Kahler

Coordinator: Dave Robinson

Cover photograph: Tony Spina

Photographs: Dick Tripp, 1, 15; Craig Porter, 53; Mary Schroeder, 105; Daymon J. Hartley, 193.

Special thanks: The Old Ball Park, Novi; Julian H. Gonzalez; Andrew J. Hartley

Printed in USA on recycled paper

Detroit Free Press Inc. 1993
321 W. Lafayette
Detroit, Michigan 48226

ISBN 0-937247-57-X

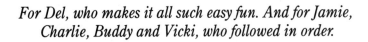

*For Del, who makes it all such easy fun. And for Jamie,
Charlie, Buddy and Vicki, who followed in order.*

INTRODUCTION

When Tom Harmon died in 1990, George Puscas noted in his obituary that "some of my earliest football memories involve Harmon." As a kid among reporters, Puscas wrote, he attended Michigan practices when Harmon played in Ann Arbor.

"Even a novice could see Harmon was not a good practice player. When it didn't count, he didn't punt very well, or run so powerfully, or throw with such precision."

A friend was skeptical. How could Puscas have seen that? He wasn't old enough to attend practices when Harmon played at Michigan in 1938-40.

Not so. From the time he was 11, George Puscas was getting rides from Detroit to watch the Wolverines and Harmon, their Heisman Trophy winner.

It was the beginning of a career that took Puscas to major sporting events in Detroit and around the country, reporting on some of the most famous athletes and coaches since the Great Depression.

In 51 years at the Detroit Free Press, Puscas saw Hank Greenberg hit with power and Al Kaline field with grace at Tiger Stadium. He covered the Pistons' first game at Olympia Stadium, and the Lions' last NFL championship when Joe Schmidt was carried in triumph off the field.

He also watched Johnny Unitas lead the Baltimore Colts to the only NFL title won in overtime, Muhammad Ali knock out Sonny Liston, and Billie Jean King make a statement for women's lib by beating Bobby Riggs on the tennis court. But Puscas didn't write exclusively about big shots and big events. Sandlot football, tough-luck boxers and bowling alley tough guys captured his attention as well.

"George Puscas covered, observed, reported and wrote about sports in Detroit for a half-century and did it with his own special kind of warmth and gentleness," said Free Press publisher Neal Shine, a native Detroiter. "In place of harshness and stridence he gave us insight and wisdom. It's that unique quality that endeared him to generations of Free Press readers."

Puscas began working at the Free Press as a copyboy in 1941, when he was 14. He didn't leave until 1992, after a career as a reporter, columnist and executive sports editor. Puscas, 66, lives in semi-retirement in Birmingham, Mich., where he still writes a weekly column for the Free Press.

This collection of stories captures the flavor of 50 years in sports, much of it in Detroit — the grit, the warmth, the revelry. The title — "Dandies, eh?" — comes from the kicker Puscas adds to his popular Love Letters columns, which have aired readers' opinions for 30 years.

These stories, though, are more than dandies. They are treasures. ✦

TABLE OF CONTENTS

1950s

1960s

1970s

1980s

1990s

THE '50s

A pride of Lions in their glory days, from left: running back Tom Tracy, coach Buddy Parker, quarterback Bobby Layne and running back John Henry Johnson.

1 9 4 5

Demands of World War II plague once-mighty Cooley

(George Puscas' first story in the Free Press contained the following editor's note: This article by George M. Puscas, sports editor of the Cooley Cardinal, may not wholly explain the Cooley slump, but it's a nice try.)

C all it lack of interest or lack of athletes, but something has happened to Cooley High School's athletes.

The once high-flying Cardinals have hit rock bottom during the past year in competition with other Detroit high schools.

War jobs and fewer hours of freedom, which had previously allowed athletes to compete in high school sports, have forced the Cooley coaches to piece together teams that are in direct contrast with past squads.

Chief among the piecers is coach Claude Snarey, Cooley's omni-champion track mentor. He has fielded the only outstanding Cooley performers during the past year, but even he is running into trouble in obtaining trackmen. His outstanding difficulties are in the pole vault and high jump. In previous years Snarey has boasted champions in both of these events. In the outdoor finals last year, John Harrower vaulted 11 feet, 7½ inches for a city record. Snarey will have nothing like that this year. Cooley will open its indoor season March 8, and he still is searching for pole vaulters and high jumpers.

Snarey isn't the only Cooley coach to add a few gray hairs, however.

When six veteran backs returned to Cooley's football team last year, coach Don Fitch was expected to produce another powerhouse 11. But linemen were lacking, and the Cardinals finished in a five-way tie for third place and lost three games. This was in sharp contrast to the Cooley grid squads of six previous years, which had dropped only one of 37 league contests.

Coach Dave Gates found trouble with the baseball squad. City champions in 1941 and 1942, Cooley dropped out of the playoffs in the first round.

The basketball team fielded by coach Don Brownlee sent the Cardinals, whose athletic teams had earned the respect of all high school coaches in the city, running to the showers. Cooley hit one of the city's low marks when it encountered the Central Trailblazers and scored only one point in the first half and wound up with a 41-9 walloping.

Mute evidence of the lack of competitors can well be supplied in view of the recent cancellation of the annual Cooley boxing show. Scheduled for March 2, the program had to be called off because of a shortage of boxers.

It appears that the Cardinals' reign as the terrors of the west side is at an end — temporarily, at least. ✦

1948

With war over, Detroit finds its Olympic spirit

R elaxed holiday celebrators may not care for the thought, but tension continues to mount in Olympic-conscious Detroit.

With the first session of the Olympic swimming trials just 48 hours away, anxiety and curiosity are getting the best of some of the hundreds of onlookers and even the contestants who turn out daily at Rouge Park's Brennan Pools.

Among the younger crowd, the Olympics represent some fabled athletic contests. Check with a few of them and you'll find they know more about the origin of the Games than they know about what happened during the 1936 Olympiad in Berlin.

The 1948 Games are the first after a 12-year layoff. That period of Olympic inactivity has created an odd state of affairs for some of the youngsters entered in the swimming trials. They can't remember the last Olympic Games.

Youngsters such as Jimmy McLane, 17-year-old freestyle ace from Akron, Ohio, couldn't be expected to remember Jesse Owens' triple victory in Berlin. After all, he was only 5 at the time.

Like most of the entries in this week's trials, McLane's Olympic background begins somewhere in a Greek mythology class in grade school.

The glamorous history of the Games serves as one of the modern athlete's greatest incentives.

For some of them, the Olympics are something of a fable, something they vaguely remember and still something entirely new. Better yet, as far as creating interest goes, Detroiters find the trials in their back yard as competition begins for the 11th modern Olympiad since 1896.✦

Detroit divers make a splash at Olympic trials

J eanne Stunyo, with one simply incredible dive, and Barbara Gilders, her pal and roommate, became Detroit's first women Olympic swimming team members since 1928.

Barbara finished second and Jeanne third behind two-time Olympic champion Pat McCormick of Los Angeles in a magnificent climax to the three-meter springboard finals at Rouge Park's Brennan Pools.

They earned positions for the Melbourne, Australia, Olympic Games coming up in November shortly after Bill Yorzyk of New Haven, Conn., had set a world long-course record of 2:22.2 in the 200-meter butterfly preliminary. Barbara and Jean are both petite blonds coached by Clarence Pinkston of the Detroit Athletic Club.

Incidentally, it was Pinkston's wife, Elizabeth, the 1928 platform champion, who last represented Detroit on the Olympic swimming team.

The last of the 10 required dives saved Miss Stunyo, a 20-year-old University of Detroit sophomore, from perhaps the greatest disappointment of her life. She had led the field of 12 entering the finals. But in the first three of the final four dives, she was far off form and fell off to fourth place behind Mrs. McCormick, Barbara and Paula Jean Myers of Los Angeles.

When the last dive was called, Jeanne seemingly had no chance to make the team. She still trailed Miss Myers by 11 points.

Then Jeanne's final dive was called. Technically it was referred to as a 1½ backward somersault with a 1½ twist. She did it almost flawlessly.

She whipped into the air off the gleaming white tower, her tanned form arched against the sky, then twisting and spiraling like a top she aimed for the pool below, opening up as cleanly as you please to enter the water with little more than a ripple.

The awed crowd of 4,000 exploded. It was the most astonishing single dive of hundreds performed. Judges agreed.

They gave her a full 60 points (the best for winner McCormick was 55), and that was enough to overhaul Miss Myers and give Jeanne third place on the Olympic team.

Jeanne couldn't believe it. She disappeared from the pool edge and only when all the diving was complete was she located again for the photographers. Even then, the pictures were of a tearful, shaken young woman who somehow had done the impossible.

The finish by Miss Stunyo actually shoved into the background a brilliant performance by Miss Gilders. The two have been rooming together at the

Gilders' home at 9576 Burnett so they might get to practice together.

Barbara's diving was the finest of the finals. She whipped through her somersaults and twists with such crispness and precision that she vaulted from fourth place in the preliminaries almost into the No. 1 spot. Barbara, 19, is a June graduate of Mackenzie High.

Mrs. McCormick, a Los Angeles mother who won both the platform and springboard titles in the 1952 Olympics at Helsinki, Finland, piled up 464.1 points against Barbara's 457.3.

Miss Stunyo had a final tally of 427.4, and Miss Myers 421.1.

For the Gilders family, Barbara's feat tops anything her more noted brother, Fletcher, had ever done.

Fletcher is the former city and national diving champion from Northwestern High and Ohio State. In his brilliant career, he also set a national interscholastic pole vaulting record.

But Fletcher never made the Olympic team. Now married and a father of two boys, he tried at Brennan Pools but finished sixth in the men's field.

✦ ✦ ✦ ✦ ✦

The long-time ambition of Clarence Pinkston, an Olympic champion and husband of an Olympic champion, has been to coach an Olympic champion.

Pinkston's dream neared reality when Barbara Gilders and Jeanne Stunyo, two of his young proteges, qualified for the Olympic Games in the women's springboard final.

America's divers long have been dominant in the Olympics, and qualification in the trials virtually assures Misses Stunyo and Gilders of finishing first, second or third in the Olympics.

That's the way it has been since the day in 1920 when Pinkston won the men's platform diving championship, and the day in 1928, when his wife, Elizabeth, won off the high tower.

Pinkston has been a coach, really a social secretary, at the Detroit Athletic Club almost from the day he won the Olympic title. But his job has nothing to do with coaching divers like Barbara and Jeanne.

His coaching is merely a personal sideline, but it's a sideline to which Pinkston has devoted much of his spare time.

In other years, the graying, balding Pinkston has looked futilely for Olympic prospects. He had Virginia Fitzgerald in 1948, but she couldn't make the grade. Since 1952, he has had Jeanne and Barbara under his wing, and now both are on the way to Australia.

Fittingly, Pinkston, meet director of the trials at Brennan Pools, has also been named coach of the women divers in the Olympic Games.

When Barbara and Jeanne made the first three places in the finals, Pinkston was almost as emotionally disconnected as they.

"They both showed they had great heart," Pinkston said. "I've never been so pleased by any of the athletes I've coached."

(In the 1956 Olympics, Pat McCormick won the springboard and platform gold medals. Jeanne Stunyo won the springboard silver; Barbara Gilders missed the bronze by less than a point.) ✦

1 9 5 7

In their finest hour, Lions win title in a rout

Our Lions had just lived their finest hour. They trudged up the underground ramp leading from the Briggs Stadium turf to their locker room.

In single file they came, dirty and bloody — all curiously silent but all with a strange childish grin like the old cat-who-swallowed-the-mouse bit marking their rugged features.

They had won the big one. Perhaps the biggest single victory in Detroit's magnificent football past.

Yet their 59-14 rout of the Cleveland Browns failed to produce any unusual reaction among George Wilson's world champions.

An occasional war-whoop, smiles and pats for each other, handshakes by the score, and that was it.

The Lions had reached the crest of a great, breathtaking campaign, and the end was purely anticlimatic.

Tobin Rote lived it up ... a little. But even Rote, whose work against the Browns was the finest field generalship Detroit has seen in a long time, would not concede this was his best game.

"Maybe it has to be my best because it was such an important game," Rote said. "It certainly feels great.

"But I'd have to rank that San Francisco game last week and one I played against the Los Angeles Rams a year ago along with it."

Wilson disregarded the final score. Not until the final minute, he said, was he able to relax.

"It certainly wasn't until then," he said, "that I thought we had the game in the bag."

Some among the dozens of newsmen, cameramen and outsiders who sneaked into the room snickered at the coach's words.

"Don't laugh," Wilson said. "I've seen it happen too many times — we've done it too many times to others — that games which seem secure are taken right out from under you."

Wilson called it a "hell of a game," gave great credit and sympathy to the Browns and their coach, Paul Brown, but acknowledged that the breaks had decided the game.

"It was the breaks," he said, "and we got them early. At the half, I warned our guys not to forget that Cleveland could come from behind and take us.

"I don't know if there was a decisive moment in the game; the breaks kept coming our way, and that did it for us."

Wilson said the two-week layoff Cleveland had while waiting to play the Western Division champions might or might not have hurt the Browns.

"There's no way of telling," he said. "But Paul Brown is one of the finest gentlemen this league has ever had, and a great coach, too."

Wilson called it a "team victory for the Lions, just like last week's game with San Francisco."

"This is not a one-man club, or a club where a small group carries the load," he said. "Everybody makes a contribution, and I think we're champions because of that."

It was suggested that this close-knit relationship of the Lions might have become stronger because of Wilson's run-in with former Lions coach Buddy Parker in Pittsburgh a month ago.

Wilson frowned. "I don't think we have to say anything about that," he said. "I wish you wouldn't."

The fake field goal attempt by Jim Martin in the second period, on which Rote threw for Detroit's third touchdown, was practiced last week, Wilson revealed.

"We got it ready — but Tobin called it," Wilson said.

Rote said he disregarded bench orders in calling the play, which caught the entire stadium by surprise.

"The play came off the bench, and we were supposed to try for a field goal," Rote said. "Some of the fellows thought we ought to go for broke, so I changed the play in the huddle."

Rote said he was mighty happy the play worked — "I'd be in the doghouse. No, that's wrong, really. Wilson is a gambler, too. He would have gone along."

The scene outside the locker room and on the playing field was marked by wild confusion. The corridor was jammed by youngsters and Lions followers seeking merely to touch the champions.

On the field, fans hung around for a half-hour after the game, hoisting defensive leader Joe Schmidt on their shoulders for the national television cameras and trying to wrest down the goalposts.

Schmidt eventually made it to the locker room, and the goalposts won again. ✦

1 9 5 7

With the NBA, it's a whole new ballgame

P rofessional basketball, having taken an 11-year break between seasons, returns to Detroit this week, considerably improved financially and competitively.

The Detroit Pistons, who have been making so much noise you would swear they've always been around, make their debut at Olympia.

You would hardly recognize the pros now from the days immediately following World War II, when the swish and slap of the roundball echoed through lonely Olympia.

Now there is stability — as much stability as Fred Zollner's millions can lend to the game — respectability, great talent and a set of rules designed to afford action and attract people.

There is a great difference between pro basketball and the college variety. The one resemblance is the 13-foot foul lane.

From there, the NBA branches off into rules all its own; rules, by the way, which are looking better to college legislators all the time.

Like hockey, the NBA prefers to soft-pedal fist fights among the athletes. Yet it's obvious that much of the attractiveness of hockey and professional basketball is the prospect that somebody will get decked. Unlike college basketball, the pro game absolutely demands size, strength, cunning and continued wariness. The NBA's answer to unrestricted warfare among the players is a system of fines. A player, for instance, can be fined $25 for muttering dissent over a bad call.

Action in pro ball, however, is so intense, the rivalries so strong, that not even fines have been deterrent enough. Such is the St. Louis Hawks-Pistons rivalry in the Western Division. This should be a hot winter.

When the Detroit Gems failed here in 1946, pro basketball was in its infancy. For five years thereafter, every town and hamlet east of the Rockies made an attempt at supporting pro basketball. In 1949-50, 17 teams were packed into three divisions.

Eight teams remain, and this season two are relocated. The Pistons, of course, are one. The Royals of Rochester now are the Cincinnati Royals.

The eight clubs are broken into two divisions, with Detroit, St. Louis, Minneapolis and Cincinnati forming the Western, and Boston, New York, Philadelphia and Syracuse making up the Eastern Division.

At season's end, all but the last-place teams enter a postseason playoff. Boston won it over St. Louis in seven games last spring. The series alone so excited St. Louis that the city is regarded as one of the strongest in the NBA.

Obviously, the Pistons hope to duplicate the St. Louis magic. ✦

Pistons' five-hour debut spoiled by champion Celtics

Searchlights played it up and a 13-piece band jazzed it up, but the Boston Celtics messed it up for the Detroit Pistons last night.

The world champions hung a 105-94 defeat on the Pistons as 10,965 enthusiastic, but weary fans sat in on the five-hour debut of the National Basketball Association teams at Olympia.

The two-game program, marked by a fist fight, speeches and other matters of little importance, carried on until 12:10 a.m. By then many had tired and gone home.

Scarcely half the crowd was around at the end when the Celtics, led by Billy Russell and Bob Cousy, caught up with the Pistons and left them far behind, giving the Celtics their second victory in two days.

In the opener of a twin bill, the New York Knickerbockers defeated the St. Louis Hawks, 112-95.

The Pistons, effectively bottling up the high-jumping Russell through the late stages of the first half and in most of the third period, suddenly lost control with 14 minutes to play.

Boston moved ahead then, 73-72, on a shot by Bill Sharman, ending the third period, and gradually pulled away.

Detroit, bothered by heavy fouling, could do little in the closing 12 minutes, especially after losing its scoring ace, George Yardley, and Walter Dukes, the man who was supposed to stop Russell, midway through the period.

Sharman and Tommy Heinsohn led the late Celtics splurge, and Heinsohn wound up with game-scoring honors at 25 points.

(The 1957-58 Pistons finished 33-39, typical of a franchise that didn't have a winning season until 1970-71.) ✦

1957

Opening night brings punches, falls, boos

V illains were quickly established, problems were immediately encountered — and the reaction was terrific — as professional basketball made its debut at Olympia.

Obvious villains were the St. Louis Hawks' hulking 6-foot-11, 235-pound Charlie Share and coach Alex Hannum.

Share and the New York Knickerbockers' skinny 6-11 Ray Felix played a game all their own, throwing hips and elbows in skirmishes under the hoop. Finally Felix had enough and took a poke at Share.

They traded punches in a manner seldom seen at Olympia these days, until they finally crashed to the floor. Both benches emptied, penalty shots were awarded, Share and Felix converted the throws, and peace was restored.

Share, who looks like a wrestling refugee from Fairview Gardens, took much razzing from the fans.

Hannum simply went looking for abuse. His reactions to calls by officials brought a warning. Then, finally, in a burst of anger, Hannum stripped off his suit coat and flung it with a flourish to the floor. He drew a technical foul and replaced Share as the fans' target.

The problem that cropped up was an old one. Despite an outlay of $12,000 for a new floor and a special covering that is supposed to prevent the Red Wings' ice from seeping through, the court quickly became treacherous.

Officials frequently interrupted play to wipe water off the floor. Players moved cautiously; the more daring took hard falls.

Gov. Mennen Williams, council president Mary Beck and representatives of the Tigers, Red Wings and Lions appeared to welcome the Pistons in their debut.

It probably is significant of nothing (Ha!), but the Lions were cheered, and the Tigers and Red Wings — Jack Adams in particular — were roundly booed.

The fans had no patience with the opening ceremonies, and when their catcalls prevented the speakers from being heard, the ceremonies were abruptly terminated and the game began. At that, it was 45 minutes late, starting at 10:15 p.m. ✦

1958

Layne sent to Steelers in biggest trade ever

B obby Layne, the golden Texan on whose dash and cunning the Detroit Lions built a gridiron empire, was cast away yesterday.

In a swift trade that shocked and disgusted some members of the team, Layne was sent to the Pittsburgh Steelers for Earl Morrall, former All-America quarterback at Michigan State. Detroit also acquired high draft choices in 1959 and 1960.

The trading of Layne approached in dramatic suddenness the resignation of Buddy Parker as the Lions' head coach just before the opening of the 1957 season. Parker subsequently went to coach the Steelers.

Lions coach George Wilson said Parker, who had coached Layne here from 1951-56, readily agreed to the trade when he broached it via telephone at 10 a.m. yesterday.

It was the boldest move made by a Detroit team since the Tigers traded outfielder Hank Greenberg to the Pittsburgh Pirates before the 1947 season.

Layne's departure came as a complete surprise, even though the defending champions have been sagging miserably below their form of a year ago.

Since the Lions' rise to pre-eminence in professional football a half-dozen years ago, they have been known as "Bobby Layne's team."

If he was that good, why trade him?

Wilson, the coach, and Edwin J. Anderson, president of the Lions, had different answers.

There was a suggestion that the Lions' front office is convinced Layne is over the hill, that his playing days are near an end, that he could be of limited value for only a short time to come.

There was a hint, too, of dissension, though Wilson has consistently sought to soft-pedal reports of friction between Layne and Tobin Rote. Rote, acquired by Detroit a year ago, has been the other half in a two-quarterback system employed by the Lions. Wilson said he is convinced the system does not work.

"The two-quarterback idea simply has too many drawbacks," the coach said. "After working with it awhile, I became convinced of it.

"Most teams are going with a plan where they have one experienced quarterback, like Rote, and another young understudy, like Morrall."

If the Lions wanted to keep only one veteran quarterback, why was Rote retained rather than Layne?

"Bobby is older," Layne said. (Layne will be 32 in December.) "Besides, if I ever traded Rote after the way he won the championship for us last year, I'd be run out of town."

Wilson recognized that there would be strong reaction in some circles.

"I know certain people are Layne fans and others are Rote fans," he said. "But a decision had to be made."

Anderson wasn't as hesitant as Wilson to point up the problem of trying to juggle and satisfy two outstanding stars at the same position.

"Openly they got along fine," he said. "But they must have had some resentment of each other. Each thought he should start every game. How wide the breach was no one knows, because they never discussed it."

Although he was plainly chafing under the Lions' failure to win in their first two games of the season, Wilson said his decision to trade Layne was not connected with the quarterback's play in Sunday's shoddy, 13-13 tie with the Green Bay Packers.

"Actually, I've been thinking this over since our preseason training camp opened in July," Wilson said.

The Lions' coach informed Layne of the trade by telephone. He reached him at Detroit Metropolitan Airport, where Bobby was waiting for the arrival of his wife, Carol, from their home at Lubbock, Texas.

"This was the toughest job I ever had to do," Wilson said. "I hated to tell Bobby he had been traded. He's been a friend of mine for years.

"I thought I would see him earlier in the day when he stopped in the office for his paycheck, but he didn't show. Luckily, I was able to reach him at the airport just before the announcement of the trade was made.

"I'm not blaming Layne for our record. But the quarterback is the one who has to pick things up, and we certainly haven't been moving this season."

Wilson said the trade was the most important in the history of the Lions.

"Maybe it is the most important in the league's history," he said, "for Bobby is the biggest name in the game." ✦

1 9 5 8

In a game for the ages, Colts beat Giants in OT

N EW YORK — The Baltimore Colts, a football team of the ages, defied the miracle and the destiny of the New York Giants yesterday and seized the world professional championship with an unprecedented, 23-17 overtime victory, which turned Yankee Stadium into a raging sea of humanity.

Alan (The Horse) Ameche, the former Wisconsin fullback, plunged through right tackle from the 1-yard line with the winning touchdown after eight minutes and 15 seconds of sudden-death play.

The move came as a pounding climax to one of the most fantastic games in the 39 years of the National Football League.

Steve Myhra, Baltimore guard, forced the sudden-death period of play by booting a field goal from the 20 with a mere seven seconds remaining in regulation time.

So caught up in the unbelievable turn of events were the 64,185 who roared through the game that for more than an hour after Ameche's run, thousands still roamed the Yankee Stadium turf, yelling, screaming, shooting firecrackers, parceling out shares of the goalposts.

It was a game of games, an incredible swift-turning contest that the Colts, champions of the Western Division, won, then lost and then by some fantastically cool method won again.

Above them all stood Ameche, the man with power legs; Johnny Unitas, the Baltimore quarterback; and Ray Berry, an end who caught the passes that had to be caught.

This was a game almost too much to ponder. You have to dissect it, take it in stages, for it changed so rapidly and so many times that to consider, say, even the finish would not do it justice.

The Colts' winning drive was a stirring thing, which several times seemed ready to bog down. The Giants had won the toss and chose to receive the overtime kickoff, but they failed to make a first down and punted to the Baltimore 20.

Unitas was to use 13 plays in covering the 80 yards to the other end of the field. He threw one pass to Ameche for a first down on his 40.

Then he found Berry alone at the left sideline and shot him a pass, which reached the Giants' 43.

Here came Ameche. Throughout the game the rugged Giants line had seemed almost impenetrable, but this time Ameche took a quick handoff from Unitas, burst up the middle and landed on the Giants' 20.

You suspected then that the Giants were through. The crowd roared deafeningly. Maybe Unitas would be content with a field goal from there. It would do the trick.

Instead he shot another pass to Berry and Baltimore was on the 8. A pass to Jim Mutscheller reached the 1, and here came Ameche again.

He barreled cleanly through the right side, and he no sooner had landed than the goalposts at both ends were thrown down and thousands poured from the bleachers.

There was no need for the extra point. The one yard by Ameche meant so much — $4,718.88 for each winning Colt, compared to $3,111.33 for each losing Giant.

Ameche's plunge was at the end, but much had gone before. Unitas brilliantly pushed the Colts 73 yards in the final 2½ minutes of the fourth period, setting up the tying field goal.

This rush against the clock and seemingly certain doom was made almost solely by Unitas and Berry. Unitas shot Berry three passes in a span of 65 seconds for a total gain of 62 yards.

The first came from the Baltimore 25 and reached midfield. The second moved to the Giants' 35, and the third, with the clock already ringing the final seconds, hit Berry on the left sideline and carried 22 yards to the Giants' 13.

Unable to call time, the Colts hustled up their field goal-kicking team, and Myhra booted sure and true, tying the score with seven seconds left. ✦

THE '60s

Hungry Lions feast on Green Bay Packers quarterback Bart Starr during a 26-14 Detroit victory on Thanksgiving Day, 1962. The Lions' rush sacked Starr eight times.

Patterson makes history
by stunning Johansson

NEW YORK — Floyd Patterson, the hermit of Newton, Conn., regained the world heavyweight boxing championship last night, the first man in history to do so, with an astounding fifth-round knockout of Sweden's Ingemar Johansson.

The end came after one minute and 51 seconds of the round with Patterson, a much-maligned fighter, having firmly established himself as a heavyweight of real merit. He was magnificent this time.

His victim, the popular Johansson, lay in his corner, as a crowd of more than 35,000 at the historic Polo Grounds broke into a near riot hailing Patterson's return to the championship.

For more than four minutes Johansson lay there, out cold, while the announcer and fanatics proclaimed Patterson's greatness one year — minus six days — from the day he lost his title to the Swede.

It was last June 26 that Johansson's right hand became the most famous right in recent boxing history.

It was a right to fear; the power it carried evinced awe from all — Patterson included.

Yet it is not Johansson's right hand that the fistic world beholds in wonder. It is the Patterson left, the left that laid the Swede bare on the canvas of the ring, stripped of his crown.

Two Patterson lefts, both long, powerful and telling, brought about the savage, dramatic end to a fast-moving, electrifying bout. Both were good enough to knock Johansson off his feet and stretch him on the floor.

Except for perhaps two minutes of the second round, after Johansson had staggered him with a right, Patterson was in command, seeming to know full well what to do.

The fourth round was the least exciting of the bout, and when the fifth began, Patterson strode from his corner, met Johansson quickly and began with a series of lefts, trying to open the Swede's defense. They went into a clinch and Patterson banged Johansson with a hard right.

Then, suddenly, with Johansson stepping away from another punch, leaning far back in his peculiar way, Patterson lashed out with a long, hooking left. It caught Ingemar flush on the lower jaw.

The Swede collapsed on the floor. It seemed for a brief moment that he was finished; finished perhaps as dramatically and suddenly as he had finished Patterson last June in another New York ball yard.

But Johansson was still alive. He gathered his senses, and as referee

Arthur Mercante tolled nine, the champion regained his feet.

No one seemed to recall, later, when last they had seen Patterson in so savage a mood. But few have been punished as much as the 25-year-old ex-Olympic champion, youngest man ever to win the heavyweight crown (at 21), and now the only one to regain it.

With a fury, Patterson tore after Johansson, flailing him with lefts and rights, catching him with bold, carefree rights and lefts, battering him to the ropes in a desperate drive to end it all right there.

Johansson, staggering about the ring, briefly seemed able to hold on.

But Patterson tagged him with a right, moved away to measure his man, then came up with a final blow — another long, punishing left hook.

This one, too, caught Johansson flush on the jaw. It toppled the Swede backward and, in an instant, the crowd sensed that Johansson would not get up again. He didn't. He lay unmoving in the corner, his head only a few yards away from Cus D'Amato, Patterson's delicensed manager.

Hundreds of Patterson's followers jammed ringside, tipping over press row seats, stretching to get a hand on the reborn champion.

He had a long walk to his dressing room from the ring, and more than two dozen policemen barely were able to get him there, safe from his admirers.

It was a good fight, a spectacle worthy of the more than $800,000 poured into the coffers, and a tribute to the great determination and zeal of Patterson.

He had been deeply affected by the almost constant criticism of him while he reigned as champion, and he was more deeply hurt when friends abandoned him after his loss of the title to Johansson.

Because of that, Patterson went into seclusion 10 months ago in an abandoned roadhouse, deep in the woods eight miles outside Newton, Conn.

It was a hermit-like existence. Once a week he went into town to see a movie. Every couple of days or so he would phone his wife and kids at home in Rockville Centre, N.Y. All the while Patterson labored with one purpose — to regain the championship.

Patterson conceded his respect for Johansson's right hand but insisted that he could survive, given this new chance. Patterson took charge quickly. Soon after the opening bell he was busy darting lefts at Johansson, straight lefts, then hooking lefts, then a combination of lefts and rights. Once he caught Johansson with a left that staggered the Swede. Before the round was done, he had opened a wound under Ingemar's left eye.

If Patterson was growing overconfident, he soon learned to be more cautious. For Johansson and the right nearly finished him in one swing in the second. Johansson began the round sticking his left in Patterson's face, fending him off. He tried a combination or two, but they were futile efforts.

Then, with no warning, Ingemar lashed out with his right. It caught Patterson on the jaw, not solidly, but hard enough to stun and stagger him. Later, Patterson admitted he was almost gone there.

But Johansson let the glassy-eyed Patterson walk away undamaged, giving him time to regain his senses. From then on it was Patterson's fight.

The Swede had missed his great chance. ✦

1 9 6 0

Seven days after surgery, swimmer chases Olympic dream

One week ago the young ex-Navy officer lay upon a hospital bed, groggy from anesthetic, his stomach stitched and bandaged, his world and dreams shattered.

From such impossible circumstances, Jeff Farrell, the world's fastest swimmer, returned yesterday to win the acclaim of rivals and admirers alike as the U.S. Olympic trials opened at Rouge Park's Brennan Pools.

Only hours free from Ford Hospital, his stomach heavily encased in protective tape, the gallant Kansan entered and survived early eliminations in the 100-meter freestyle. On each stroke of his flailing arms, America's hopes for the Olympic Games soared. Despite his handicap, he was the swiftest swimmer. He led a group of eight into the freestyle finals in 55.6, less than a second off his American record.

Farrell's stunning return from an emergency appendectomy overshadowed two developments in the first day's activity.

The University of Michigan's Ron Clark, the collegiate record-holder in the breaststroke, was disqualified for dipping a shoulder while making a turn in the eliminations of the 200-meter event.

Michigan coach Gus Stager, who also is serving as head coach of the United States Olympic team, angrily charged that officials "are getting mighty technical."

On the heels of Clark's heartbreaking elimination, Ohio State's Sam Hall and ex-Detroiter Gary Tobian became the first members of the U.S. team. They finished 1-2 in the three-meter springboard diving.

But this was Farrell's day.

In the best of condition, Farrell can win the Olympic 100. He could help the United States in Rome later this month in other events, too.

But first he must earn a place on the American team.

Few athletes have faced the challenge Farrell faces to come back from the emergency appendectomy, which floored him seven days ago.

Two days ago Farrell, having shaken the gloom brought on by his operation, secretly swam in the Ford Hospital pool, determined that he would make a try for a place on the team. His doctors did not discourage him. Farrell arrived early at Brennan Pools on race day and took a test dive.

"It hurt like the devil," he said, grimacing over the pain in his healing stomach. "The longer I swam, the more it hurt."

But Farrell was not ready to pull out. When the 100-meter heats came up, he was ready.

The crowd of 1,000 that ringed the racing pool was plainly aware of Farrell and his problem. While rivals shouted encouragement, the spectators sat silently as the 23-year-old flash stood poised on the starting block.

He seemed to get off late with the gun. And he raced uncertainly through the first 50 meters. But on the return leg home to the finish, his power and speed took over. He won the heat in 55.9, which is 1.1 seconds lower than his American record, but the second-best time posted in the trials.

Wearily, Farrell pulled himself from the pool. The crowd hailed him in the manner it might receive an Olympic champion.

"It didn't hurt a bit," Farrell insisted. "Not a bit."

But, said Yale coach Bob Kiphuth, Farrell's mentor: "It hurt like hell. Every inch of the way."

In the evening, with a crowd of more than 3,000 urging him on, the newly confident Farrell churned strongly over the course, beating off the challenges of Lance Larson and George Harrison.

"I know of nothing like it in sports," said meet director Clarence Pinkston of the Detroit Athletic Club.

"He did it on his own," said Ford Hospital's Dr. Richard Collier, who watched the performance with interest.

Farrell's courage and strength face yet another stern test before he earns a spot on the team. Coming Wednesday is the final of the 100 freestyle. If he can win it, the slender ace will have gained a special niche in swimming lore.

(Jeff Farrell did not qualify for the Olympics in the 100 freestyle final, but he did in the relays. He won gold medals anchoring the 400 medley and 800 freestyle teams.)

♦ ♦ ♦ ♦ ♦

Three days later George Puscas wrapped up the swimming trials and examined Detroit's Olympic spirit.

When the great sportsmen of the world next meet to award the Olympic Games, there will be $60,000 worth of new evidence that Detroit can stage, promote and sell amateur athletics.

The most successful meet in swimming history was concluded at Rouge Park's Brennan Pools with the naming of 37 men and women to the 1960 U.S. Olympic swimming and diving teams.

For years a small group headed by industrialist Fred Matthaei has sought without avail to have the Olympic Games brought to Detroit. It was with that in mind that the Olympic swim trials were first staged here in 1948.

Each of three final trials, the 1948 meet, 1956 and 1960, has been more successful than the one preceding it.

The $60,000 represents the net receipts of the amount Detroit's Olympic committee will turn over to the U.S. Olympic Committee as evidence of the city's interest in the international Games.

(Detroit made seven bids to stage the Olympic Games, but all failed. The first presentation came in 1939, the last in 1963. After Mexico City was awarded the 1968 Games, Detroit no longer was a contender.) ♦

1 9 6 2

Weep for the child
of a boxing tragedy

As most tragedies do, this one began innocently enough.

Bored, largely ignored at home, the preacher's son wandered into the streets of Chicago.

It was 1943. Johnny Bratton was 14 years old, a cocky, showboat kid, instinctively disliked by others.

But Johnny had something going for him — fists that could win instant respect and admiration.

Within weeks, roaming the streets, challenging the neighborhoods, Johnny found his way to a gym and slipped his hands into boxing gloves.

There the boxing world had itself another fighter — and there the pages began to turn on a sickening adventure that produced one of its final chapters in Detroit yesterday morning.

The life of Johnny Bratton is one of the great wastes of the sports world. The fault is not all his, perhaps not mostly his. But waste it is, a sad commentary on the poor boy grown rich, the insignificant becoming important, the young moving too fast, living too "old," maturing too slowly.

Within a year of his first wearing of the gloves, Johnny Bratton fought and won his first amateur fight. Two years later, he was Golden Gloves champion of Chicago. He turned pro. Before long he was fighting main events in Chicago Stadium, suddenly the hero of the teeming south side.

His manager was Howard Frazier, a 285-pound giant who had spied Johnny on the streets. Frazier was wise; he moved Johnny cautiously.

In nine fights in 1946, Johnny earned $31,000. Big money came quickly. In the first four months of 1947, he made another $21,800.

In pursuit of it came the first tide of moochers, bootlickers, hustlers — the leeches who prey on the naive.

And Johnny was naive. He was 17, owner of a big, black Cadillac, a sport in expensive clothes. He hired a liveried chauffeur to drive the car, married, fathered a daughter and divorced within a year.

Shortly he met Joanne, then 15, who later was to bear him a son, Ricky.

Johnny was a big deal. This was the era of big-money television fights, and Johnny Bratton was a steady star. His fight career progressed. Though his fists were small, Johnny possessed a devastating two-handed attack, had catlike agility and awesome courage.

He lived the life. Stylishly dressed, an impassioned spender, he banked cronies at $200 a clip, lost heavily at poker and dice, borrowed constantly.

First sign that the world was not gold-crusted came in 1949, when Johnny,

20 and growing distrustful, sought to rid himself of Frazier.

The Illinois Athletic Commission wanted to know why. Under constant questioning, the manager admitted that he had bet Johnny's purses on the outcome of fights, and when fights were lost, he was unable to make good.

They say most problems begin with money. Soon, Johnny's ex-wife hauled him into court for non-support.

Within the same month, March 1951, Johnny fought Charley Fusari for the world welterweight title. He won, but the government took his purse of $39,000 to pay delinquent income taxes.

Johnny continued fighting. He made money fast, played faster. He had two more title fights.

The second is remembered as one of the most brutal, vicious fights of the last 20 years. In it, the world darkened, perhaps forever, for Johnny Bratton.

It was the 11th round at Chicago Stadium. Bratton had been holding up well against bolo-swinging Kid Gavilan.

Suddenly, Gavilan cornered Bratton, rained repeated blows to his head. Bratton was hurt. Gavilan punished him severely — 10, 20, 30 blows to the head. Bratton never hit back.

Ringsiders recall it as the most dreadful punishment they have witnessed. Seeing Bratton helpless, Gavilan paused, expecting the fight to be stopped. The referee made no move.

The blows came again, 10, 20 and more.

"They were to the head," said one veteran fight writer. "I counted 60 in all — and Bratton never was able to swing back."

Perhaps because of his cockiness, the fight crowds loved to see Bratton beaten. And probably because of that, he refused to quit. The punishment continued for four more rounds.

It was the turning point in the life of the preacher's son. A champion no longer, he was no more a center of attention.

And he began to act queerly. Friends tell how he went on reefer kicks, indulged in a variety of excesses, frantically embraced the Muslim religion and suddenly started grieving inside.

At the age of 10, Frazier explained, Johnny was accidental witness to the infidelity of a loved one. Frazier said this troubled Johnny constantly.

In March 1955, Bratton was knocked out by Del Flanagan. He never fought again.

Within a few months, his mind began to slip, and soon Johnny was taken aboard a van and carried to Manteno State Mental Hospital outside Chicago.

This was September 1956. In the years since, the preacher's son has been largely unknown and unknowing.

Last week, a young mother who once might have expected much, brought a handsome son, ill of infection, to Detroit's Children's Hospital.

In two days, he slipped into a coma, soon passed away.

Ricky Bratton, 11, a child of tragedy, was buried yesterday morning in Detroit's Memorial Cemetery.

The preacher's son sits, unknowing. ✦

1962

Past imperfect when it comes to bowling

I dreamed I bowled 300 in my Jockey shorts.

Later, with my pants on, I wasn't quite that good.

But I can bowl 300.

I've got the arm, the brain, the heart. And I know where 300s are waiting.

If we were fishing, I wouldn't tell you where the big ones are. But bowling, well …

Big ones await at Fort Park Recreation, a neat little spot in Lincoln Park that thrives on the unnatural. This is the place that had its lid lifted by a tornado six years ago, the place where Ernie Babcock shot his back-to-back 300s last month, where Phil Trapani, Ern's teammate, hit a 300 last week.

How did they do it? Well, they too have the arm, the brain, the heart. Some have it, some don't. We've got it, Ern, Phil and me.

Lanes 13-14 at Fort Park are the ideal alleys to take your bowling physical.

They test the arm. You've got to wing the ball, pal, let 'er rip.

They test the brain. And let's hope we haven't lost you yet, friend.

You have to forget your hook. The sooner the better. It just won't take on 13-14. In the vernacular, 13-14 are known as "stiffs" or "nonrunners." Roll down the middle of one of 'em and the ball will buzz along without a bend.

Confession: It took three games to quit the middle.

"These are extreme outside alleys," counseled Trapani, who wandered in to relive his moment of perfection. "Get to the right corner, and let 'er roll in from there."

Brain.

It worked.

Right from the corner. Halfway down, the ball starts taking, moving in on the headpin. Three feet from the wood triangle, you know it's there, solid in the pocket.

WHAM! Not a pin left.

Do it again. Wham! And again. Same old stuff.

Ha. This is simple. Great. Wrap up 13-14, manager, I'm taking 'em home.

Whoops. What went wrong on 14 that time?

"Well, it's a little bit different than 13," Trapani said. "The ball doesn't take quite as much. Move in from the corner, just a bit."

Nuts. A split.

"You moved all right," the coach said, "but then you gave the ball an extra twist. Gotta throw the same ball all the time."

Sure.

Oh, no. Now 13 has gone haywire.

"You moved in on 13, too. Stay in the corner there, but move in on 14."

How am I supposed to remember all this?

"Some do, some don't."

OK.

Say, that's not bad. A 200 game.

First serious try for 300, and here I am, two-thirds perfect.

Forty million games will be rolled in Detroit this year, maybe 20 will be perfect. One of 'em will be mine.

Heart.

"Stick with it," Trapani said.

Sure, sure. But right now, I've got to go to work.

"With luck, you might get a 300 someday."

Luck?

What's luck got to do with it? ✦

1 9 6 2

When betting, don't trust the horse or the driver

The harness racing fan cries constantly of screwy things happening on the tracks.

Essentially, however, he has two pet villains.

Horse. Driver.

He has confidence in neither, and there might be some foundation for this. By nature of the sport, a harness trotter or pacer cannot be as reliable as a thoroughbred racer.

Unlike the thoroughbred, harness horses must maintain certain gaits. A horse that breaks off his gait almost invariably loses the race.

And breaking is painfully common. Scarcely a race is run, locally, without one or more. Obviously, once his bet has been wiped out by a breaking horse, the bettor is going to be angry.

He might have good reason to be. For the quality of horses running at Hazel Park Harness Raceway during its completed meeting was not good.

"Of 1,000 horses barned at Hazel Park," said state steward Dan Gilmartin, "180 were on the stewards' list."

A horse is placed on the list for one of three reasons — habitual breaking, poor performance or lameness. Roughly, then, one out of five horses at Hazel Park was cited during his stay as unfit for racing.

Is the figure high?

"Yes," Gilmartin said. "It is high."

Yet despite the horses, which track owners admit are not the best, public wrath falls heaviest on the harness driver.

It is the driver who controls the horse; it is the driver who is blamed for breaking and suspected constantly of collusion with other drivers.

"You can't tell me these guys don't know who's going to win which race," a disgruntled bettor insisted. "They get together and decide among themselves. One for me, one for you."

The criticism is harsh and when applied to all drivers is doubtless unfair. Yet it reflects the public image of the driver.

Don MacFarlane, president of the Hazel Park Harness Racing Association, and Pres Jenuine, head of the powerful Western Harness Racing Association (Santa Anita, Hollywood Park), both defend and criticize the drivers.

"You hear the loudest complaints," MacFarlane said, "when a horse breaks. But I guess you have to know something about harness driving to understand it. The last gimmick a man would resort to if he were trying to throw a race would be to break his horse deliberately.

"It would be dangerous to the horse and extremely dangerous for the driver. You'll hear that drivers are pulling back on the reins, holding a horse back. Well, here again, it's a matter of knowing. The driver must keep tight control to prevent horses from running beyond their capacity. Otherwise, a break would be certain."

It might be well to interject here the comments of Eddie Wheeler, a young driver, the new breed, who rates among the top 20 in the United States.

Wheeler cannot understand the mistrust of harness fans.

"I've worked the thoroughbreds and among the harness people," he said. "There's far more conniving among the thoroughbreds than you'll ever see in harness racing. For instance, I've never heard of entering a horse in a harness race for exercise, as they do among the runners.

"Listen to the way they talk. The thoroughbred owner says, 'My horse won and paid $13.80.' The harness horse owner says, 'My horse won a $4,000 purse.' Maybe that's simplifying it too much. But there is a real difference in the approach."

Jenuine does not question the integrity of harness drivers, owners or others connected with the sport.

Yet as a top harness official he is pointedly critical of several facets of harness racing.

And the drivers are one of his targets. Their conduct on and off the tracks, and the impressions they leave before the public, are harmful, he says.

"These are things which breed skepticism among the public and cause distrust," Jenuine reasoned.

Jenuine himself points up a few actions of drivers that arouse public suspicion.

"They should consider," he said, "the conclusions formed by the public when they look at the odds board when they parade their horses; talk to other drivers on the track; talk to the public at the paddock.

"Or when they go into long huddles with owners and other drivers in the paddock, or come back at the end of a race laughing and talking to other drivers, or engage in barroom huddles and loose talk."

The obvious public conclusion is that something is going on — a deal is being cooked up — among the drivers and owners.

Thoroughbred racing and other sports — football, baseball, basketball — all have strict rules against fraternization.

Local authorities are not unaware of these activities. All of it has happened repeatedly at Hazel Park and other area tracks in recent years.

Gilmartin and Hazel Park stewards cracked down recently on driver Jim Carrivau and banned him for the remainder of the meeting for "loose talk."

"He was complaining in the barn area how a race had been run," Gilmartin said. "If there's a protest to be made, it should be made with the stewards.

"This is the sort of thing which has been damaging to racing — loose talk."

It is the sort of thing that slowly is bringing harness racing into disfavor. ✦

1962

Mighty Liston batters Patterson in short order

CHICAGO — Sonny Liston won the world heavyweight boxing championship last night, his mighty fists destroying in just two minutes and six seconds one of the cherished fables of our times.

Liston, the bald-man challenger, Liston, the deadpanned braggart, was right. His crushing power was too much for champion Floyd Patterson.

In the very first round, he smashed Patterson to the ring floor at Comiskey Park, left him lying dazed and immobile, and ascended to the championship as 35,000 sat, stunned to silence by the brevity of it all.

Referee Frank Sikora finished his 10-second knockout count over Patterson and only then did the hysteria that accompanies dramatic events take hold of the ballpark.

The ring was mobbed by so many Liston friends and Patterson followers that to this minute, Liston has not been formally pronounced from the ring as the new heavyweight champion.

Patterson was finished by four blows, the first a jolting right hand that sent him against the ropes near his corner, the other three powerful left hooks.

The last of the lefts tumbled him to the floor. He lay there on his left side for a moment, rolled and propped himself on an elbow, aware that he must get up but unable to do so.

Sikora signaled the end of his count — the fight was done, the world had a new champion — and only then could Patterson regain his feet.

It was so short, so quick, so decisive, that the first reaction at ringside was sympathy — not for Patterson but for thousands who paid $5 million to watch what had been built up as the classic fight of our day.

But it was far less than that. Virtue does not always triumph; the good do not always prevail, and Patterson, the nice guy champion, did nothing in the limited time available to him to suggest that he might handle Liston, now or any other time.

Only three heavyweight championship fights in the long history of boxing have been shorter, or ended so abruptly.

They were James Jeffries' 55-second knockout of Jack Finnegan in Detroit in 1900; Tommy Burns' 1:28 knockout of Jem Roche in 1908, and Joe Louis' vengeful 2:04 knockout of Max Schmeling in 1938.

Patterson was surprising in a way. He did not, as most figured he would, try to run from Liston, to use his greater speed to elude the far-bigger man who had claimed Floyd could not last more than five rounds.

Instead, Patterson came out at the opening bell, met Liston in the middle of the ring and quickly stuck a left hand in his face. If nothing else, it showed that Patterson was unafraid. Perhaps he should have been more wary. He had reason to be, as the seconds passed.

Liston, plodding ahead, coming to Patterson constantly, unwavering in his intent, threw a right hand into the champion's body, and Patterson grabbed, pinning Liston's arms. Boldly then, Patterson reached for Liston's stomach with a sweeping right, missed and collided with him in a corner. It was the last strong move Patterson made.

Four seconds later, Liston caught him near the ropes, threw a straight right hand that caused Patterson's head to drop. Not even Liston seemed to realize Patterson was hurt.

The champion grabbed the top strand of the ring rope with his left hand, tried to swing himself away from Liston but was too slow about it.

Liston followed with a left hand — people who measure such things say it is the best left since Louis — which caught Patterson on the forehead. Patterson seemed to sag. Another left caught Patterson a glancing blow on the head, then the third came hard and true, flush on the jaw.

And at its impact Patterson sank backward to the floor. Liston himself was startled by the quickness of it. He hesitated, then, at referee Sikora's urging, retreated hastily to a neutral corner.

The count went on then, and a new champion was born.

Liston, outweighing Patterson by a muscular 25 pounds at 214, disappeared among a mob of well-wishers who clambered into the ring. One of the first and most conspicuous was Detroit middleweight Henry Hank, who has known Liston since Sonny's early TV fights at Motor City Arena and remained his fast friend despite Liston's repeated conflicts with the law.

There have been a good many unsavory characters connected with boxing and some boxers whose pasts are almost as sordid as Liston's.

Jack Dempsey was one. Perhaps Liston's reform is complete now with the championship in hand.

Liston, who learned to box in prison while serving a term for armed robbery, had to overcome his criminal past to get a chance at the championship.

New York refused to license him, and the bout was moved to Chicago.

Now that he wears the crown, it's unlikely there will be objections anywhere to having Liston about and on display.

As for Patterson, he was a forlorn and disgusted champion standing dazed in his corner, shaking his head in sadness and apology for his futile effort. He retreated from the ring with his wife on his arm.

They will meet again, these two fighters. Liston and Patterson have a binding contract to meet again within a year.

This time, however, there will be a more equal sharing of the loot from the fight. For this night of work, Patterson will receive nearly $2 million, Liston about $400,000.

Next time, they will get equal purses. ✦

1 9 6 2

When Lions' gamble fails,
Packers pull out a plum

GREEN BAY, Wis. — It seemed a cinch, a literal cinch. But wise ones do not gamble, not even with cinches.

The Lions gambled yesterday, gambled with the world in their hands, and lost a crushing, 9-7 decision to the Green Bay Packers in a game that ultimately could mean the pro football championship of 1962.

Under dark and weeping skies, glamour boy Paul Hornung kicked a 21-yard field goal with 33 seconds to play, lifting the champion Packers over the Lions before an almost unbelieving throng of 38,669 at City Stadium.

It looked like sheer giveaway. It was the Lions' game; they had it locked up, 7-6, their fourth straight victory, command over the Western Division race — until the last 90 seconds.

Then they went looking for catastrophe, daring fate, and it came tumbling down on them. They were trying to run out the clock, waste away the last threatening seconds of this rain-, mud-marred showdown, after having stopped the Packers as no team has stopped them in the last few years.

The Lions were at midfield, with third down and seven yards to go, when the fateful decision came. They dared to pass, hoping to pick up another first down, to keep the ball, not let the Packers have another chance with it.

You could see it coming. Quarterback Milt Plum stepped back behind his protective wall as Terry Barr shot down the right side, for about 12 yards, turned and ... oops, slipped.

Here came the pass. Before Barr could regain his balance, fleet Herb Adderley, the former Michigan State halfback, cut in front of him, picked off the ball and raced down the sideline to the Detroit 18 before the stunned Lions could collar him.

Seconds ticked away, but the roaring stands and the Lions knew what was coming. The Packers ran two idle plays into the Lions, then took time out and called Hornung for his field goal.

The kick was hard and true, smack through the uprights.

With it went the game, a truly great effort by the Lions despite adverse conditions, and perhaps a lot of the heart that the Detroit club had put into its early season surge to title possibilities.

Was it a foolish gamble? Was it a reckless move, this calling for the pass when victory beckoned, when the least error on the play might mean defeat?

Well, you can debate that into eternity. A sound case can be made for calling the pass play, especially in view of the fact that the Packers needed only a field goal to win.

But the Lions probably will be second-guessing themselves and wondering why, oh, why, this foul blow had to fall on them at this instant.

They did a whale of a job against a team that had scoffed openly at them.

The Packers won without a touchdown. Hornung, greatest scorer in professional football, gave them all of their points on three field goals.

It was the first time since 1959, before the Packers ascended to the world championship, that they and their crushing ground game had not crossed a rival's goal line. Hornung earlier had kicked two 15-yard field goals, one in the first period lifting the Packers to a 3-0 lead, another in the last seconds of the third period, as Green Bay closed to within a point of the Lions, 7-6.

The Lions had shoved across their only score in the second period on a six-yard dash around end by Danny Lewis. This score followed recovery of a fumble at the Packers' 34.

From the time of the Lions' score until the very end, Detroit fought the Packers to a standstill, cutting them off abruptly whenever they pressed close to the goal. Opening the third quarter, the Packers found that not even Jim Taylor, their punishing fullback, now could make reliable, steady gains through the Detroit defense.

But the Packers desperately went to the air, pressed to the Detroit 23, only to be stopped by an interception by Carl Brettschneider, the big linebacker. It was one of two pass thefts by the Lions, who also collared two fumbles to help curb the champions.

Despite Brettschneider's move, the Packers, though trailing, still were dominating the play. On the next try, they went in for Hornung's second field goal, pulling within easy reach.

In the fourth period, both Hornung and the Lions' Wayne Walker missed on long field goal kicks, and it was after Hornung's try went awry that the Lions came out trying to save their slender edge.

Six minutes remained when the Lions opened from their 22. Twice in third-down situations Plum went to the air and put across passes that kept the attack going and kept the Lions in control of the ball. The clock had faded away to a minute and 46 seconds. The pass gamble had been tried twice before and succeeded. Try it again?

The Lions decided to gamble.

Had they not gambled, they probably would have had to punt to the Packers. Green Bay possibly would have had the ball deep on its own ground with perhaps a minute to play.

A gambling team, a team that thrives on risk, died with this one.

Weather and playing conditions had much to do with the waging of the war between the two best teams in the West. The field was wet and soggy; rain fell intermittently. The Lions had to abandon much of their passing offense because their receivers could not break on the treacherous turf.

Green Bay, which relies more on a ground attack, did not suffer as much.

In the end, the Packers won with another Lions slip — the slip that sent Barr to the ground and let Adderley take the pass that ruined the Lions. ✦

1 9 6 2

Lions get revenge, give Packers the bird

R emember it as the 20 minutes that rocked the football world … 20 minutes that frowned on gridiron history … 20 minutes in which the Lions thrust themselves among the great teams of gridiron lore.

On this chill, windy Thanksgiving Day, as tough and as brutal a team as ever strode on a gridiron smashed, wrecked and left in ruin the pride of a team that had come to be known as the greatest of all time.

Detroit 26, Green Bay 14. The Packers are human, after all.

From the opening kickoff through the first few minutes of the second quarter was all the Lions required to deal these Packers their first defeat of the season, break their run toward a second straight world championship, and bring the Lions themselves closer to their title dreams.

For sheer force and emotion, not many games compare with this one.

A roaring crowd of 57,598, second-largest football gathering ever crammed into Tiger Stadium, sat enthralled and then driven to near hysteria by the overwhelming might and dominance of the vengeful Lions.

Millions more across the nation watched via television the destruction of a Packers winning record unmatched by any team since 1942.

No one Lion emerged as the conquering hero in this one, but there were two who stood clearly above the rest. They were Gail Cogdill, surely one of the great pass catchers of recent times, and ponderous Roger Brown, 303-pound defensive tackle.

Launching the rout of the Packers, Cogdill snared touchdown passes of 34 and 27 yards from quarterback Milt Plum for the first scores of the game.

Brown led a vicious, unstoppable Lions rush that overpowered, then brought to frustration and collapse a Packers offense that stood as the very best in pro football.

How great was the rush? It produced nine points that rocketed Detroit to a 23-0 lead after just 18 minutes and 16 seconds of play.

Sam Williams ran six yards with a fumble for a touchdown, and Brown tackled Packers quarterback Bart Starr in the end zone for a safety.

How great, really, was the Lions' rush?

Starr, attempting to pass, eight times failed to get the ball away; he was thrown for 110 yards in losses. Seven other times, Packers runners were tossed for losses.

The Packers were never in it. Detroit's lead went to 26-0 early in the third quarter. Not until the final period did the Packers get closer to the goal than the Lions' 37.

Green Bay's touchdowns followed then, both tainted by Lions errors.

Plum, chased back from his 28 while trying to pass, threw into the hands of Bill Quinlan, who then fumbled into the Detroit end zone, where Willie Davis fell on the ball for a touchdown.

Just six minutes before the end, Ken Webb lost a fumble to Davis at the Detroit 14, and Jim Taylor scored the Packers' second straight touchdown from the 4.

These two errors by the Lions were part of a flood in the game. Detroit lost the ball on three fumbles and two pass interceptions. The Packers were identically loose with the ball.

Two of the Lions fumbles were by halfback Dan Lewis in the first quarter. Neither was damaging, but the first of them served to trigger and reveal the kind of muscle the Lions would apply to the Packers.

After taking the opening kickoff at their 29, the Lions moved on two passing strikes by Plum to the Packers' 32. Lewis fumbled and Hank Gremminger recovered for Green Bay on the 17.

The Packers moved out to their 47, but then came the first of the Lions' telling defensive blows.

Alex Karras, who with Brown, Darris McCord, Joe Schmidt, Carl Brettschneider, Sam Williams and Wayne Walker blew through the Packers' line like wind through a tunnel, smashed Tom Moore for a loss.

Starr was belted for a loss, then chased and belted again for a 15-yard loss. The Packers had to kick.

Boyd Dowler got away a weak 15-yard boot, which went out of bounds on the Packers' 39.

Three plays later, Cogdill went streaking down the left sideline, ran away from luckless Herb Adderley, slipped around Willie Wood and made a fingertip grab in the end zone of a 34-yard pass from Plum.

The huge crowd erupted, perhaps in realization that this Lions team, not nearly so potent a scorer as the Packers, did have weapons to score.

It stood at 7-0 through the remainder of the first period, despite a fumble lost at the Lions' 44. The Lions regained the ball on the next play when Moore was jarred into a fumble by Brown.

From that start at their 46, the Lions moved to their second touchdown.

Crisp, jolting blocks cutting down the Packers' own vaunted defense sprang Tom Watkins loose for 31 yards in three runs to the Packers' 27.

Then along came Cogdill again, this time on the right side of the field, angling toward a corner of the end zone.

Plum pitched a high, arcing pass; Codgill left Adderley in his tracks and took the ball over his shoulder in the end zone.

It was 58 seconds into the second quarter, the Lions ahead, 14-0.

In the 2½ minutes that followed, the Packers' ambition of a defeatless season, an easy run through the year and to the championship, was shattered.

Following the kickoff, Starr saw the need to pass in an effort to put his team quickly back into contention. He had no chance.

Surging through the Packers' line, supposedly the best in the NFL, the Lions gave chase to Starr. Brown caught the retreating quarterback at the Packers' 7 and jarred him loose from the ball.

Williams picked it up at the 6 and charged unchallenged into the end zone for a third Lions touchdown and 21-0 lead. Only 21 seconds had passed since Cogdill's second scoring catch.

The Packers seemed to panic with that. Adderley fumbled, but recovered, the kickoff at the Packers' 10.

Then Jim Taylor, best running back in the NFL — he ran for a minus three yards on eight first-half carries — tried the Lions' line and was thrown back on the 6.

Starr then tried to pass again, but Brown burst through and grabbed the quarterback as he stood in the end zone, under the goalposts.

With their swiftly earned 23-0 lead, the Lions might well have put the Packers to a more embarrassing rout.

That they did not score more can be blamed on two Plum field goal kicks blocked by Bill Quinlan and Adderley, and a third-period pass interception, which stopped Detroit at the Green Bay 30.

Opening the second half, Night Train Lane intercepted a pass by Starr at the Detroit 42; Plum followed with a 47-yard field goal, which gave Detroit its last points and a 26-0 lead.

There was no coming back for the Packers. The Lions' defense was unrelenting. Not once did the Packers show ability to organize a march.

The defeat was the Packers' first in 12 games overall — including the 1961 NFL championship game. They had won 11 straight league games, a record unequaled since the Bears of 1942 won 12 in a row. ✦

1 9 6 3

Lions cry double-cross after NFL gambling inquiry

Those six punished Lions feel strongly that they have been betrayed.
They were identified among the players involved in betting on
football games, and they thought they would remain anonymous.

So they're planning a meeting with an attorney to consider all
avenues of appeal and rebuttal to NFL commissioner Pete Rozelle.

"Rozelle told them just a couple of weeks ago that there would be no
suspensions and that nobody would be hurt," one source close to the players
told the Free Press. "Now there's this, where he has come out and
condemned them all without any explanations.

"Well, they want to tell their side of the story, too."

In New York, Rozelle insisted he had never made a "firm promise" that
player names would not be mentioned.

He said he never intimated that their admissions would help Alex Karras,
or that there would be no suspensions.

He revealed that he sent letters to all players involved, advising them that
under NFL rules they were allowed to appear at a formal hearing to contest
any charges against them.

"They all returned the signed waivers of a hearing, indicating that they did
not want to contest the charges," Rozelle said.

NFL rules make it clear that there is no appeal possible from the $2,000
fines levied against Joe Schmidt, Wayne Walker, John Gordy, Gary Lowe and
Sam Williams, and the indefinite banishment of Karras.

"They scared the hell out of a couple of the kids," the source said. "A
couple of them insisted on taking lie detector tests."

Schmidt, captain of the Lions, did not take a lie test. He openly admitted
making a $50 bet on the Green Bay-New York title game last Dec. 27, figuring
it would help Karras.

"Rozelle told Schmidt he was one of the most respected people in football,
and that no names would be mentioned when the investigation was finished,"
the source said.

Lie detector tests, it was learned, were given in Detroit and New York to a
handful of players during the last three months.

Players on at least six other of the NFL's 14 teams also submitted to tests
in the investigation.

Schmidt had been captain of the Lions for the last six years and is the
team's delegate on the NFL player representatives committee.

In Philadelphia, Pete Retzlaff, the Eagles end who heads the players committee, said, "Schmidt should have known better" than to place a bet on a football game.

Unlike Walker and Karras, Schmidt was not talking. The word was that Lions management had ordered all players involved to refrain from comment.

The case developed more than a year ago, when a special detail of the Detroit Police Department began keeping tabs on athletes associating with known gamblers in old Greektown.

Last August, police commissioner George Edwards reported, a bus with some gamblers aboard was driven to the Lions-Pittsburgh Steelers exhibition game in Cleveland.

Karras and guard John Gordy rode back to Detroit on the bus. A car belonging to Walker trailed the bus back to Detroit.

Coach George Wilson later was informed of the incident but apparently did nothing about it.

On Dec. 27, Edwards forwarded his entire report to Rozelle. Included were charges that Lions players frequented the Lindell Bar, owned by brothers Jimmy and John Butsicaris. The report said gamblers also visited the bar.

One week later Rozelle and Lions general manager Edwin J. Anderson met with Karras.

Karras, who had invested $40,000 to become part-owner of the new Lindell, said Anderson ordered him to "get out of the bar business." Karras refused.

At the same time, Chicago Bears owner George Halas said a league investigation of gambling was under way.

Then Karras, while preparing for the Pro Bowl game in Los Angeles last January, went on a network television show and admitted he had bet on games.

"But it was only for cigars and cigarettes," he insisted later when Rozelle summoned him to explain.

The resulting investigation showed it was something more.

In the weeks since, Karras has not avoided the limelight.

Three weeks ago, while playing on the Lions' basketball team, he became involved in a fracas with a Belleville, Mich., player, who charged Karras slugged him in the game.

Karras said he had been hit three times by the player and warned him to lay off. The incident brought no reaction by the Lions.

Karras, meanwhile, has been busy as a bartender at the old Lindell on Cass Avenue. The new location, at Cass at Michigan, is ready for a grand opening.

But the Michigan State Liquor Commission has not granted a license to make Karras a legal partner of the Butsicaris brothers. ✦

1 9 6 3

The little guy
Big Daddy left behind

"A man's dying is more the survivors' affair than his own." — **Thomas Mann**

The little guy sat quietly now, his head cradled in the mother's arms. The tears were gone. Can there be wetter tears than those of a little guy, 6?

But he cried no more. The preacher stood alongside the flag-draped gray coffin and said: "He did some good, he did some wrong…."

"Yes, yes," the mother answered chokingly. "He was good, he was good."

This was Big Daddy's last day. The little guy cried. Big men cried.

On a football field, Gene Lipscomb was a crowd by himself. But now more than a thousand people — friends, relatives, employers, former employers, fellow players — were in the crowd.

They packed the chapel at the House of Diggs Funeral Home on East Grand Boulevard to give final tribute to the huge Pittsburgh Steelers tackle.

Men he had played for and against were there: Art Rooney, owner of the Steelers, and his son, Dan; Don Kellett, general manager of the Baltimore Colts; Bud Erickson and Bob Nussbaumer of the Lions.

"How do you begin to replace a tackle like him?" Art Rooney said.

And men he had played with and against: Lenny Moore, Jim Parker, John Sample. Tom Tracy, Jim Gibbons, Erich Barnes, John Henry Johnson.

"He was as good as tackles come," said Tracy, the Steelers' fullback.

And people he had loved and grown with in his 31 years — the grandfather, Charles Hoskins, 65, who reared him; three ex-wives; a little guy, Raymond, 6; a daughter Eugenia, 10. And the Detroit schoolteacher, Billy Jean Plumber, who was to become Lispcomb's fourth wife in about two weeks.

"At one time in his life," said the Rev. H.E. Owen, "he could not have gotten these people together no matter what he did. Now there is not enough room to hold the many who had come to know him."

It was a fine tribute to Big Daddy.

The procession to Lincoln Memorial Cemetery at 14 Mile and Gratiot was a long one, led by a green hearse, the family car with the grandfather, mother and daughter, and the little guy, 6, perched on the lap of Big Daddy's fiancee.

Lipscomb's death was attributed in Baltimore to an overdose of heroin.

"He couldn't have been on narcotics for long," insisted young Dan Rooney. "He had a thorough physical exam two weeks ago, and the doctor says he would have spotted the needle marks then."

Big Daddy, you should have known there's no greater kick than a little guy, 6. ✦

1 9 6 4

Minnesota Fats feeds off a steady diet of suckers

O nce upon a time, or so the story goes, there was this kid who was good to his dog, worked hard, saved his money, never fooled around with girls and struggled unhappily ever after.

And then there is Minnesota Fats, who has never worked a day in his life.

There he stood laughing at the side of the big green table, surrounded by the bigs and swells at the Detroit Athletic Club, seeming to prove that wizardry and a fast tongue beat hard work every time.

That's the way it is with Minnesota Fats. He gets away with it.

He is a round guy of maybe 5-feet-7, 260 pounds, with a belly that balloons and jiggles 50 inches, but this just hides the real meat of Minnesota Fats.

He is strong and steady of hand, keen of eye and mighty sharp with a cue stick.

He'll be kicking around the town's pool halls for the next few days, and the next month he'll be back again looking for new challenges.

From the time he was a kid (he's 52 now), Fats has made his way and weight with the stick. Around some tables, they might even call him a hustler.

In fact, Jackie Gleason made him rather widely known a few years ago in a movie labeled "The Hustler," the story of a fat pool sharpie. Fats claims Gleason was portraying him.

But if that is true, Fats is being outhustled for perhaps the first time. He was not paid a penny for the movie, and so he has a $30,000 suit going against Gleason and 20th Century Fox Studios.

"It's a cinch, a mortal cinch," blared Fats who, like Cassius Clay, occasionally runneth over at the mouth.

"Everybody knows there has been only one Fat Man. Gleason was playing me and, in fact, I could have done a better job."

Long before Gleason, the name Minnesota Fats or Chicago Fats or New York Fats was almost legendary among pool sharpies.

Fats' real name is Rudolph Walter Wanderone, but he can't recall the last time he heard it. Perhaps when he was a kid, living on 49th and Broadway in New York.

"New York, Chicago, Minnesota — it don't matter — I'm Fats, the one and only," he boasted.

"Like right now I'm Detroit Fats. I just adopt the name of the city I'm hanging around in, and that's how people know me."

There is some question about Fats' stature among the recognized greats of the billiard table. But Fats scoffs at titles ("Who needs 'em?") and the men long accepted as the best of tournament billiards, men like Mosconi, Greenleaf, Caras, Hoppe.

"Oh, nuts. You name 'em all and I've played 'em all and beat them," Fats said. "Why, if Mosconi came in the room and saw me, he'd start quivering. I've played him 20 times and never lost."

Fats is an accomplished trick-shot artist, which is great stuff for exhibitions, but his money game is one pocket. A player breaks and concentrates on only one pocket of the table. His opponent must play the opposite pocket. First player to pocket eight of the 15 balls is the winner.

"It's 100 times harder to run eight balls in one pocket than 100 in every pocket," Fats said in a slur at Mosconi, the polished, long-time pocket billiards champion.

Fats' ego overflows when he speaks of his conquests on the table.

For nearly 12 years I was in semi-retirement," he said. "You know why? I couldn't find no action. I'd walk into a room and the players would freeze. They know I'm the greatest."

He told of the night he walked into a pool room and a player "built like a big bird, all hunched over," hustled him.

The player said his name was Cornbread Red and he wanted to play one pocket for $500, best four of seven games.

Fats said: "Son, I'll play you for one game for $500 or $5,000. When I get through with you, they'll call you No Bread Red."

They did.

"I could make a thousand bucks blindfolded," he said. "But I don't want to work. They want a game, I give 'em a game."

Beats work every time. ✦

1964

Good guy, good coach
gets the shaft from Lions

I f he were an ordinary man, there would not be this haunting sadness, for the world is full of ordinary men who suffer daily misfortune unnoticed by the rest.

But George Wilson is no ordinary man, nor was he an ordinary football coach, and his departure from the Lions leaves a special void his successor cannot hope to fill.

True, they might win more games some years and they might win a championship again someday. But it will not be the same.

There was a special quality about Wilson unrecognized by the public, and it was the thing that won him friends wherever he went and causes so many to damn the circumstances that brought about his resignation.

He was a decent guy. Now that might not sound like much, except if you look you'll find there really aren't many around.

He was the only thing the Lions had that amounted to public relations, the art of making friends for the organization. It came naturally to him. Never too big, never too busy.

He had his problems — far more than most coaches ever encounter.

Remember that until this year the Lions were owned by 144 people and most of the time the factions within were at each other's throats, and here was the coach, caught in the middle.

Wilson had to ride the fence, satisfying one boss or another until his own decency forced him to take one side.

Edwin J. Anderson had saved his job once, so he helped save Anderson in the 1962 proxy fight. He went with the company team headed by Anderson, which really meant Bill Ford, and now Ford has given him the squeeze. There ought to be a moral there somewhere.

Wilson has had much professional and personal misfortune during the last two years, though few would know about it because he never complained. The gambling scandal of 1963 embarrassed him for it forced him into a new attitude with his team.

Decent? Well, remember that those involved in the gambling scandal had been roundly condemned by the National Football League and no one around the Lions was ready to say an official word in their behalf.

It was Wilson who ordered up a public statement reflecting the Detroit Football Co.'s faith in the integrity of its employees.

Perhaps that was the unhappiest of his 16 years — eight as head coach — with the Lions because nothing went right. Week after week, the coach was taking his team apart in the locker room, in the press, in the screening room, and then Scooter McLean got sick.

They were closest of friends within the organization, and when Scooter died this year there was a change. Wilson had no one to talk to, not the way he talked to Scooter, his old Bears teammate.

They were confidants with mutual trust and the two of them doped things out their own way. Not that they were always right. Not that the other assistants weren't valued or trusted.

But there was this special thing with Scooter and when it ended, Wilson, in a way, was alone.

Looking back, I recall a colleague saying during training camp last summer that the atmosphere seemed different somehow at Cranbrook. Nothing you could put your finger on. But different.

And then there was the gossip — perhaps unfounded, perhaps not — that someone within the Lions called Bobby Layne to ask whether he would return as an assistant coach because jobs were opening.

That was a few months ago, and now all the coaches are gone and the impression here is that George Wilson was jobbed. Knifed, if you will.

They led him through a ridiculous sequence of staff reorganization last week, and finally it dawned that they were telling him he'd had it. They could have done it more decently.

Almost all his players will bemoan his downfall, and a few of them should hide. They never had it so good. If they were unhappy under Wilson, they will be miserable under his successor.

Not often do you view a man over a period of years and retain an admiration. Wilson has been right and he has been wrong, but either way, I mostly liked the way he did it. ✦

1965

He could hit hard, but boxing hit harder

For a few years, they talked of Sonny Banks as a new Joe Louis.

He had it all — a big, beautifully developed kid, lithe and quick with an air of innocence and massive arms and fists that could crack a wall.

They said of him that no one could hit harder, not Sonny Liston, perhaps not even Joe Louis in his day.

He lived to fight, and it seems that he will die because of it.

Sonny Banks lingers near death in a Philadelphia hospital, his brain damaged, the surgeons unable to do more.

Barring a miracle, they must list him soon as one more victim of the ring.

But it is difficult to think of Sonny Banks as a mere statistic, the fifth man of his cruel trade to be felled in 1965.

He was a good kid. Gentle, intelligent, devoted.

The swaggering gals who follow the fight champs do not know him. Sonny gave them no time; he never tasted smoke or alcohol.

It was evident, or it became evident, that Sonny was not the heralded "new Joe Louis."

He was too good too fast, and there was no way left for him to learn all that he needed to learn of ring warfare.

He was too tough for the club fighters and too dangerous an unknown for the good ones to risk defeat.

He never fought as an amateur, and it was this gap in his experience that distorted his ability.

He had come here with a dream from Tupelo, Miss., in 1958, leaving behind his mother and father and three brothers, who since have moved to Detroit.

Sonny's first fight was as a professional in 1960 and he was raw and awkward, but he was powerful, and his strength alone won him the decision.

"That showed me something," he said once. "I never believed you could be so good in the gym and so bad in the ring."

Subsequent fights masked the real weaknesses of Sonny Banks while creating the impression that here was a near-heavyweight marvel.

He scored three straight knockouts, was knocked out himself when he blithely turned his head to look for corner instructions.

Then began a magical chain of knockouts. Seven straight heads felt the thundering power of Sonny's fists, and his gym mates thought he was on the way to the big time in boxing.

They sent him into New York's Madison Square Garden to fight another kid, Cassius Clay.

Not surprisingly to those who had watched him here, Sonny caught Clay with a left uppercut in the first round and dropped him to the canvas.

Clay, who was to become heavyweight champion of the world, had not been off his feet before, or since. He came back and belted out Banks in the fourth round.

Sonny was musing about that only a few months ago.

"All those early knockouts I had was the worst thing possible for me," he said. "They made me think I was all that good. But I'm learning. Every fight I'm learning."

Most of the others, Clay in particular, had 200 and more amateur fights preparing them for the day when their livelihood would be earned in the ring.

Sonny lacked that. His lessons were learned the hard way, against seasoned pros.

Three months after the Clay fight, in May 1962, Banks was knocked out again, this time by fat Jack Johnson, later to be knifed fatally in Harlem.

It was then that the fight crowd began to sour on Banks. They said he couldn't take a punch, had no heart. Worse, they said he would never make it because he had a "glass chin."

In a way it seemed to be true. Sonny never seemed to take a stiff punch cleanly, without a wobble.

But Burns Stanley, a tax expert at Ford Motor Co. who fostered Sonny's career, never believed it.

"The kid is all heart and that glass chin idea is nonsense," Stanley said. "What slowed Sonny after his fast early start was that he had to meet better fighters, and his inexperience began to show.

"He simply did not know how to handle himself when he got into a difficult situation in the ring."

Banks' last fight for Burns was in July 1964, when he lost on a knockout to Cleveland Williams. His record reads 19 victories (16 by knockout) and seven losses (five by knockout).

But Sonny was his own magnet. He desperately wanted to fight, and the urge was compelling.

"I want to be somebody," he said once. "It's all that simple. I've pumped gas, worked in Ted Ewald's collision shop and in the foundry at Ford's.

"But I'm nobody and have no chance at being anybody until I get in the ring.

"When I make it, I'm going back to Mississippi to take care of my momma and my daddy."

It was a dream to haunt a memory. ✦

1965

Peaches' climb began on a wall in Hamtramck

In the heart of old Hamtramck where little Poland once thrived, Berras Street runs maybe 400 links of kielbasa east off Jos. Campau, then ends abruptly against a high, blank concrete wall.

From the kitchen window of the neat white frame home at street's end, the wall is an ugly but inviting symbol of a better life.

It was on that wall, stretching 60 feet across and nearly 20 feet high, that Peaches Bartkowicz, who lives in the white house, became the finest tennis player in Michigan, the best her age in the United States.

She is a mere 16 years old, but already the wall has carried her to England, Puerto Rico, Mexico, Jamaica, Colombia, most of America's major cities — and 110 tennis championships.

Peaches is a tall, trim and muscular teenager who feigns the fluffy bouffant hairstyle of her set and has been seen to rock a bit to the raucous beat of the jukebox.

But otherwise, Peaches is quite unlike the other girls at Hamtramck High or other schools.

She has spent most of her life belting a tennis ball against that wall, then carrying her lessons onto the adjoining courts at Memorial Park or wherever there is competition to be had.

Such unwavering devotion to a game and purpose has left its mark.

A relaxed Peaches, taken away from the tennis courts, is not a young girl who caresses a telephone, gossiping of dates and boys and styles, or palling with friends in a sweet shop. Dates are few and social life is limited outside the tight little band of coach Jean Hoxie.

The result is predictable. Peaches, who has played before princes and queens and showed her great talent on the finest courts, is painfully shy and withdrawn, almost uncommunicative. The words come slowly and quietly, unsure, almost as if they had not been bounced off that wall often enough.

She is amazing, though. On a tennis court, or on that wall, no young girl speaks clearer, stronger, more dominantly than this latest protege of Mrs. Hoxie, who for 26 years had tutored the working man's sons and daughters in the art and manners of one of sport's most difficult and nicely-nicely games. Peaches does not remember exactly when she became aware of the wall, which stands only a lob away from her bedroom window.

Her father, John, a 51-year-old machinist, came to the United States from Germany with his wife, Eugenia, a Russian native, in 1948, and the next year Peaches was born. Three years later, the family landed on Berras Street.

"I must have been 5 or 6 when I first knew what the wall was about," Peaches said. "There were always kids playing tennis in the park, I remember that."

No kid so close by could possibly escape Mrs. Hoxie. She already had Billy Bartkowicz, now a 21-year-old junior at the University of Detroit, in tow, and Peaches was next.

Everyone begins on the wall. Whether 6 or 16, the daily regimen calls for novice and star to practice stroking a tennis ball to the wall, keeping it in motion without error.

From the beginning as a 7-year-old, Peaches was a natural. Five years later, after already having claimed a handful of juvenile championships, she set several wall records, which Mrs. Hoxie challenges the world to beat.

"It was 1,775 consecutive shots," said Peaches, a smile showing for the first time. "I could have gone on, I think, but it took almost an hour."

"Don't forget the volley record," Mrs. Hoxie said.

The volley record requires that the ball be kept in the air continually, from racket to wall, without touching the ground.

"That was 980 shots in a row," Peaches said.

There are no medals or trophies for wall performance, this being mere routine. But wall efficiency does reflect devotion and developing skill — and no championship ever was won without it.

The record shows clearly what the wall meant to Peaches. She won her first national championship when she was 11, won the U.S. title for 14-year-olds when she was 12, took the title for 16s when she was 13.

Always it has been a fight against girls more mature in years, if not in tennis.

"When a youngster can win against older players," Mrs. Hoxie said, "you know you have a champion. That's the way champions are made."

Except for California and the Deep South, most tennis players are shut out, idled, for a crucial four to five months a year by weather. This is not so for Peaches or the others in Mrs. Hoxie's gang.

On a chilly day in April, they began the outdoor season at Hamtramck. But the Hoxie troupe had labored winter-long on indoor courts arranged in gyms of Hamtramck schools. As a result, at first public showing, they are always in midseason form.

"I went a week once without tennis," Peaches said. A week once, in nine or so years.

"I was sorry I did. If you miss it that long, it takes a week-and-a-half to get back where you were."

Surely, though, the boredom must weigh heavy, tennis and the game, day after day, weeks and months and years endless, to play the game, labor through the routine.

"Oh, sure, sometimes it happens," Peaches confessed. "But it doesn't last that long. A day maybe.

"I'll take a day off. But then the next day I want to go out and play again."

In a way, it is puzzling what drives Peaches and her young counterparts on so relentlessly. At 16, they must have other games, other interests.

"Remember," Mrs. Hoxie said, "that what young people want most is an identity, to be somebody, to be important. Well, these kids get that.

"They play the best clubs; they meet the best people; they travel and see places they might not otherwise ever see."

And there is this, too:

"They know what has been done for others before them. We've had more than 100 kids from our tennis group go on through college on scholarships.

"Very few of their families could have afforded to send them to schools like Michigan, Michigan State, Notre Dame, Indiana. But this is one way for them to get there. I pound that into them."

Peaches Bartkowicz is neither the first nor the last of the Hoxie prodigies. Just before her, remember, there was June Stack, a powerful swinger who for years lived the same life thrust upon Peaches.

"I'm sorry I spent all that time at it," June said several years ago on the Eastern Michigan campus. "I mean, I never dated or did things like other girls do in all that time, not until I got to college and away from tennis."

June Stack has not been noticed in competition since.

That story was repeated to Peaches. It had no effect.

"Maybe by the time I get to college," she said, "my outlook will change, too."

"She has nice boys to hit tennis balls with," Mrs. Hoxie countered.

Peaches — they never call her Jane — is at the turning point of her career. She is 16, pushing into the last major bracket of junior play, and there are some girls here, in the 18-and-under bracket, she has never played or even seen.

The U.S. Lawn Tennis Association ranks her fifth, behind the likes of Mary Ann Eisel of St. Louis and California's Cathy Harden. The day is coming when these will have to be met.

Peaches will be thrust into the U.S. championships this summer at Forest Hills, N.Y., the citadel of American tennis. Mrs. Hoxie, following her never-too-young philosophy, is convinced Peaches is ready for it.

Before that, however, Peaches already will have had a taste of scrambling among the very best distaff players in the world.

At Wimbledon last summer, she drew wide recognition by conquering leading junior girl players from throughout the world. This June, Mrs. Hoxie will take her back to the island and send her after the women's championship.

Peaches herself thinks eventually she can go all the way to the top. An experience in Mexico City last February convinced her of it. She was matched against Australia's Margaret Smith, the best woman player in the world. She lost by scores of 4-6, 6-1, 6-3, but the method of the defeat showed her something.

"I think I can beat her," Peaches admitted.

If she can, that wall will stand as a memorial and a symbol for thousands of other hopeful young athletes. ✦

1 9 6 5

The greatest? Clay leaves little doubt

LEWISTON, Maine — True to his boasts, Cassius Clay, a young zealot who reigns by "divine right," achieved the almost unbelievable last night.

He knocked out Sonny Liston in just one minute of the first round of their long-awaited rematch, retaining his world heavyweight championship as cops and Black Muslims swarmed around the Central Maine Youth Center arena.

It could not happen, not quite this way. But it did — one of the fastest knockouts in the history of heavyweight title fights.

A short, darting right to the jaw, the only really solid blow of the fight, finished Liston.

He dropped to his knees, rolled over on his back, his arms stretched wide to his side.

Timekeeper Francis McDonough, on the opposite side of the ring, began to toll. But referee Jersey Joe Walcott, the former champion, did not hear it.

He tried to get an eager Clay into a neutral corner. He was still trying as McDonough struck 10.

Liston, stunned and obviously hurt, rose up on his left knee, then tumbled back to the canvas.

Even then, Walcott, Clay and Liston did not believe it was over.

Liston finally made it to his feet, and Clay came at him again, banging viciously with rights and lefts in a needless barrage.

McDonough finally caught the referee's attention, yelling that Liston had been counted out, and Walcott pulled the fighters apart, raising Clay's hand in victory salute.

The crowd of about 3,500, including nearly a thousand newsmen, was as stunned as Liston.

Clay, with both arms raised, marched around the ring, shouting, "I'm the greatest. Now do you believe?"

There was, in truth, no other choice.

The 23-year-old darling of the Black Muslims was swarmed over in the ring by his entourage, the Muslim's Fruit of Islam, here to guard him against a threatened assassination attempt.

More than 200 police ringed and infiltrated the arena on the lookout for vengeful followers of the late Malcolm X, murdered several months ago. Three Muslims have been charged in the crime, and Clay supposedly is living in danger of retribution.

No incidents were reported. The only gun revealed here was that flashing right hand of Clay, who earlier in the day preached that "this is my private, sacred day, a holy day."

For the few seconds the fight lasted, it seemed to be moving according to plan, Clay moving away from the power of Liston's left hand, Liston pursuing, striving to catch him.

The early seconds belonged to Clay, who at 206 spotted Liston 9½ pounds. He shot a long right to the head at the very outset, came back with another left to the head, all the while pulling away and out of danger.

Liston caught Clay then with a glancing right to the head and followed it with a long left hook.

Clay retaliated with a right cross to the head, then Liston, switching his attack to the body, threw three long rights that Clay caught on his ribs.

Then it happened. In a neutral corner — to the right of Liston's, the left of Clay's.

Liston tried a right to Clay's head. He missed. His momentum left him wide open, at Clay's mercy.

Cassius lashed out with that right, and down went Liston.

Timekeeper McDonough said later that his count actually had gone to 20 before Liston managed to regain his feet.

The showing of Liston, collapsing so ignominiously before the young champion, almost surely finishes him as a fighter of note.

His was a sorrier showing than that of Floyd Patterson, from whom he had won the crown in 1962 and defended it successfully in '63 — both with one-round knockouts.

It was sorrier, perhaps, than even his seventh-round loss of the title to Clay in Miami on Feb. 25, 1964, when he sat on his stool refusing to answer the bell.

For this one minute of activity, Liston and Clay each earned something like $650,000 from gross receipts, which probably will top $5 million. An estimated 600,000 poured into 258 U.S. theaters to witness the action via closed-circuit television to homes via the Early Bird satellite.

In the Youth Center itself, which holds merely 5,000, hundreds of seats were vacant. But cops were in every aisle, every exit, watching for any signs of trouble.

It never came. Clay left in triumph, as he solidly predicted he would. Liston left in despair, unbelieving what this young star had done to him.

Liston had been on the floor only once before in 37 fights. Marty Marshall of Detroit knocked him down in a fight in St. Louis in 1955. Liston got up to knock him out.

Before his first encounter with Clay, Liston had lost only one previous fight, that to Marshall on a decision at the old Arcadia in Detroit in 1954.

Clay's victory, his 21st straight and 17th knockout, stamped him finally as a man with a real knockout punch. Despite his record, no one had accepted him before as a knockout artist.

Now they must. ✦

1 9 6 5

Although Liston went down, fight was on the up-and-up

Our good Sen. Phil Hart is a grand and gracious fellow who always has seemed a touch above the muck-muck of politics, so it was astonishing to see him leap blindly into this latest mess of the boxing world.

He did jump blindly. Just as all the other pols who are screaming for an investigation of the Cassius Clay-Sonny Liston heavyweight fight the other night jumped blindly, with their mouths open.

The senator has a boxing bill awaiting action in Washington, and maybe it is a good bill, but he has done it a disservice by joining the false cries of fraud. His bill couldn't have changed this fight.

Boxing is always fair game for politicians and do-gooders and even the sports writers. It is a cruel and vicious sport, peopled by the worst elements in our society, and the voices heard in its defense are few because boxing is mostly a rotten game.

There have been plenty of opportunities in the past and more will be available in the future for lawmakers to whip up interest and a following to wipe out the sport or bring stiffer controls.

But not this time, baby. You picked the wrong time and wrong fight to make your pitch, Senator.

The world screams of fraud and fix in Liston's one-minute knockout. But the world had a better case working when Liston sat like a coward on his stool in Miami 15 months ago, or when Benny Paret was beaten to death on TV in 1962.

After months of waiting, we all expected to see something more than Clay and Liston provided. But the same was true of the two Liston-Floyd Patterson fights, which ended in one-round knockouts. They screamed fraud then, too.

What people who watch these fights must understand is that a $100 ringside ticket or a $6 theater seat does not guarantee an evening's entertainment.

All it actually buys is maybe 11 seconds — long enough for one man to land a punch and the other to be counted out.

Anything beyond is a bonus.

That might not be much, as it was with Clay and Liston and Liston and Patterson, three of the last four heavyweight title bouts — that two men will appear in the ring for at least 10 seconds.

To believe otherwise is to suggest that fights be required to last a specified period of time, that no knockouts be allowed before, say, the fifth round, after everybody has seen enough and is prepared for the kill.

It might not be a bad idea, at that. Sort of like the bullfights, where the matador teases and parades and only when the crowd is aroused and satisfied does he dare dispose of the bull.

While we're at it, we might as well fix up a few other sports. Nobody will be allowed henceforth to score six runs in the first inning and finish off the Tigers so early; no horse can be left at the post; no wrecks will be permitted on the first lap at Indianapolis.

I mean, we've got to get a run for our money before the decision is rendered, don't we?

No, Senator, the intent of Clay and Liston the other night was to take each other out at the first opportunity, and that opportunity just happened to come too soon, long before we had seen enough. But that's the game, isn't it?

A flood of ridiculous comments has come out of this fight, and there's an explanation for it. Many ringsiders did not see the right hand that dropped Liston.

But many others did. Section B, ringside, to the right of Clay's corner, had a clear view of the blow, almost in profile.

On the opposite side of the ring, others either missed the blow entirely or, their vision obscured by Clay's turning shoulders, saw it only partially.

The television picture more often than not is unreliable. Once here we tried covering the weekly fights via television, but gave it up because they did not jibe with the on-the-scene reports.

A man or camera can be at only one angle at the knockout instant, and the camera was unlucky this time.

Was Liston hit with a really hard blow? Well, who knows, except Liston? He was down almost long enough to be counted out twice and he was wobbling when he finally arose.

Perhaps the TV cowboys can take a dozen haymakers and come back strong. But if you've ever hit or been hit, you know it doesn't happen that way.

The rest of it, of course, was ludicrous. Jersey Joe Walcott, the referee, was futile, unable to handle Clay, unable to pick up the count, and it was this bit that turned the fight into a fiasco. A more experienced man was needed.

Sen. Hart and his colleagues are calling for a full investigation, but an investigation of what?

If Liston went in the tank, what had he to gain? His knockout cost him at least $1 million in future earnings; it cost the promoters perhaps 20 times as much.

But stick around, Senator. There'll be another fight someday, and the chances are reasonably good that you'll have cause for an investigation. Not this time. ✦

1966

When Campbell roared, Tigers knew who was boss

I t was spring in Lakeland, Fla., and trouble was ahead. Superstar had not signed his contract; he was not going to sign it, either, unless more money was forthcoming.

For five days Superstar, no favorite among his teammates, held out, becoming increasingly embittered, until finally he yielded in anger, accepting his old salary.

"I'll never talk to that —— again," Superstar announced.

He didn't. But at the end of the 1963 season, Rocky Colavito, darling of the dolls, the town's biggest home run hitter in nearly two decades, was shipped away.

Jim Campbell became boss of the Tigers with that move.

He had, in fact, been general manager of the baseball club for nearly two years, though much of the time he seemed merely another in succession of seven such men who in an 11-year period attempted somewhat feebly and indecisively to lift the Tigers from the mire.

"There was no bitterness," Campbell insists. "Rocky had some valid points, and I had some."

"Ho boy," says another in the Tigers organization. "If Campbell hadn't handled Rocky then, he would have lost all control here. The team was split and in serious trouble. Campbell showed everybody who's really boss around here."

There's no question that Jim Campbell, a man groomed, if not born, to his job, is the one most important man — more than Al Kaline or manager Charlie Dressen — in the Tigers organization.

In a sense he shows the world two faces.

Within the stadium confines he is a tough, exacting administrator, as the Colavito case reveals. To the front office at the ballpark he lends an air of crisp organization and efficiency.

To the outsiders who know him, however, Campbell comes across quite differently — a quiet, shy, almost colorless sort.

The smiles come across readily enough, splitting a wide face and creasing a forehead that reaches back beyond his ears. But in a crowd, Jim Campbell is mostly just another guy.

This is a town that can blow its smokestacks, if properly encouraged, about baseball and the Tigers. In such a town, Campbell, married but childless, is Nut No. 1 each day of the season.

Beginning in April and ending in October, he dies 162 times with the

Tigers. He will perch in the press box, staring blankly at the playing field below, unmoving, as if transfixed, inning after inning.

Press box strangers wonder occasionally whether Campbell has just lost his job or is mourning the departure of a dear friend. Too often that's true, as when the Tigers lose.

When that happens, the mourning becomes almost fitful, tying the general manager in such knots that he cannot eat. Some suspect that a nine-game losing streak several years ago really led to that diet that stripped 25-odd pounds off his frame.

At 41, Campbell is one of the youngest men in a major job in sports, and for it the Tigers pay him something like $40,000.

Some would knock Campbell for a lack of background in one essential baseball phase, that of judging player talent.

He admits to no basic ignorance there, referring to his early Tigers years as farm club director. But it is typical of him that he prefers to rely on his experts — the scouts — for judgment.

"I was grateful that my bosses gave me opportunities and responsibilities," he explains, "and that's what I like to do with my people here."

Campbell is not without a competitive past. Short and stocky, he was a footballer at Ohio State in the late 1940s, went on to the Navy and emerged in 1949 looking for a future.

"I had always been a sports nut — football, baseball, track, anything," he says. "I knew I was too old to think of playing anymore, but I wanted to stay in sports."

A friend put him in touch with Billy Evans, then general manager of the Tigers. Evans gave him a job as business manager of the Tigers' Class D farm club at Thomasville, Ga., in 1949. Campbell then was merely 25.

His team's first game was nearly its last. The ballpark burned down.

"I got a phone call about 4 in the morning," he recalls. "I looked out the window and it seemed the whole town was burning. Everything went — the players' uniforms, their clothing, all the equipment."

Surely, there must have been a temptation to re-enlist in the Navy.

"No, the team went on the road with borrowed uniforms," Campbell says. "We bulldozed away the debris and strung ropes along the field, putting fans on an honor system to buy tickets. They were great about it."

From then on, Campbell's future with the Tigers was assured.

Though he rose and prospered with each change, Campbell is convinced that the constant top-level shifts caused the club to flounder through the decade.

"We had five different ownership set-ups in that time," he says.

The club also had six general managers, seven field managers, with two more following into the 1960s.

In 1962, John Fetzer, having gained full ownership of the team, named Campbell, then 38, as the new general manager. The command was to bring a settled and efficient state to the Tigers' house.

Campbell has done that. Essentially a business-type executive, he runs the ballclub as a business, requiring regular and detailed reports from each of a half-dozen departments.

The Colavito episode was an early and serious threat to Campbell in his new job. Rocky had become a tail wagging the dog; the Tigers' clubhouse was split into factions.

To quell the factions, Campbell was determined to hold Colavito's salary in line the following spring. Though he finally signed a contract, Colavito was not content.

Bob Scheffing, then the Tigers' manager, was reluctant to take up the front-office's battle with the star outfielder or "step on" the players.

For that — as some tell it — Scheffing was ousted in June 1963, and in came Charlie Dressen.

Like all the others before him, Campbell recognizes the necessity of producing a winning club. This year the Tigers embark on the 21st season since their last American League pennant. The town no longer is impatient; it's angry and derisive.

Old fans accustomed to losing Tigers teams scoff at the faint suggestions that it somehow might win. Pessimism runs so deep that the Tigers are booed on Opening Day.

Campbell offers more than a suggestion that the Tigers will improve. He offers a promise.

"We have the potential to win the pennant," he insists.

He pauses then to look the startled listener in the eye.

"If not this year, soon," he continued. "We have a good, young developing club. We're moving.

"The American League is better — better balance all around. Five, maybe six teams could win the pennant this year. Look at Minnesota.

"The Twins were picked for seventh and eighth place last year and they won it. They did it because their players all came up with a good year together. That's the secret. To have everybody moving at the same time. You've got to have that; I think we can do it." ✦

1967

Tigers fall one game short on final day of the season

D etroit's long wait for an American League pennant drags on for another year. The tightest, most stirring championship fight in baseball history ended yesterday with the Tigers sitting numb and in tears in the clubhouse at Tiger Stadium. They could not manage one last, vital victory, and so the team that had lived for weeks, wastefully at times and usually on the brink of disaster, finally succumbed.

California's Angels ruined them, 8-5, in the season's final hour, after the Tigers had fought them off, 6-4, in the opener of a televised doubleheader that gripped the nation.

With that final Detroit defeat, the Boston Red Sox, who three hours earlier had whipped Minnesota , 5-3, became the American League champions.

In staid old Boston, Red Sox worshipers erupted in wild celebration. Thousands flooded downtown streets, hotels and bars on the most joyous fling the city has seen since the end of World War II.

In contrast, it was a silent, somber crowd of 38,398, that filed out of Tiger Stadium in keen disappointment over the Tigers' narrow miss.

"My boys are champions in my book," said Tigers manager Mayo Smith, fighting off tears. "They went down battling to the end."

Boston, a ninth-place team a year ago, was a 100-to-1 shot in the 1967 pennant race. The title was the Red Sox's first since 1946.

The Tigers slipped to a final second-place tie with Minnesota. Their last pennant came in 1945.

In the end, pitching inconsistency crushed the Tigers' hopes — pitching failure and the heavy hitting of the Angels.

After Joe Sparma and Fred Gladding had set down the Angels in the opener, Smith turned to Denny McLain in the decisive nightcap.

McLain, shelled five times this month, idled by a foot injury the last two weeks, could not handle the Angels. A 3-1 lead built on a two-run homer by Jim Northrup was wasted. Seven other pitchers followed McLain in Smith's frantic juggling to contain the Angels while trying to mount a Detroit attack.

They gave it a good shot in the fading moments. In the seventh inning, with the crowd roaring on every pitch, Dick McAuliffe singled home two runs, pulling Detroit within three of the Angels.

They had one last chance in the ninth inning, after putting two men aboard with none out. But the final stroke came from McAuliffe, who grounded into a double play — something he had not done all year long — ending the season. ✦

THE '70s

It's a happy homecoming for Magic Johnson and his Spartans teammates following their 75-64 victory over Indiana State in the 1979 NCAA basketball final.

1 9 7 0

Powerful men met their match in Jean Hoxie

J

ean Hoxie is dead. A thousand men who thought they were her one special man mourn.

She was the most loved woman this town had ever seen in her time.

She was short and stout with a face weathered by 71 years of summer sun. She had a voice loud and gravelly and a manner brash and demanding.

She was beautiful.

She had nestled in her palm men such as Bill Ford, George Romney, Ralph McIlvenny and Soapy Williams, and countless others who reacted to her whim.

You had to wonder why.

She was frequently outrageous. She would stroll noisily into the sports department here, plant a kiss on my cheek, announce that her tennis kids were upstairs getting their picture taken.

"I'm leaving for South America in two days," she would say, "so make sure the picture is in the paper tonight. I want to take the clipping with me."

She got away with it. Invariably.

She was an out-and-out tennis huckster. No game has known a better one. She taught her game, preached it, sold it.

But she was something more.

She was Old World discipline with a hard-as-a-hammer exterior and a marshmallow heart.

That's why the guys loved her. The girls, many of them, were not always so sure.

Memorial Park in Hamtramck sits alongside Jos. Campau in an area that once was rat-a-tat-tat and booze and broads. It was that way when Jean arrived in the 1930s.

Occasionally, she'd tell about it.

"There's nothing fancy about this neighborhood now," she would say. "But in those days, it was much worse. Kids were hungry and aimless and so were their parents.

"It all seems so simple now. But remember, in those days and in that area, kids were embarrassed to be seen with a tennis racket in their hands.

"I won them over by collaring the gang leaders and forcing them to play against my kids. When they saw how futile they were, they'd lay off. Some of them even joined us. They know who they are."

Over the years, the Hoxie Hamtramck tennis crew won more than 100

All the sting of the Lions' comeback dissipated, and the Lions went down to a 28-23 defeat as the ambulance wailed in the distance.

Lyall Smith, Lions public relations director, kept outsiders posted.

"It looks very, very bad," he said. "The players and coaches are inside, praying."

Long minutes passed. Smith returned several times with word from the hospital. Finally he returned again, speaking haltingly with tears in his eyes.

"The news is the worst," he said.

Thompson later emerged from the locker room.

"His heart had stopped on the field," Thompson said, "but we were able to get some brief signs of it before we left for the hospital."

Thompson said it was not possible immediately to know the cause of death. Asked whether it could have resulted from a blow, such as on the tackle three plays before his collapse, Thompson replied: "It's possible.

"At the moment, though, we don't know whether it was a heart attack, a brain hemorrhage or rupture of a major artery. This is the first time I've ever experienced anything like this on the field of play, and it is a shock."

Shortly, the Lions assistant coaches emerged, heads bowed, walking briskly through a waiting crowd of reporters and a gathering of players' wives and friends standing on the corridor outside the locker room.

Minutes later, they were followed by Lions owner William Clay Ford and general manager Russ Thomas. Both were clearly shaken by the tragedy.

"What can you say about a thing like this," said Ford in a halting voice. "It's unbelievable."

✦ ✦ ✦ ✦ ✦

Chuck Hughes died of an acute heart seizure, an autopsy determined the next day. The examination indicated that Hughes died from a heart attack, which stemmed from the clogging of an artery by blood clots.

The official cause of death was "arteriosclerotic coronary artery disease with acute coronary thrombotic occlusion."

Drs. Edwin Guise and Richard A. Thompson, Lions team physicians, explained at a news conference the cause of death.

"He had a hardening of the main artery supplying blood to the heart," Thompson said. "A clot had formed in this artery, shutting off the flow of blood." Hardening of the arteries is unusual in a young person, although not uncommon beyond the age of 50.

Thompson, who attended Hughes on the field following his collapse, said the player was "unresponsive from the moment we got out there except for trying to get a breath."

"One dies officially when one is pronounced dead," Guise said, "but in my heart I feel Chuck died on the field."

Guise said the death stemmed from "a degenerative disease of the arteries that was coming on for years. There's no way to detect this.... I know it will be of concern to parents and other football players, but this was an old man's disease in a young man's body." ✦

1 9 7 1

After taking shots from Layne, Karras finally gave one back

(By Alex Karras as told to George Puscas.)

On my first day of practice with the Lions, after having played against them and insulted them personally in the 1958 All-Star Game, I was scared to death.

I had reason to be, and I was right to feel that way because they got on me right away.

"Listen, you punk rookie … " one guy would say.

And they would hammer me.

"You wise-guy rookie creep … " another would say.

And they hammered some more.

I just kept my mouth shut, which proves how scared I was, I guess.

They had me shining their shoes, fetching towels, running all kinds of errands for them.

It was the sort of hazing common for rookies in those days, and it wasn't all bad. It took the starch out of some fancy All-America kids.

Most guys go along with it. But Hopalong Cassady never did in his rookie year, I'm told, and it took Hoppy a few years to really win his way among the guys.

I must have sung the Iowa fight song 60 times a day — on top of counters, tables, in the bathroom, whenever anyone thought I ought to be singing it.

Then Bobby Layne got hold of me. He said, "Listen, rookie, you think you're hot stuff. You're nothing but a rookie who don't know enathang."

I said, "Yes, sir, Mr. Layne."

"From now on, you just follow me around like a puppy; you understand, you're my puppy."

I said, "Yes, sir."

He liked me from the start. He started calling me Puppy, and then he changed it to Tippy; that's how I got the name "Tippy Toes."

So I used to chauffeur him around. I was scared to death of him.

Following the afternoon practices in that 1958 summer, he used to holler out in that harsh Texas drawl, "Tippy, Tippy, let's go get some Cutty."

And I'd drive him in his old Pontiac to a place called the Bar-B-Que, which later burned down, or to the Town and Country in Pontiac, and he'd drink six, seven Cuttys, mostly on the rocks.

I'd take him back to camp and we'd eat the evening meal, and we'd go out again and have six more Cuttys, then back to camp for the evening meeting.

The worst thing was, he made me drink the Cutty. I never drank Scotch in my life. I was just a beer drinker. Three drinks of Scotch and I'm drunk.

This went on, day after day after day, so that I'm getting really worried. I'm drunk all the time.

He'd come out of his evening meeting and he'd holler through the dorm, "Tip … py! Tippy! Let's get going downtown!"

I'd hear him and I'd just say to myself, "Jesus, oh, God, I can't take it anymore," and I'd hide under my bed, but I was always scared, and I'd be out from under there by the time he showed up in my room.

At night, we'd hit about six places. One was a black and tan on John R called the Flame, and when we'd walk in they'd holler out: "Mr. Layne's here, Mr. Layne is in here," and the people would go crazy. Mr. Layne and his flunky.

I'd go over and get his table for him and say, "OK, Mr. Layne, sit down right here, sir," and he'd sit down and say, "All right, let's have a ball. Let's have a ball!"

Then he'd take those knockers like they have at nightclubs and he'd sit there banging on the table, tossing off one Cutty after another. Twenty was an easy night for him.

The band would be ready to take a break and he'd holler out, "Keep on playing," and they'd say, "But, Mr. Layne, we're tired."

So he'd get up and throw a $100 bill in a horn and say keep on playing, and they'd say yes, sir, and they'd play on and on and we'd sit there and drink and get drunk and sick.

I'd have the booze lined up in front of me and I'd ditch it on the floor because I just couldn't take it anymore, and we'd do that till 4, 5 in the morning.

He'd say something like, "Well, we've got two more weeks to the opener. That's when Layne's gonna shine." And I'd say, "Yessir, Mr. Layne, that's what you're gonna do."

He used to tell me, "I don't like the dark. I'm scared of the dark. I don't want to go to sleep."

I heard a story about him once. I don't know whether it's factual, that when he was about 7, he was riding down a Texas highway with his father and the car rolled over and his father was killed. They weren't found for two days. If that's so, I can imagine why the dark terrified him.

Of all the guys I met in football, Layne and George Wilson were the guys I'd most like to copy; Layne because he was a free soul who thrived on the competition of football but enjoyed life away from it, and Wilson because he was just tremendous with people, a really fine man.

There were many nights when Layne and I'd get so darned sick I couldn't drive, and he'd drive back to training camp.

One night we're going back and he's really happy. He's driving and singing "Ida Red." That was always his favorite song, and he'd sing it over and over again, the same two or three phrases. "Ida Red… ."

In my stupor I looked up and saw him, and he had his right foot up on the dashboard and something jammed in the accelerator, I don't know what it was, and the other foot straddled out the window, the damnedest sight I ever saw.

I checked the speedometer and we're going 100 down the expressway, and the car was shaking apart and he's singing "Ida Red, Ida Red," and I got down on my knees and absolutely begged him to stop the car; I begged him to stop and he wouldn't.

This sort of thing would go on every night. He never required sleep. It'd be daylight when we rolled into camp, and while I'd try to sneak in an hour's sleep, he'd be in the shower, still singing.

When he hit the practice field, it was just unbelievable. He perked up like a robot. I couldn't understand it because I was always so sick, throwing up all the time.

I don't know why they kept me my rookie year except maybe George Wilson liked the idea that I was one of the guys. Really, I stank the place out, mainly because I was learning, but also because I was sick all the time.

Layne threw some big parties, win or lose. He'd get the whole team together and somebody would have a guitar and Buster Ramsey would sing and Wilson would sing "Cut down the old pine tree," his favorite.

We just had a ball, drinking and singing. There was never a team so close-knit.

I didn't play much in the early exhibition season, but then I caught on a little bit and played against the Bears in Dallas. I'll never forget it. It was the first and last time the Lions and Bears played each other in an exhibition.

Jimmy David got all his teeth in the front knocked out; somebody dislocated an elbow; David broke Harlon Hill's jaw; then the Bears had a fumble and some poor kid picked up the ball and Gil Mains hit him from behind and completely compounded his ankle, just twisted it all around.

It was the fiercest game I've ever played in. Eleven guys were hurt and many of them were out for weeks after, and the Bears' PR guy died on the plane home.

That was a real eye-opener for me as far as what pro football is all about. It really scared me, and I said, well, one year, then I'll quit.

There were stories about Layne acting different that summer, not really hanging with the guys, but as a rookie, not having been there before, I paid no attention.

Frankly, I'm worried about my health now. This guy has got me so drunk all the time. I'm worried about making the club, too.

I wasn't aware that the coaches were unhappy with Layne. When he got on a football field, it was his field, and there's never been anybody like him in my time.

He'd get up and say in practice to the coaches: "Instead of a post pattern heah, y'all tell that end to break it off about two more yards, then bring it down."

Or he'd say, "George, tell that boy over theah when he takes that outside, take it about fahv more deep."

And the coaches would; they'd go along with him because they understood that nobody knew quarterbacking like Layne.

The great thing about him was that he could break down a rival team, dissect it, in three quarters. They said he was a great two-minute man, but the reason was that he knew where he could go to get his points when he absolutely had to.

Often he would throw to one side or the other with short passes, not really caring whether he completed the pass or not, just to see the defensive reaction.

That's why he looked so bad at times. And then when he needed, he knew just where to strike.

We were 3-2 in the exhibition season and played a decent opener against Baltimore but lost it when Layne scuffed the pitcher's mound on a field goal. The next week we tied Green Bay in a lousy game, and the next day he's gone, traded to Pittsburgh.

A lot of things have been said about his trade, that he had been gambling on the games and the Lions either had to get him out of town or he'd be put in jail.

I don't know what happened and I don't even want to go into it, but it was probably the biggest shock I've ever seen a team go through.

At the time, Layne to me was sort of a pacifier, my blanket. When things went wrong, I'd say, well, Bob will take care of it. The whole club felt that way about him.

The club never got over it that year. We were defending champions, but we finished 4-7-1.

I never saw or heard anything from Layne until two years later, when we're playing Pittsburgh in an exhibition game.

On the field, he said, "Hi ya, Tippy."

And then later in the game we were chasing him and I clobbered him on the sideline after the play was over. I really clobbered him. I don't know why I did it.

He liked that. I liked him. ✦

1971

Lions, Karras haunted by what might have been

(By Alex Karras as told to George Puscas.)

Once in a lifetime, maybe, if you're lucky, if the wind blows right and the tide comes in when it should, you happen to come across a guy like George Wilson.

What a beautiful man. A simply tremendous person.

He could bull with the best of 'em and he could be as mean and tough in his talk or as mean and rotten physically, from what I'm told, as any man who ever walked.

But he had this simply great feeling for people, for ballplayers, for anybody he happened to like and even with people he didn't particularly like. He made everybody feel good.

Maybe only once in a lifetime do you come across a guy like him, only once maybe, because I've never met anybody quite like him. I'd like to be like him and I'd think anybody would. But I'm not.

For most of my years with the Lions, Wilson was our coach, and I don't think he was all that great as far as making X's and O's on the board and technical football stuff.

He knew the game thoroughly, though, as far as understanding player reactions, because he played it beautifully with the Bears — tough, mean, shrewd, emotionally.

George, I think, lived by his feelings and emotions, and it was contagious because he got you that way, too, and you'd swing with him, go all the way with him.

He gave the Lions the best years they've had in the last 15 years or so, in my time, anyway.

Wilson had been an assistant coach with the Lions and took them over in 1957 when Buddy Parker walked out, and he coaxed the team to another championship that year.

I showed up the following season, when George for some reason or other — that would be interesting if somebody directly connected would ever say why — traded away Bobby Layne.

We went downhill in 1958 and 1959, the first year because the Layne trade shattered the team, and later because the team was aging and Wilson was rebuilding.

I shouldn't say "we" because the first couple of years with a team you don't really feel you're that much a part of it. When you're that new and struggling to survive, you have no idea, no thought, about what the front office is doing, the pressure on the coach to win or anything like that.

It wasn't until long afterward that I realized George Wilson almost got fired in those years. That's how it is with young players, they just don't relate to the outside.

Anyway, in the winter and summer preceding the 1959 season, Wilson brought in new guys such as Dick (Night Train) Lane, Carl Brettschneider and Sam Williams.

Our draft began paying off, too. I had some experience, so had Wayne Walker. And Dick LeBeau, Roger Brown, Gail Cogdill and a few more came along, and Terry Barr was converted to flanker and Nick Pietrosante and Pat Studstill joined us.

That 1959 season was a turning point for me and for the whole team, and I think it all happened in one game, about the third game of the season.

It's odd. I don't even remember whether we won or lost. It doesn't matter.

The point is, from that time on, I was going to be a good pro.

You know how it is? All of a sudden your confidence swells and you know no matter what comes around, you'll handle it.

It's a great feeling when it comes, and you can spot people who've had it happen because they've got a bounce about them like they've got the world hanging at the end of a yo-yo string.

What happened is, Johnny Unitas went back to pass and I wrestled away from the outside and went almost parallel along the line, and he took off running and was almost in for a touchdown, and I knocked him down and we took the ball.

That's all there was to it. Just that. Maybe it sounds silly, but I'll bet that anybody who's good at anything has had something like that happen, one moment, one accomplishment, that just lights the whole way for them.

As it turned out, the next three years were successful years, the best for long years to come. But they were the years that haunt the Lions to this day.

With a break here or there, a little bit more, any kind of luck at all, we could have won championships all three years.

Instead, Vince Lombardi was winning the titles at Green Bay and we were finishing second, three straight years of frustration.

Turn it the other way around and the world wouldn't even know Vince Lombardi existed.

It's pointless to recount the games and those years except for a couple of incidents that illustrate the peaks and valleys of football life.

I don't think there's been a wilder finish to a game than the one when we beat Baltimore, 20-15, in 1960.

We're leading with only 13 seconds left and Unitas throws his pass down the right sideline, and Lenny Moore skids 10 yards on his belly into the end zone with Night Train Lane riding his back like a toboggan and catches the ball, and Baltimore goes ahead, 15-13.

Those people in that town are nuts anyway, but they go absolutely berserk. They're all over the bench, screaming, yelling, climbing over our bench, and that jackass cheerleader of theirs is riding his horse like crazy all over the field.

Our bench is just stunned. We can't believe what happened, and so many thousands are on the field we can't tell what's going on.

All of a sudden, two strangers grab me and this one guy pulls a knife. I had my helmet off, and I hit his hand and knocked the knife loose and then started chasing the other guy.

We're going 'round and 'round in circles, dodging around George Wilson and other guys, and I'm chasing him like an idiot when Jim Gibbons takes that pass from Earl Morrall and goes 65 yards, and we win on the last play, 20-15.

I never saw the play. The first thing I know is that place is quiet like a graveyard except for our team and our guys who are simply out of their minds.

There was never a darker moment than the 9-7 loss to Green Bay in 1962.

No single loss ever cost a team so much. It cost us the championship, and there was absolutely no reason for that to happen. The bitterness that set in later cost us our quarterback, tore the team apart and eventually cost George Wilson his job.

We were ready. Lord, were we ready for Green Bay that day! We all felt the Packers were wearing championship rings that should have been ours, and we tore them apart.

I mean, they go 58 minutes and they can't pass or run or do anything against us, and the best they get is two field goals, and with 90 seconds left we're ahead, 7-6.

We've got the ball on about their 45 and it's third-and-seven, and all we need is to run one more play and let Yale Lary kick it into the end zone and we're home free.

I remember Joe Schmidt and I are standing on the sidelines together congratulating ourselves when we look up and see Milt Plum back to pass, and we said: "My God, he hasn't passed all day, why do that now?"

And he throws the ball and Terry Barr slips and Herb Adderley intercepts, and three plays later Paul Hornung kicks a field goal and we lose, 9-7.

I was absolutely violent. Joe Schmidt was absolutely violent. The whole defensive team was absolutely violent.

We hit the locker room and everybody is asking: "Who in hell called that play?" And nobody would answer.

Joe Schmidt started yelling and screaming at Milt Plum, asking who called the play, and Milt says: "None of your business" or something like that, and when he said that, I just went completely mad. I threw my helmet at his head and missed him by maybe two inches, and guys are cursing him and spitting at his feet and I am so mad, the maddest I've ever been, I could have killed someone.

Finally, I backed off. Milt said nothing. He was just petrified.

Later, Wilson took blame for having called the play and later Aldo Forte, the offensive coach, said he called it.

Well, OK. But that was typical of Milt's attitude. Here the defense is, busting its can for years and the best he can give us is, "It's none of your business."

Whoever called that play had to be the biggest, dumbest jackass imaginable. It really brought the team down so that the idea with everybody was that we can just never win a championship; a coach or some player or some bad luck or some sheer stupidity will blow it all for us. A hopeless situation.

On the plane home, guys were still crying, the coaches were crying and it was such a bad scene that even a couple of the newspaper guys who are usually like pallbearers with us are trying to cheer us up.

Later that season, on Thanksgiving Day, we sacked Bart Starr, actually beat the breath out of him. There are some classic pictures of our front four and the linebackers smothering Starr that day, and we whipped Green Bay.

But sure as hell, they won the championship again. ✦

1 9 7 2

Walking tall,
the Bill Mihalo way

I always used to say that everybody has a bit of the Bill Mihalo Syndrome buried somewhere within, and with any luck at all, it would remain buried.

I stopped saying that because everybody forgot who Bill Mihalo was, if they ever knew. But here comes Jim Ryun, and it is clear to me that what troubles Jim Ryun is the Mihalo Syndrome.

If you've been around here any time at all, you will remember Bill Mihalo as a Detroit milkman back in the late 1930s and through the war years.

More than a milkman, he was a competitive walker, almost the only one in the Midwest.

He would walk against runners, three times around Belle Isle, and he would beat them.

He'd have exhibition walks any given morning. He'd walk from City Hall to Eight Mile Road and back before most guys were finishing the morning coffee break at the office.

I remember Claude Snarey at Cooley High threatening to break the legs of Bill Mihalo's milk horse if Mihalo did not stay away from his cross-country team. Mihalo wanted to make walkers of them all, so devoted to his sport was he.

Bill Mihalo would walk around Belle Isle faster than any man before or since, and it was a tragedy that the war canceled the 1940 and 1944 Olympic Games because, surely, Mihalo would have been there.

Middle age was creeping up on him when it became clear we would have the 1948 Games in London. In the few years leading up to those Games, Mihalo cast aside all else to prepare himself for the once-in-a-lifetime walk.

He walked miles. Hundreds of miles. Thousands. Against anyone, anywhere. And he was ready when the final trials for the 1948 U.S. Olympic walking team came along.

He hitched a ride down to Cincinnati where the trials were being held, and he was a favorite to become the star of the team.

Off they went down the highway, 150 or so walkers seeking the three positions available on the team. At the head of them was Bill Mihalo.

He stayed there, for the first mile, the second, the third, and his lead grew so extravagantly that soon the rest of the field was out of sight and Mihalo was walking alone.

Along the highway came a motorist. A careless, unthinking motorist. He hit Bill Mihalo, knocked him heel and toe into a ditch and fractured his swinging hips.

Bill Mihalo walked no more that summer. Gone were the Olympic Games and a lifetime dream.

So, to me, that's what troubles Jim Ryun. The Mihalo Syndrome, the little black cloud that floats overhead.

When Jim Ryun, who has run the mile and the 1,500 meters faster than any other man alive, trips and falls while running next-to-last in a race and does not even finish a qualifying race in the big Games, what else can you say, except that it just was not meant to be.

Onward and upward, Jim Ryun.

Bill Mihalo? Oh, he turned professional. A professional walker. And then he moved to California, where they appreciate that sort of thing. ✦

1 9 7 3

Don Shula's super success began on Lions' sidelines

R ight from the beginning, almost everyone knew that Don Shula one day would become a great football coach. Just ask any one of us.

Today he is that, and it is most unfortunate that he is doing his thing for somebody else.

Today Don Shula is just about as big as coaching talents ever get. He is a threat to the Lombardi legend, for one, and the hottest non-playing property in all of sports.

Winning the Super Bowl with the unbeaten Miami Dolphins — and winning more games in 10 years than any other coach ever — has done that.

He is so hot that colleges call, asking him to make their commencement address.

He is so hot, or so it is said, that he commands something like $4,000 for one simple guest speaking engagement. He makes more in a week of speaking than the Lions paid him for an entire season of assistant coaching back in 1960-63.

Well, he's not going to get anything like that at all Monday night.

Shula will be in Detroit as the guest speaker at the annual Michigan Sports Hall of Fame dinner at Cobo Hall.

This is the night the late Olympian Lorenzo Wright, former Michigan State football great Johnny Pingel and basketball pioneer Cincy Sachs are hailed for their achievements.

Shula is coming back, at far less than the going price, I'm told, because this is where it all began for him. Many memories, many friends.

I mentioned that everybody knew Shula someday would become a very fine head coach in pro football. There's no jest in that, really.

Edwin J. Anderson, who was general manager of the Lions then, mentioned several times in those days that here was a young guy who would do it all someday. Shula then was a mere 31. The skids had not yet been greased under George Wilson, so in 1963 Shula went to Baltimore and at age 33 became the youngest head coach in pro football.

I don't know what it was that Anderson saw in Shula, but Ben Dunn, who was covering the Lions for the Detroit News, and I had our own ideas.

We used to play catch on the sidelines with the young assistant while Alex Karras, Joe Schmidt and the guys of that period did their practice calisthenics.

One day, in exasperation, I guess, Shula said: "Is there something strange about all newspaper people, or just you guys? You both have trouble seeing the ball over your left shoulder."

To this day I remain impressed. Even I didn't know at the time that Ben had a glass eye, and that my own left eye soon was to be covered with glasses.

Shula moved on shortly to become head coach at Baltimore (where Lions coach Don McCafferty held on as one of his assistant coaches). It was there that he got the stamp as the new young genius, although with Ben and me he remained "boy coach."

One of the finest coaching jobs I've seen in any sport was his work preparing Baltimore for the 1965 championship game against Green Bay after injuries had sidelined quarterbacks Johnny Unitas and Earl Morrall.

Without a quarterback, in one week's time, he converted Tom Matte, a heady halfback, into his signal-caller. Except for a bad reading on a sudden-death Packers field goal kick, he would have won the title that year, I'm sure.

Matte's play that day surprised everyone, but I've always thought that Matte was simply being what Don Shula might have been — a star quarterback.

In his days as a defensive halfback at Baltimore, Shula was the backup quarterback to Unitas. But he never really got the chance to throw until he came across a pair of sports writers who had trouble catching over the left shoulder.

Since taking over at Miami three years ago — replacing old favorite George Wilson — the world has opened full bloom for the onetime boy coach.

He has been to the Super Bowl twice in that time, and the last trip culminated in an unprecedented all-winning season and the world championship.

He has been on the cover of the big magazines, his face is regularly on network TV, and when I look back I have to admit that it was about the time he left here that everything started falling apart for the Lions. ✦

1 9 7 3

Wings won't have Gordie
to kick around anymore

G ordie Howe, Detroit's finest athlete in a quarter-century and more, has
fled.

Gone to Houston. To another town and clime, to a new life and a
reborn hockey career.

Gone to the money, too.

A million bucks, plus or minus a bit, with some for Gordie, some for
wife Colleen and, not incidentally, still another bundle for budding stars Mark
and Marty Howe, his young sons.

The public figures are $1.8 million for the Howe family to play and serve
the good game of hockey for the Houston Aeros of the World Hockey
Association during the next four years.

Gordie's switch to the fledging WHA was far from unexpected. His sons
had signed contracts two weeks ago and his own commitment awaited only
legal details.

Then at noon yesterday under a huge battery of cameras and lights at a
downtown Houston hotel, it became final.

"You'd thank the first man from the moon was finally landin' here," came a
strange voice over the phone. "Everybody's heah for this."

In Houston, at least, they knew what they had in hand.

Who would blame Gordie Howe for pulling up stakes, forsaking all that
came before, and moving on at age 45 to start anew?

Good luck, No. 9.

Still and all, it hurts. It hurts to lose a man who has graced the arena for
so long, played his game with such magnificent skill and carried himself with
such honest humility. Too few remain.

Charlie Gehringer is still in our midst. Joe Louis pays us regular visits.
Even Bobby Layne comes back once in a while. These are names and faces
that enlivened and enriched the town in the good years.

Gordie Howe is as big as any of them, more familiar than all, and his
departure is a matter of strange and twisted circumstance.

It would not have happened without creation of the WHA, a new league
struggling for a place in the sun. Openly the Aeros intend to use the Howe
name and reputation and what skills remain for pure profit.

"They were willing to pay what I felt I had to have," Gordie said, "and my
name and reputation are a part of me."

It would not have happened without the bitterness that enveloped Howe's
two retirement years in a meaningless job with the Red Wings and Olympia,

a bitter discontent that swelled in recent months.

"I talked to Ned Harkness just the other day," Howe said of the Red Wings' general manager, "and he said he wished he'd known my feelings. He would have given up as GM and been my assistant. At least that's what he said.

"I simply told Ned that I didn't see eye-to-eye with his thinking. That's no great crime, but I wasn't contributing much there or learning much, and then the feeling grew that there were a few people who didn't really want me there.

"So, well, I can't be a hypocrite, so the thing to do, I thought, was to get the hell out. So here I am."

Nor would it ever have happened if the Houston Aeros had been unwilling to sign both of the Howe youngsters, too.

"That's very important to me, to be able to play with them," Gordie said. After his signing, he said: "I'll be a protective father."

Left unsaid, but just as important, was the fact that Marty, 19, would be able to look after Mark, who's 18, in the club's travels throughout the country.

"Well, it's done," Gordie said, "and I'm really happy and so is my family."

One obvious question is whether at his advanced age, despite his early brilliance, can even Gordie Howe come back to active hockey and play with dash and daring?

"That is a question, isn't it?" he said, laughing. "I don't know. I hope so. I haven't been on skates since March or so, and even then I was really bushed.

"I'd guess it will take me about two months to get in really good shape. I'll start serious work in early August when I'm on vacation in northern Michigan, and I suppose camp will start for me in September.

"I don't even know that much about it. They just told me to have some fun and they'd call when they're ready for me."

When he ended his playing career with the Red Wings at the close of the 1971-72 season, having played longer and scored more than any other man, Howe was sick at heart, disillusioned by repeated upheavals within the team and management.

He was distressed, too, by his own physical skills.

"There's nothing wrong now; my wrist is fine," he said. "We'd thought it might take three years, but I've tested it and there's no more pain."

Gordie's wife, Colleen, long active in Detroit junior hockey, was a surprise fourth party in the contract signings.

"They're developing a junior program here, and I will be active in that," she said. "Now that the two older boys are taken care of, we have to be concerned about Murray, who is 12."

The Howes plan to move to Houston in the fall, but even that shift is contingent on Murray's being able to find competition that befits his talent.

And his name. ✦

1 9 7 3

Now it can be told:
How I fixed the '64 Derby

W ell, they got me. Forget the lie detector. No need to summon the grand jury.

I confess.

The Pinewood Derby at Greenfield Elementary in the spring of '64 was not on the up-and-up.

Come get the ribbon, Mr. Scoutmaster. Be kind, judge.

I mean, the kid brings home these four rubber discs and a block of wood with instructions to whittle it to the size and shape of a race car, and in a few weeks the Cub Scouts will have their big race day.

Understand, it is for me one of the great challenges of fatherhood. I cannot effectively operate a screwdriver. But there is no way that kid will be poorly represented in the grand competition.

So appeals for help were made and out of a collision shop on the east side came a couple of uncles who in two nights whittled and perfected the fanciest, slickest Pinewood Derby entry ever, sprayed with eight coats of lacquer, hand-rubbed with 50 coats of wax, and, well, you know what happened.

What happened was that it was fifth in the race behind two Ford engineers, a Chrysler stylist and a plumber, but first place, no less, for looks.

I learned a lot that day. I learned, for instance, where Gaylord Perry keeps the grease on his greaseball. He keeps it hidden on the axle support of his Pinewood Derby car.

I learned, too, about a plumber, and how he could pour a shot of lead into the nose of a car for acceleration as it comes down the long, sloping track.

What I learned mostly, though, was that in any group of 30 kids, 28 or maybe 29 fathers will offer something more than good counsel and thereby steal their minor triumphs.

The kid learned not a thing. He still endangers himself with a butter knife. So there you are.

What we are really talking about here, as you might guess, is not the Pinewood Derby, which is strictly little kids' stuff, but the scandal of the Soap Box Derby, which brought all this to mind, and the myriad of kids' activities — baseball, football, hockey, all of it — spawned and nurtured by well-intentioned people.

In Akron, Ohio, the people's prosecutor is considering a delinquency warrant against the kid who won the Soap Box Derby with a juiced-up car.

Well, nuts. I have never seen a Soap Box Derby car created and constructed by a kid.

This one had electrical wires embedded in the Fiberglass fuselage. If a 13-year-old kid truly managed that, they should give him the scholarship prize, for here is a budding genius.

Well, you know who did it, don't you?

Sad to say, it is merely one more example. Once snared in a kid's game, the old man and the real purpose is lost.

It happens always. Once involved, you see, the old man won't let go.

His leisure time, his social life, his money, indeed his pride and status, are poured into the kid's life.

It is truly amazing, for example, how many guys go boffo over Little League baseball. I would like to congratulate the Birmingham Federal League for reaching the World Series of their game at Williamsport, Pa., last week.

Yet, I know, too, that to have a team of 14 boys ready for that grand elimination, the flyweight championship of all of baseball, the rest of the league had to end its season by July 4.

And so, master planners that they are, the good fathers of Little League have no baseball at all for thousands of sons through the last two months and more of summer.

It is not only the fathers but sometimes the mothers who ork out over kids hockey.

Hockey is such that it turns people on anyway, but scarcely a month passes in season that we fail to hear of a bare-knuckle blast among parents or are asked to arbitrate some dispute.

Show me different and I might renege a bit, but offhand I say that whenever big people get too involved in activities of little people, the latter have less to gain.

I tell you this with the vow that I have written my last sixth-grade book report. ✦

1 9 7 3

Billie Jean teaches
Bobby Riggs a lesson

HOUSTON — Just don't think this changes anything, Maude.

Remember whose name is on the paycheck, babe, and don't get any wild ideas.

I mean, those floors are for scrubbing, those pots are for scraping and the kids got to eat. But do not fret about it, 'cause the laundry will keep your fingernails clean.

Besides, there is no other candidate but you, ol' girl, so don't go looking around the room.

That Bum. The absolute ham bum. How could he do this?

Defender of the faith, he says. Warrior of truth, he says. Savior of tradition. Ha. The bum.

How could Bobby Riggs, with everything he had going for him, lose at tennis to this Ms. Billie Jean Moffitt King?

He had it all. He had Malehood, is what he had, and what else do you have to give anybody? And yet he lost.

He is 55. That is all I can tell you. I hate to tell you that because there are a lot of 55s who still fight a good fight.

But there is a question now, isn't there, whether a 55 can fight the good fight against such as Ms. Billie Jean Moffitt King.

Bobby Riggs certainly is not the one, and if not him, who else? Likely there is no one else. This gal has too much speed, too much savvy, too much of the competitive fire for an ol' geezer to handle.

He looked awful. Early in the play, he looked awful. He looked worse as it went on, and at the end, after his stunning 6-4, 6-3, 6-3 rout was done, he looked ready for a hospital bed.

He sat on a chair at courtside, his head bowed between his legs as thousands of gals yelped and whooped and hollered for the things Billie Jean King had done to him.

By the handful, he grabbed chips of ice from a bucket and almost frantically rubbed them into the back of his neck, over his forehead and face. Then, with both hands, almost desperately, he took more ice and rubbed it hard into his legs and chest.

He was a thoroughly beaten man, embarrassed and humbled by a competitor he had ridiculed without restraint, and now it had come home to him.He gave her full credit for what she had accomplished.

"She surprised me, she really did," he said. "She has surprising quickness and reflex at the net. She took the net and she kept it.

"I knew right away I was in trouble. I wasn't getting my first serve in at all, and that let the pressure off her.

"But there's no denying her anything. There was nothing fluky about the way she won. She won it fair and square and that's the way it should always be, and there's no kick coming from me."

For more than a half-hour after, Bobby remained closeted in his locker room, unavailable to anyone, while just outside his door, queen Billie Jean held court with the press and beamed her satisfaction. She did not gloat, and goodness knows, she had reason, if she chose to do so.

"I just can't believe it," she said. "I never in the world thought it could be straight sets against him.

"But I had a plan put together by three men and me, incidentally, and it was the right plan. It worked for me all the way."

The idea, she explained, was to force the action at Riggs, keep the ball low and force him to hit up so she could cut off his returns right at the net and put the ball away.

It worked to perfection. Time after time, there was Billie Jean, up at the net, punching away with forehand and backhand and whaling her overhead past Bobby.

"A big thing, too, was to keep trying to hit the ball behind him," she said.

And that worked, too. Countless times Riggs would be going in one direction, and Billie Jean would place the ball in the area he had just vacated. It's a near impossible shot to retrieve, and Bobby made few efforts at it.

For his own, Riggs had neither the stroking power nor the speed afoot to combat this gal.

He was simply outmaneuvered and overwhelmed, a sharp contrast indeed to his 6-2, 6-1 dismantling of Margaret Court in May.

If she allowed herself any boasts of self-satisfaction in her stunning triumph it came merely in the expression of the good that can result for women's tennis.

"Tennis had been my life," she said, "and I have long felt that it was too much for the rich and not enough for the blacks and other underprivileged people.

"I promise you'll find more of the poor and disadvantaged coming into tennis, because the women will make sure of that.

"A lot of nonsense has ended with this match tonight, and for that I am thankful."

Billie Jean included in the nonsense "all the quotes you've heard from Bobby Riggs about women's lib and women in general. Maybe he will be happy to hear that the thing I want most to do right now is to drink a few beers and just relax. Just like one of the guys."

Say, Bobby, ol' pal. Dash into the kitchen, would you, and bring the lady a beer. Bring her slippers, too, and the paper. Don't you know she's tired from a long day of work?

Get up, you bum! Things are going to be different around here — for a day, anyway. ✦

1 9 7 3

Ann Arbor always a winner
on football Saturdays

This is before the fact, so what I tell you might not really have happened yesterday at all.

But for sure it did, for it is always so on the special football Saturdays in Ann Arbor, Mich.

For years and years it has been the same, and I could have told you a month ago, or more, that on Saturday, Oct. 20, 1973, I had a simply glorious day.

Who else could tell you that in advance, and be sure?

The scheduled brides of Oct. 20 could not tell you that, because they could not be sure (could they?) how the day would go and end.

Or the kids with birthdays, or the guys and dolls on big dates. They could never be so sure, in advance.

How many people could tell you for sure about tomorrow?

Do not be surprised — there are 80,000 and some who could tell you. Saturday was a glorious day.

These thousands are the Michigan football nuts, the boffos who in good years and bad clog the streets and restaurants and yards of Ann Arbor to go to the Michigan football game.

They are not necessarily Michigan people, U-M people.

I count among them a friend who holds no diploma, to show you it is not an old-school tie involved here. He has missed two games in 30 years, once because of a war — he had to work overtime — and once because he almost died of something or another.

He goes to Michigan games, which are the real glory days of the year, he says, because, with everything else, he dearly loves dinner at the Elks Club.

I add another among them who has this thing about apple cider and donuts, which abound on the streets surrounding Michigan Stadium. Through the summer he talks of the days we will go the Michigan games and of apple cider and donuts, along with everything else, though in truth he rarely drinks the cider and donuts do him ill.

I give you another who will not go to the games unless he can chauffeur. It is part of the game, you see, to gather and transport the party.

Still another mans the tailgate bar, dispensing in the fashion of a Julia Child, just the right touch, you know.

One more must emcee the parking lot, another must ingratiate himself to all the ladies, still another must hassle the passing long hairs.

"How do you tell a boy from a girl anymore?" the latter says, each year, every game. "Ha, ha. Hey, girls, how can you be sure anymore?"

It matters not so much in this group what the football game is all about, whether Michigan will win or lose, whether Bo Schembechler will not throw a pass again and thus bore the pants off the press box.

And I suspect it is so through much of the Michigan crowd, for in the lean years, too, before Schembechler, through those years when Michigan football tradition was being insulted, the crowds numbered almost the same.

What I'm saying is that there is something more to a Michigan football Saturday than what transpires down in the bowl.

It is true. Perhaps it is true in other places, at other games. It must be so because other schools pack them in; other crowds have pursued their teams for years with an ardor of their own.

Stanford had a flavor much like it until a few years ago, until the kooks took over. Ohio State has a fever all its own. Texas-Oklahoma is wild. Notre Dame is a religion. Michigan State tries.

But Michigan, Michigan has something special, a lure, a magnetic atmosphere that all but assures Saturday will be one fine day, sun or storm, win or lose.

The old grads come home and some of them cry as they sing "Hoo-ray for the Yell-oh and Blooo," and some get drunk and look at other guys' wives and they say, boy, ol' Harry didn't marry too well, did he?

They look at all the young judys walking around and they are jealous, to be sure, but it is Michigan, Michigan, always the leader and the best.

Where else, they tell you, do you find a school with a stadium like this, 101,701 seats, not a bad one in the lot, where else a band like this, its capes, its caps, its drum major, its style unique.

Where else a team that looks like this, with its winged shield headgear, a color called maize, a team that has existed almost a century and won more than almost anybody, certainly more than any of its neighbors and rivals.

Long after the game, they linger in the stands — where else do 35,000 people sit watching band music long after the game — and they follow the band out of the stadium, across the railroad tracks, down the narrow streets of the campus, and then they disappear.

To the Elks Club for dinner. To the cider stand. To the tailgate. To who knows where to await another Saturday, another game.

It is a grand and glorious day, to be sure. It always is.

Often I have wondered, would it be the same, or more so, if Michigan were my school. ✦

1 9 7 4

When the lights go out,
Secretariat left at the gate

I give you fair warning.

Send the kids to the movies, to the store, send 'em anywhere, but get them out of the house.

Draw the blinds, close the drapes, lock the door, for what we are seeking is a few minutes of privacy, away from inquisitive little minds.

Sex is the subject today. Sex as it concerns the breeding thoroughbred horse.

You know the story of Secretariat?

Secretariat, the wonder horse, six million bucks worth of flesh on the hoof, big and powerful and beautiful and all, but a royal bust at stud.

I tell you true, for a while I laughed and smirked at the irony of Secretariat, this great stallion, being unable to, to, to … well, striking out with the bases loaded, if you will.

His plight is such that it inspires much mirth among the public and considerable consternation among his owners, but nowhere around do I see much sympathy for Secretariat himself.

It is as if this horse that has it all really has nothing much when you come right down to the things that matter. Know what I mean?

I got to reading up a bit about Secretariat and his problem, which they say is immaturity, maybe, and I found it absolutely amazing the things that have gone on in the horse barns.

I mean, being a sidewalk kind of guy all my life, I am shocked by the transgressions of the horse farm.

Do you know, for instance, that there was a Chilean horse named Olhaverry II who won the Santa Anita Handicap and many other big races and looked for all the world as if he would make a wonderful horse daddy, and then the worst befell him?

They sent him to the barn, and he was kicked in the head and killed by the female in his company. I guess all Latin lovers are not all that smooth.

Tom Fool, a mighty big winner on the tracks, too, was a notoriously shy guy once they led him to the barns. Only after much pampering, by what method I do not know, was his interest in girl horses developed. Maybe they showed him stag movies or such.

Assault, the Triple Crown winner of 1946, was a washout in the barn, so you can see an unfertile Secretariat is not without precedent.

Assault was a crushing blow and disappointment to Robert Kleberg, whose fabulous King Ranch stable in Texas soon dissipated for lack of first-rate horse heirs. It goes to show you something. I'm not sure what.

Horse people worry much about making advantageous matches of stallions and mares, and they gamble considerably that the matings will pan out, much as families of the Old World did with their sons and daughters not too many decades ago.

Sometimes, they succeed fantastically, better than they even hope or plan.

Charlie Keller, who played outfield for the Yankees and Tigers years back, went into the breeding industry and sold one of his products, a trotting mare named Fresh Yankee, for $900.

Charlie did not know what he had. The horse won $1.25 million and has retired to produce offspring of her own.

The late M. H. Van Berg, who raced in Detroit and was the country's leading owner-trainer until his death in 1971, tried to breed his classy mare Estacion to a top-ranked Kentucky stallion. The fee was $20,000 with no return privilege, which means you get one turn at it, and good luck. Van Berg said nuts to that, resorted to his own collection of stallions and came up with a big winner named British Buddy.

In horse racing, as you know, bloodlines are the thing. What it amounts to is winners beget winners, and so demand is heavy for the stud performance of champion horses.

Bold Ruler, a champion of the 1950s, is acknowledged also as the champion sire of his time, his progeny accumulating $10 million in winnings at last count.

He has 333 sons and daughters running about, and one of his yearlings brought a record $600,000 at the Keeneland sales last July.

Secretariat is one of the sons, which seems to prove that Bold Ruler did not transmit all of his attributes in this case.

I cannot tell you what was wrong with Olhaverry II or Tom Fool or even Assault for that matter, but I have a suspicion. I suspect the horse people put too much pressure on studs to perform these days.

Take Secretariat, for example. Before he was even sent to the farm, one of his owners turned down a $100,000 fee for what is known as a standing with Secretariat.

A standing is a blind date with a lady horse.

You know how blind dates are. Who's ever at their best on blind dates?

With Secretariat there is something more.

Because of the fabulous price his owners demand for his dates, there are always newspaper guys and radio guys and television cameras around, watching everything.

"How'd it go today?" they ask. "Did it, uh, did anything happen?" "When's the next one?" "What'd the doc say?"

At cocktail parties people joke and laugh, and around the racetracks the horse people shake their heads and say, hey, it's too bad about Secretariat, eh?

With that sort of thing going on, what can you expect out of poor Secretariat?

I mean, given the same circumstances, what could you do? ✦

1 9 7 4

Kaline did the right thing better than almost anyone

W ell, nuts. He means it.
He means it, and they mean it, and so what else is there except to believe that is the way it will be.

Al Kaline is gone from rightfield. So long, baseball. Not for a while will you intrigue me so again.

It is not really a surprise; they have talked of it for many months, how they would make Al Kaline exclusively a hitter, but always I thought that when the season began Kaline would be back in rightfield.

Alas, there he sits on the bench, maybe the greatest-fielding rightfielder the game has ever known, and the passing of the finest phase of his career is accepted almost casually, by him and so many others.

I called him on it. I dug him out of the training room in Baltimore. "What's the point of my going to the ballpark," I said, "if you will not play rightfield?"

"Well," he said, "maybe you will be able to see me bat more often."

Which is true enough. Al Kaline is full-time designated hitter for the Tigers and should be in the lineup every day.

But it is not Kaline's batting, which is impressive enough, I know, that dragged me to Tiger Stadium in years when I cared not a bit to watch the rest of them play. It was his fielding. Rival benches would spend the day simply watching Kaline field, to show you.

Among keen baseball observers, there is no player of his time rated higher in all-around fielding brilliance, not Mantle or Mays, who were mighty fine indeed, not Oliva or Jensen, who were recognized as fly-chasing thoroughbreds.

Among baseball men, you get little argument when you say Al Kaline and Joe DiMaggio, for all-around fielding brilliance, are unmatched in recent generations and rate among the dozen or so very best outfielders in the history of the game.

We are talking some hallowed names, you know: Sam Crawford, Tris Speaker, Johnny Mostil, Harry Hooper. Do not tell me about Willie Mays' catch in the '54 Series, or Joe Rudy's miracle grab last fall.

Ask me the greatest play I ever saw an outfielder make and I will spot you all the catches you ever saw, and they can't beat one throw Al Kaline made.

It is a day when Mickey Mantle bombs one off the roof and out of Tiger Stadium and the crowd is still talking about it two innings later when the Yankees put a runner on third with one out.

A fly goes deep into the corner, along the foul line in right, and it is high and deep enough so that everyone can anticipate the run will score after the catch, but that Kaline will try to prevent it anyway.

With the baseball professionals, it is almost unanimous that nobody ever got better position on a ball, in stride, in rhythm, in position to throw the instant the ball is secure, than Al Kaline. It was never truer than here.

He came flying over toward the foul-line barrier, then slackened his stride, timing his approach, preserving the momentum because he would have to pivot and throw instantly.

I remember glancing at the Yankee on third, and he is literally in a crouch, like a trackman at the starting blocks, and he is watching Kaline, realizing it will be no trot home, even though Kaline is almost against the rightfield wall.

Kaline made the catch in full circling stride toward the plate and threw with a fury that lifted him off his feet.

I have never seen a throw like that one. I can see it now. I see it every time people want to talk about the great plays they have seen in sports.

That ball is never more than eight feet off the ground during its flight, and Norm Cash looks it in the eye as it streaks past first base, whirring, whistling in the bright sun, and it pops right there into the catcher's mitt, right at his shoe tops.

There is a mighty collision at the plate and the dust flies, and the umpire throws his fist into the air, and nobody can believe what they have seen.

It is a mighty close play indeed, and all the Yankees leap out of the dugout, but they do not scream at the umpire. They stand there in front of the dugout looking to rightfield, because they saw the throw, too, purring as it rocketed past their eyes, and they know only a howitzer could have propelled a ball 300 feet and more like that.

A few of them wave to Kaline. Some shake their heads in disbelief, but they will not debate the call at the plate.

It was a moment to treasure, or so I thought, until I asked Kaline about it.

"No, I don't remember it," he said.

"C'mon now," I said. "It is a day Mickey Mantle hits one off the roof and out of sight and — "

"No, I really don't remember that one," he said. "What I remember mostly is throwing out a guy at second while sitting down in rightfield. It was against the White Sox, I think.

"I remember another day, too, years ago, when I threw out three guys in one game. In those days you had guys like Minoso and Rivera and guys like that who could really fly, so that was something that stuck with me."

He says he can't do it anymore, not as he used to. The arm went with the legs. Some of his velocity and spring did not move through the calendar with the rest of Al Kaline.

Even so, a Kaline who can't do everything he used to, who can't reach the balls he once handled so gracefully and surely, is better than some of the butchers I have seen periodically in his place in rightfield, that is for sure.

He is not tempted. Not at all. He seems pleased to have escaped the field that was his alone in his time. ✦

1 9 7 5

After Russia, there's no place like home

From the dance hall off in the woods comes the raucous pounding of a rock band. Several hundred yards away thousands are gathered in an outdoor movie arena, and the whine of rockets on screen pierces the air.

Music from the carnival midway, off to the right, attracts the four of us as we wander, confused and lost in the dark, unable to find anyone who can help us.

Finally, Billy Williams, a biggie among bowling operators, halts us.

"Think for a minute," he says. "Just a few hours ago, we were home, comfortable, with anything a person could possibly want to make life enjoyable.

"Now you have me in a hotel that smells so bad I choke, with food I can't eat and people I can't talk to.

"So somebody tell me now what the hell we are doing in Gorky Park, in the middle of Moscow, at 10:30 at night, looking for a bowling alley?"

I have been away for a spell, and that's where I was, in Moscow, of all places. Do not ask me why Moscow, of all places. Except for simple curiosity, I cannot tell you why we went to Moscow. But it was worth it.

It was worth it because one comes home changed, maybe forever. No matter your burden, friend, it is better than we saw it.

Over the years, I have met Russian athletes and such touring here. The impression they leave is that all Russians are in college, studying to become engineers, scientists, doctors, that Moscow U. is the seat of the world brainpower, a mecca for all Russians.

Moscow U. has 30,000 students. Wayne State has more; a half-dozen schools in Michigan have more.

Would you believe it if I told you that, aside from the arts, there likely is not a single thing in all of Moscow, so probably Russia, that is not excelled in abundance in Detroit itself?

We board up and tear down better homes than are theirs; our markets would not dare display meat and fruit that shows on the tables of some of their best restaurants.

Billy Williams and I were traveling with our Polish princesses, and within a few hours, they were frustrated. The Russians do not understand Polish, as the ladies had thought, and they were feeling ridiculous, playing charades before them, imitating the bowling delivery, hoping someone in Gorky Park would understand what we sought.

"I hear them — the bowling alleys are over there, beyond those trees," says Virginia Williams. "I'd know the sound of pins falling anywhere."

She's right. Behind a barbed fence sits a canvas, air-supported dome housing the only bowling lanes in the Soviet Union. Brunswick Corp. installed them six months ago, hoping to create a market.

We are to meet Comrade Slavidinsky, minister of culture, there. He has tickets for the opening of the Bolshoi opera season, the spectacular event of the fall.

Forty-two people staff the 16 lanes, which are black with grime, as if they had not been conditioned for months. It is incredible by our standards, but typical of almost everything, as we later see. There are plenty of workers everywhere; everybody has a job, but few really work, as we know it.

Sixteen of the staff are mechanics. Seven lanes are down for repair; the lane conditioner sits in its original box. The mechanics are bowling, barefoot and bare-chested; others in the crowd wear high-heeled shoes, boots, whatever, because the 240 pair of bowling shoes disappeared within the first week.

Slavidinsky is home in bed. He will see us in the morning.

It is beyond midnight now, and the doors of the Ukraine Hotel, as other hotels, are locked. Two soldiers let us through without a word.

The first shock of Moscow still fills the lobby. A heavy, foul odor, strong enough to choke the queasy, hangs in the air.

It comes from the kitchens, which produce a shock of their own. The food is awful, worse than we had been warned.

Only twice a week can we handle a meal, and no doubt the Russians wonder about us. Americans eat only bread and butter.

The morning brings a first full look at Moscow, though no Slavidinsky.

Gnarled old women in babushkas and black shirts, all seemingly 70ish, sweep the streets and walks; in the winter they shovel the snow. We wonder why these, who lived and fought through the darkest years, hold such jobs.

Apartment complexes stretch out for miles to the horizon.

Housing is a problem; there are no single homes.

If the apartments are a reflection of the hotels, which are fairly new, too, they are awful, in disrepair, unwashed and unscrubbed, with craftmanship one might find in a beginning shop class.

Gasoline is merely 10 cents a gallon, but there are only 100,000 cars among 8.5 million people, so the wide streets, often 16 lanes across, are uncluttered.

Before we left for Russia, friends wondered whether we were wary, or even afraid. There is no reason for it.

You go where you want, do what you want, unchallenged. Soldiers do not abound. Women do. It is a feminist's city. Women run the hotels, the shops; they operate in the subways and on the scaffolding, too, laying brick on the new buildings.

My one regret is that I never managed a picture of a hod carrier. I would mail it to my pal Billie Jean King, from Moscow, with love.

The women are tough-looking, hard-eyed and stoic; they are heavy-boned, broad-beamed with solid, bulging thighs and calves football coaches like to see. To be true, it is the only place I know where the men are better-looking than the women.

Shopping is a worthless challenge; you really have to try to blow a hundred bucks. There is nothing worth bringing home, beyond souvenirs, but at the shops, long lines of jamming, cramming women fight for hours to buy what's available.

"When shoes are on sale," a guide tells us, "you buy regardless of size and hope to trade weeks later when your size comes on the market."

Everything leads toward the walled Kremlin, which is awesome historically and impressive for what it represents.

Nearly 10,000 a day stand for hours for a whisked-by look at Lenin's tomb. Within the walls is the magnificent new Kremlin theater, and we catch the Bolshoi ballet there in an incredible performance of "Swan Lake."

The Russians do not stink in art and culture, and in that regard, they are truly superb. We never see Slavidinsky, and I suppose Brezhnev or some such got our tickets to the opera.

After Moscow, Leningrad is a treat. The people are looser, friendlier, but Americans are warned not to drink the water, use ice cubes or eat anything that is not cooked or peeled. The water could ruin a visitor for months.

What saves the day is Russian champagne, which is the middle grade quality and a shame to waste brushing teeth.

Leningrad grabs you, and at last you understand somewhat and appreciate the Russians. The city was devastated during the 900-day blockade and siege of World War II. A million of its people starved or were killed in defense of the city, and they are revered.

A cemetery on the edge of town contains mass graves — huge mounds, 20 yards wide, 50 yards long, row after row. Stark black-and-white pictures of the devastation and death are on display nearby.

It is custom that the day's brides come to the cemetery to place their flowers of the graves. Thirty years after the fact, the natives, and some visitors, leave weeping.

They are proud, these people. Tips do not often bribe them to service; often kids refuse gifts of candy or gum.

"We have gum here," one teenager says, though in truth they do not, and a pack could get them three bucks on the loose black market.

They are proud and they do not complain, if they dare, and they seem content — dull and rarely smiling, but apparently content.

Twice within little more than a half-century, their land has been ravaged, the population decimated, and what they have, chances are, is better than they have known.

You come away with the conviction that, with a little help, it could be so much better for them. But it will not be, not soon.

And you come home wondering what it was that was bugging you, what you were complaining about so hotly, when you left. ✦

Many boaters snagged by Detroit River's allure

A s Jack Love reflects on his years along the Detroit riverfront, which some consider seedy, smelly and worse, he sees what north-end settlers never have, never could.

"It's beautiful here, quiet and beautiful," he says. "I grew up here. I love the waterfront. I guess I'm what you'd call a river rat."

He is sitting at the wheel of the Queen Bee, looking back over the stern and down the canal that runs along the east side on Parkview on into the river.

Scattered behind are boats in varying stages of scraping and painting, all awaiting summer's invitation.

Jack Love and the Queen Bee are just back from Ft. Lauderdale, where they escaped our winter, as has been the captain's custom. They are back to the old roost, only a block or so away from Manoogian Mansion.

"I grew up only a couple of hundred yards back there," he says. "Hell, I fell in the canal when I was 6 years old, and that's when I learned to swim. I remember selling papers all over this area when I was a kid, and old man Gregory (the boat man) running me off. I vowed then never to buy a boat from him, and I never have."

Tough luck for old man Gregory. The kid who never forgot laughs about it now — several dozen boats later.

Jack Love is 53, a smiling, portly yacht master who reminds one of Cannon, the TV private-eye.

He is from a kind of Detroit I never really knew — the close-to-the-water residents. They are different, luckier perhaps, than the rest of the natives.

You notice that east siders, particularly those from the Grosse Pointes, the Shores and along that stretch, rarely desert and move west or to the north suburbs.

I figure it's the water that keeps them there. They won't, they cannot leave it and be happy.

Jack Love says it is absolutely true.

"I can't remember when I didn't have a boat," he says. "When I was a little guy, a gang of us pulled out this boat that had sunk under the docks. It was a mess, but it could take six oarsmen.

"We worked like devils and cleaned it up, and it was great fun for a week or so — then somebody stole it. But the thing is, you grow up on or near the water and it becomes part of you, like a magnet always pulling."

Alas, it never happened to me, although, looking about Jack Love's Queen

Bee, I figure it could, given such a chance.

It is a magnificent yacht, one that has entertained the Prince of Morocco, to show you, and a collection of Hollywood hotshots and people like that.

I am with Jack Love, so you will know, to obtain rental of this dream boat for a collection of ne'er-do-wells known as the Motley Crew, with whom I carouse now and then.

The Queen Bee is for hire, perhaps the finest yacht of its type riding the river and lakes around. By coincidence, the Wall Street Journal talked about it nationwide just a few days ago.

She is 60 feet long, 18 feet across the beam, and she's powered by two 655-horsepower diesel engines, which kick up a 24-mile-an-hour cruising speed.

Below deck, she is mighty inviting — a king-sized bed dominating the master bedroom; a beautifully appointed galley and bar offering other pleasures in a sumptuous living room.

"This one is my dream boat," says Jack Love, who owns the Queen Bee. "Except for the basic hull, I designed and laid out everything here."

She is 3 years old, costing — don't fall overboard, mate — $215,000. During the winter, Jack spurned a check offering $315,000 for its purchase.

"On the market today," he says, "she's worth probably $485,000."

I would not believe that, except Jack Love is a sturdy businessman, owner-operator of a prospering warehouse-trucking firm, and he does not josh about numbers.

"I'll have perhaps two or three charters a week during the summer," he says. "Mostly the major manufacturing companies bringing in clients and that sort of people have them aboard for a chartered cruise.

"It's the way a lot of business is done — that's no secret to anybody. I've heard any number of big-money deals finalized while we're cruising about."

He figures there is absolutely no place in the United States, perhaps the world, as ideal for the boat and yachtsman as — would you believe it? — right here on the Detroit River and the Great Lakes.

"Where else can you take a really fine cruise for 10 miles, 20 miles, 50 or 200?" he says. "There's no other area like it, at least none within such an easy reach of so many millions of people."

Well, we are approaching the nitty-gritty with Jack Love and the Queen Bee, the gritty being how much it will cost to charter this palace for an afternoon or evening float.

"The fee is $120 an hour," he says, "with a minimum number of hours, depending on the day and time."

Say what?

Jack laughs. Five out of six charter inquiries end as this one does.

"This is not a toy," he says. "The Queen Bee is as fine as you can find anywhere."

Not for a minute do I question whether it is so. But you will excuse me, no doubt, while I check to see whether the Boblo boat requires reservations. ✦

1 9 7 7

Numbers game thrived long before the lottery began

Whatever happened to Felix and Dog Willie? Where are Mr. Henry, Cryin' Jake and Bobo the Dream Man?

Lordy lord, where are you now, Prophet Jones?

We need them one and all, especially now.

In this fast-changing age, when what once was sin and crime is sanctioned and encouraged, we need wisdom and counsel from the likes of these forgotten seers.

They were men of magic numbers; some booked, some touted. Every day for years on end they had one number, or more.

We are talking of a day when a hot number was not some date, necessarily, but a three-digit, honest-to-god number that might come out at twilight and bring riches to the neighborhoods.

Policy numbers, they were called.

By sanction of the legislature and the governor, with no cops or courts to fear, we are one and all into the policy racket now.

Ol' folks around must laugh themselves silly, recalling the cop wars on the racketeers — the chases, the knifings and shootings, the killings that resulted.

And now numbers is a legal game.

It confounds me, really, how official attitudes and acceptance of things can so easily change.

The most brutal man-on-man assault I have witnessed occurred years ago over the very same game I played just minutes ago so openly and casually at a downtown bar.

The cop cruiser rolled down Lumpkin Avenue in north Detroit, trapping Bobo the Dream Man against the dead-end railroad tracks. They zapped Bobo a dozen times on the head before the Dream Man fell, his policy receipts scattered in the dirt. "Damn hard head," the cop said.

For years after that scene haunted me until I came upon a blackjack. I tapped myself lightly and realized the cop was right. Bobo must have had a hard head.

The wars over policy territory were vicious. A friend's brother, a former Golden Gloves champion, was slashed ear-to-ear but survived. Several months later, his assailant was found in the shadow of the water reservoir at Davison and Dequindre. He had 70-odd knife jabs in his chest — and he, too, lived.

Now all of a sudden it is legal to bet the numbers — at the proper place, paying the right people, of course.

One can play without frown from the cops or worry from the robbers; play a hunch, bet a dream or birthday, using the electronic, computerized facility of a respected businessman, and maybe it will be your lucky day.

For years, whenever I returned to the old neighborhood, I would bet Charlie Gehringer's lifetime batting average, which everyone thinks is .321. It hit a few times, too, but then I discovered Charlie had played baseball a year too long and his average actually was .320. For all I know, .320 never ever hit.

If you happen to see an auto accident, the number to play is 518. Dream of blood and 315 is the thing to do.

Do not figure me for a tout. It is what kids learned years ago, before algebra, history and don't-say-ain't.

The churchiest guy I knew always bet 962 — that number being accepted as the "church and hard-luck roll." It was all of that. The number never hit, not in eight straight years of daily mass and wagering. Finally he said to hell with all of it.

Would you believe that I am honeymooning years ago in Quebec when an urgent call comes from Detroit. The guy needs to know what the bride dreamed last night — he wants to play the number.

One of these times, we will get into the dream books that are still around offering all sorts of numbers, some based on astrology, others on real-life incidents or just plain hunches. The innocents around need to know a bit about that, I figure, if they are going to play this game and help support our schools, the government and such.

The illegal game flourished all right — in the factories, restaurants and bars, in the streets and the neighborhoods.

Mostly, the daily winning number in the old policy racket was developed from horse race results. The Polish Bank, for instance, used a derivative of the mutuel payoff in the sixth race at Aqueduct as the basis for its daily number.

The challenge was in guessing what that number would be — and the wars were fought among the rival "banks" striving for neighborhood business.

No doubt you are wondering what Prophet Jones had to do with all this. He was the flamboyant leader of a religious group that thrived in Detroit and elsewhere — supposedly 800,000 strong — in the 1950s.

On his weekly radio broadcasts, Prophet Jones offered to the public pictures of Christ on the cross, suitable for framing, every home should have one, or more, in every room.

"These are lucky pictures," the Prophet would say. "On the back of each one are some numbers. They have nothin' to do with any kind of gamblin', but people who have sent in a donation and got a picture say these numbers have been lucky for them."

In this regard, if nothing else, the Prophet was true.

It had a peculiar charm, the old game. I'm not at all sure about the new. ✦

1 9 7 7

It's a no-win situation
for compulsive gamblers

rankie is 36, and maybe for the first time he feels good about himself.
Half his life has passed, but it is not too late for him, not the way he
sees it. At last, he can like himself and what he is.

Still, the damage has been done. Irreparable in some instances.
There's no escaping that.

He came here looking for help, not for himself particularly but for
people like him. He says there are thousands — millions, actually — yet, as
far as he knows, only 50 in Detroit seek to save themselves.

He is, or was, a compulsive gambler. He talks of it freely and openly,
ashamed of it but knowing that attention can come only by laying himself
open. So he says:

"I was always around gambling. My grandfather was a bookmaker and my
dad liked to play the horses. What I knew, what I learned, I picked up as a
kid. I was 16 and in high school when I went to the horse races for the first
time. Just like that, I picked a $105 winner and was a big shot overnight. It
was flattering; who listens to 16-year-old kids about anything? But people
were listening to me about horses. It seemed an easy thing for me.

"I was a very good handicapper, as good as anybody. I could pick winners
one out of three races. That's plenty good. But you still lose.

"I don't know when I actually went over the line and became a compulsive
bettor at the horses. But it was quick. The tracks became my life-style.
Everything I did for years and years revolved around betting.

"The compulsive bettor has a self-destruct button. He has to bet; he has to
have some action going. They punish themselves. It's an escape for them —
entertainment in a way. Deep down they know it, every one of them.

"It wouldn't matter if I picked six or seven winners one night, and the next
night too. I'd still wind up losing. It's the same with all guys like me. You
don't play to win money but to have action, always action.

"Lots of times I'd bet the last race and leave the track not knowing who
won. You need the overnight action, understand?

"There were periods, lots of them, when I was winning big, but I
remember I'd gamble it back. Guys like me always do.

"I remember hitting the twin double for $3,000 one day. The rent was due,
the bills were piled up at home, the kids were eating sandwiches but I'm
having steak at the track.

"I gave my wife $50 — I told her I'd been lucky — and I bet the rest back.

"That's the problem with compulsive gamblers. The money is like

Monopoly money — just paper. It doesn't mean anything. If you win, it's only to have money to bet the next race; you toss it around and give it back.

"It gets so you're in debt. You go to the day races and con some money to go to the night races — day after day for years it was like that.

"Of the money I won, I never had a thing to show for it ... and now I have nothing, really ... no wife, no kids, no home. Nothing.

"People think guys who gamble like that do it for fancy cars, clothes or broads. Stuff like that. It's not true. The compulsive gambler wouldn't spend his money on these things; he needs it for more betting.

"There are a lot like me — doctors, lawyers, accountants, business people. They have a compulsion to bet, shoot the load. It's like the guy betting the plantation with the riverboat gambler. Sure as hell he will lose it — if not in one game, then in a later one.

"I know a guy who mortgaged his manufacturing plant to pay a gambling debt. Now Vegas is looking for him. He owes $75,000.

"One guy put together a resort hotel. It was a phony deal; the project never existed. He sold $150,00 in worthless stock and blew it all.

"Real con artists. It's how they get their money to gamble every day. They con. They might write bad checks; if things are really pressing 'em hard, they might embezzle or steal so they can bet. They have to bet.

""Four years ago, I stole some money from my parents, I was so desperate to bet. That's when I realized I was sick. Really sick. Do you know what kind of feeling that is, to realize you stole like that? Who can be proud of that?

"My mother died before I could get straight with her, and myself. Think about that.

"I went to a psychologist. They never have been able to help compulsive gamblers because they don't understand them. It's not like alcoholics. They can go to a hospital, get rejuvenated and go back to the streets. There's no pill for gamblers. The doctor sent me to Gamblers Anonymous, and that's why I'm telling you. We need some help. People need to know about us, so we can help them.

"We know what it is to be in the sewer and how people get about gambling. The thing is, I don't believe many people know we exist, and they ought to, because there are enough of 'em suffering out there.

"Government studies say there are nine million like us, and each one of 'em affects six other people — their families, their employers, their friends."

With all of that, he had me wondering what the government is doing luring us into all sorts of lotteries and gambling games, any new gimmick that might cause us to invest regularly on chance.

"Gamblers Anonymous takes no position on that," says Frankie, who has been out of betting since 1973. "It doesn't matter what kind of game it is, you're going to lose. You can bet on that. The test is how determined are you to keep betting and lose your money — and maybe everything you have.

"Sure, the lottery and numbers can be addictive, like anything else.

"I'll tell you, I'm surprised about one thing. We're getting younger people, guys like 20 to 30. Before, they were much older. It tells you something." ✦

1 9 7 7

In sandlot football, men were men, teeth were few

I f you happen to encounter the honorable Mr. Fifi Fikadova, who is about town somewhere, do not ask what happened to his nose. He will tell you.

He is a delightful sort, actually, but for years Fifi has opened every conversation with the day his face was smashed and his nose reshaped to resemble a mountainside stream.

The nose is his trophy, a quick reminder — whenever he crosses his eyes — of the glory days of youth, of sandlot football in this instance.

He comes to mind because of a visit moments ago of several more just like him.

The Warrendale-Dearborn All-Star football team, which bloodied and stormed over rocks, glass and mud and raised such hell on fields all around in 1946-59, will be gathering for its first reunion several weeks hence.

You know how it is with such groups. There might be silver and bronze stars and a few Purple Hearts among them, but always they would talk of real battles, for neighborhood honor and superiority.

So it was with Ben Benton, who was coach-shepherd of a motley collection of guys who, by family-economic-world circumstance, either went off to work, to war, to families of their own and never had a chance at class football.

"We had some who were really fine players," Ben says. "They could have played college or even pro ball, except things didn't work out right for them."

Maybe all of the 100 or more Benton expects at the reunion will have a special story to equal Fifi Fikadova's.

What Ben says of his guys, though, seems fairly typical of players from a bygone era who never had a chance at college or even high school ball.

"We always used to play one game against Jackson Prison," Ben says. "One time we opened the season missing our best halfback. Nobody knew what had happened to him since the winter.

"We get to Jackson and guess who's starring in their backfield? It's our back. They had him for a holdup somewhere."

Ben can go on like that recalling glory-gory days of sandlot-type football.

"Maybe nobody remembers Fats Szczerba," he says, "but Fats shows how guys really knocked themselves out just because they loved to play.

"We're losing to the Jerry Lynch All-Stars, 46-0, at old Mack Park when Jackie Lowther goes on a 90-yard run with only 10 seconds left. What's it matter, one more touchdown?

"But Szczerba chases him right down into the end zone and takes a flying dive with his World War II tank helmet flapping around his ears. He hits a goalpost, straight-in, with his head."

In the goofy way sports heroes are remembered, Szczerba is enshrined as one of the great "heart" guys of the team.

Do not for a minute believe they were rinky-dinks.

"When Doc Spears was at Toledo U.," Ben says, "he invited us to a game at 10 o'clock on a Sunday morning. His team had an open date. We got 50 bucks and played behind locked gates, no publicity.

"They got off to a 20-0 lead, but they lost six players and were ruined for the year."

Ed Maples was one of the classier Warrendale-Dearborn stars, a rugged 5-foot-10, 210-pound railroader who even now looks capable of shoving a boxcar off track.

"Buddy Parker gave me a tryout with the Lions in 1956," Maples recalls, "and I scored a touchdown. But they cut me. They were championship in those years and had a lot of guys coming back from Korea."

Maples never made it through high school, illness forcing him out. But love of football, the hitting, the heavy man-for-man battles led him to play on for years afterward.

"It was that way with most of the guys," he says. "They still had the game in their system and they kept playing even without adequate equipment and facilities. They just loved the game."

Well, they will talk plenty like that, as older guys do, when they all assemble at the Monsignor Hunt Council Hall in Dearborn Heights. Art Salesky is checking them in.

Fifi Fikadova never was part of this group, but he is one of them anyway. They would recognize the nose and welcome him as a brother.

What happened to Fifi was maybe the toughest, scariest incident I have ever seen in football.

Fifi came roaring up and over the backside of this golf course bunker where sandlotters played in north Detroit — at the Oakland-Davison corner.

Often he would use the bunker as a screen from waiting tacklers or as a ramp to run up, over and through 'em. Except this one time.

"Three of 'em were waiting down in the sand," Fifi says, almost proudly, "and they caught my face with six elbows, six knees and a couple of feet, too."

He bled for hours. That wasn't scary.

Like a dog mad, Fifi went around biting everyone who had hit him.

Now that was scary. ✦

1 9 7 9

Phantom TD, miscues
bowl over Wolverines

ASADENA, Calif. — The time has come for people of great wisdom, which is to say you and me, to sit down and and solve the problem and plight of the University of Michigan.

Here is a school known around the world for its contributions to mankind, and yet it begins each new year with the populace scoffing.

It is very nice to help put men on the moon and transplant hearts from one artichoke to another, but if the football team can't win a bowl game, what have you?

Michigan blew it again in the Rose Bowl, although if you really want to be fair about it, you can't blame it all on the Wolverines.

They had help from their own conference, which sent a zebra with street fright to officiate in the game.

I mean, you don't want a guy standing on the goal line where touchdowns are scored who will throw up his hands whenever anybody says: "What you got?"

It's what happened to Gilbert Marchman, the line judge. When the referee asked him what had happened on that goal-line swan dive by Southern Cal's Charles White, Marchman must have realized what we all know.

The referee is the only man in the game with a gun.

He threw his hands in the air signaling a touchdown. It happened to provide USC with its second touchdown of the game, altered the style of play, and ultimately was enough to do it to Michigan again, 17-10.

In the afterglow, we see more clearly what a horrible decision Marchman made. A guy has to be in panic to react so blindly as he did.

Television pictures suggested strongly that White had lost the ball before reaching the Michigan goal. Still pictures appearing in the public prints show the play more clearly.

Hell, it wasn't even close. White lost the ball fully two yards short of the goal.

The decision on such tight plays is left to the line judge because he is in the best position to mark the ball-carrier's forward progress. So when he says a guy made it to the goal line, chances are he's right.

What he is not in best position to see is whether the guy has the ball when he gets there.

When the ball-carrier flips in mid-air, as did Charles White, and turns his back to the line judge, the official usually assumes he has the ball with him. He might not.

Dandies, eh?: The '70s ✦ **93**

Coaches generally are the toughest opponent of instant pictures, but you suspect more of 'em will come around, like Bo Schembechler.

Bo is for it today, although he's not so sure about tomorrow. He probably figures the officials owe him a big one and he wants to collect.

It is obvious, though, that the masterminds of football owe it to the public, if not themselves, to correct the officiating problem at the goal line.

If instant-replay pictures are so distasteful, they could simply change the rules. At the moment, a ball-carrier needs only to have possession at the instant he touches the goal line.

They could remove all judgment and doubt by saying nobody scores until he's down — with the ball in his possession, of course.

All of this has taken the heat off Schembechler and the Wolverines for having flopped one more time — make it the sixth straight time, the last four years in a row — in a bowl game.

If Michigan did not deserve to lose against USC, neither did it deserve to win.

You can't be sure what it is with Michigan, but the Wolverines are never themselves on New Year's Day. Neither are a lot of people, but these guys from Ann Arbor go to bed on time.

U-M makes more errors in a single bowl game than it makes in half a season. Take Rick Leach, for instance.

Leach had thrown only four interceptions coming here, and then threw two more, both putting up points for USC.

It's a curious thing about the U-M quarterback, but all of his interceptions have come off the same type of pass — deep over the middle. He threw three like that in the loss to Michigan State.

On all of 'em, Leach's passes sailed over the head of the receiver into the hands of a waiting safety. Noting that, you are led to wonder why that play is made available to him.

He didn't get much help against USC. The Michigan offense sputtered with dropped passes, penalties, misplayed punts — a gruesome variety of miscues you almost never associate with a Schembechler team.

Except in a bowl game. In a bowl game, you can count on Michigan to show less than its best. I'm not bitter, mind you; it's what the record shows.

The Wolverines have had three straight swinging strikes here at the Rose Bowl, and under the rules as we know 'em, anybody ought to be out and sent back to the bench.

It is time for somebody else to try. ✦

1 9 7 9

Magic, Spartans cage Bird, bring home NCAA championship

S ALT LAKE CITY — Maybe there have been more delightful moments. Perhaps there have been more delicious moments. But never ever could there have been a more wild, delirious moment in Michigan State's long athletic history than the one its magic basketball team produced last night.

The Spartans are champions of college basketball. They completed a miraculous turnabout from midseason despair to whip unbeaten and top-ranked Indiana State, 75-64, and all the joy championships can produce burst from them.

They swarmed over each other on the floor of the jammed Utah Sports Arena, pounded, hugged and even kissed each other, and up in the stands, some 2,500 who had followed them burst out in song.

"A-a-men, A-a-men!" they chorused.

They waved and tossed their green-and-white pompons in the air and danced in the aisles and seemed likely to cascade down the chairs in unrestrained celebration.

It was as wild a scene as you are likely to see in any basketball arena.

Coach Jud Heathcote and his players gathered in a circle at midcourt, knelt and seemed to be chanting a prayer of some kind. A moment of sobering thanks, so it appeared.

They sang it out like a college cheer. They spelled:

"P-O-T-E-N-T-I-A-L!" Potential.

It has been their motivation. They knew they had it in them to do great things, even when they were on the verge of collapse weeks ago, if only they persisted. Now here they had done it all, completing one of the grandest comebacks from near disaster in the history of the NCAA tournament.

They won't forget their hour here. It was an incredible scene from the instant Magic Man Earvin Johnson fired a pass from under one basket far up floor, where Greg Kelser gathered it in, took a flying leap and slam-dunked the ball for the final score of the game.

It was typical of this Spartans team. They always have been very quick, opportunistic, destructive and especially dramatic, and here was Kelser delivering the hammer blow to a proud Indiana State team that had not lost in 33 previous games.

This wasn't an easy victory for the Spartans. Far from it. There were several moments when they seemed likely to put Indiana State to the same kind of rout they had applied to all others en route to the championship finals.

They couldn't manage it. Indiana State stayed threateningly close, close enough to suggest right up until the final two minutes this game still could be plucked away from the Spartans.

As we mentioned two days ago, the one element that could ruin the Spartans in this showdown was fouling. It came perilously close to happening.

They got into foul trouble early and it restricted their play the remainder of the game. Except for some careful play by Johnson, and Kelser, too, the mounting fouls could have proved disastrous.

Most of the fouls were worth it, because the majority of 'em came as the Spartans battled heavily under the boards to control Indiana State's driving offense.

Heathcote gambled with that. There had been a suspicion he would let Indiana State's marvelous Larry Bird roam fairly free and do his thing, which is score, while shutting down all the other Sycamores shooters.

Heathcote decided to concede nothing to Bird. The sharpshooter who had averaged better than 29 points a game came away with merely 19.

The Spartans threw their scissor-tight three-man zone around Bird, shutting off passes from the front and behind. They kept him frustrated from start to finish, and that was the decisive stroke in thwarting the Sycamores.

"We won it with our defense, no question about it," said Heathcote, who had ranted on the sidelines while penalties continued to mount against the Spartans. "The penalties limited the things we could do on offense, and so we had to play conservatively, more conservatively than we like. But that's the way the game developed."

The heralded matchup of MSU's Earvin Johnson and ISU's Larry Bird, the two best players in college basketball, was clearly won by the Magic Man.

Johnson not only outscored Bird, 24-19, he produced more assists (5-2), ran the Michigan State game on offense and defense as if his every move had been choreographed, and he kept Indiana State at a distance and under control at all times.

"Coach came up with a great game plan to stop Larry Bird," Johnson said, "and it really worked. Larry's a great player, but we did a job on him."

The Magic Man was mainly responsible for that. Most of the game, he was in Bird's face, with Kelser, Ron Charles or Jay Vincent at his back, and one or the other shutting off Bird so he could not slip through their vise.

And of such strategy are championships won. ✦

Putting the jockey before the horse often pays off

I t generally is assumed by unsophisticated visitors to the horse track that race winners, if not actually preordained, are at least predictable in more instances than you know.

This is not to say they believe a fix of some sort might be working, although from time to time that has been the case at almost any racetrack.

What the innocents believe is that horses bearing a name that seems especially significant at a given moment surely will be first under the wire.

Depending on the day of the week, maybe 10 to 20 percent of all the bets will be made on such coincidence and hunch. So it is said.

I am tempted to say this is a very dumb way to bet a horse race, except I have seen it work too many times. Several years ago I witnessed a triumph that has affected my own handicapping.

Three ladies were pooling a trifecta bet. One with a hot-tempered son picked Fiery Don; the second chose My Buddy because she had one. The third picked a horse named Paleface because she alone in the group had a deep Florida tan.

The combination paid them $1,900. I haven't trusted horse racing since.

Whenever I get near a racetrack, I challenge insiders to explain the weird results we see coming out of horse racing and, of course, they can't. I always figured horses were more reliable than the lottery, but can we be sure?

Remember back in January the nation was alarmed to hear the celebrated kid jockey Steve Cauthen had ridden 110 straight races without a winner. It was more than weird, it was impossible.

Given nine horses in a race, experts can't pick that many straight losers. Riding just one horse per race, the nation's best jockey cannot lose 110.

Two years ago, Cauthen won more than anybody else, and right behind him was Wayne Catalano, the New Orleans flash who does most of his riding at Hazel Park.

I stopped by to interrogate Catalano because, truth be told, if you can't entrust a few bucks to the very best jockeys around, somebody ought to start a new game.

"It seems impossible, it does," Catalano says. "It seems tough to ride that many horses — 110 races — and not come up with a winner. You'd think one or two have got to stumble in."

An awful lot of people who don't bet horses' names bet on name jockeys, even if they're riding a mule.

They bet Wayne Catalano that way, figuring that sooner or later on any afternoon that slicker will get you home safely.

When I said that, he blushed. Not out of modesty. He was embarrassed for another reason.

"I'm just coming off probably my worst losing streak since I started five years ago," he says. "I had nine losers one day last week, then seven the next and some more before I got a win again."

I'm glad you weren't there to share it, either.

He wasn't worried or disheartened, he says, even though people around the finish line at Hazel Park were calling him something other than "good ol' Cat."

Catalano is the smoothie who has brought home a winner once every five times he has climbed in a saddle here since 1974. We've had guys at the ballpark who don't hit .200 with a bat, but he does it on horseback.

"Racing luck can go either good or bad," he says. "When you hit a slump, you just have to be realistic. There's always a reason.

"One or two of my horses in that losing streak just got beat; a couple others didn't belong where they finished. There were a few others that were going to be my ride, but they won with another rider."

Like anybody else and especially racetrack people, he does not like to talk much about losing.

"I also hold the national record for 41 straight racing days with at least one winner," he says. "You know that?"

Of course. It was how I became rich in 1977.

Despite the losing streak, Catalano is running away as usual with the jockey race at Hazel Park. Before another winter arrives, he will pocket maybe another $250,000 for his work on local tracks.

His success perpetuates itself. A top jockey generally will be asked to ride the very best horses. Ergo, both are most likely to win.

Horse experts say Catalano wins because he is possibly the hardest-working jockey — at the track at 5:30 every morning to say hello to horses, even the ones he does not ride — and because he is smart and bold and gifted with "great hands."

He is not sure what they mean about his hands, except they are powerful yet sensitive hands, and he finds horses respond readily to him.

"The handicappers say I'm worth 10 lengths in a race," he says. "I don't know. That's an awful lot extra to expect out of a jockey."

He paused and thought about that.

"Hell, I'm a cinch for five."

Me, too. No matter the horse's name. ✦

1979

Joe Louis, Thomas Hearns: Moments in the sun

L AS VEGAS, Nev. — For the past several days, interrupting routine which is vital to finely tuned athletes, Thomas Hearns has gone off on his own special pilgrimage.

He walks out of the shabby gym where he sweats and trains for his biggest hour in boxing. He abandons the Gold Strip of this hard-hearted town and drives off to the edge of the desert scrub to pay his respects to a failing old man.

The young Hit Man from Detroit's east side takes time to see Joe Louis, who came out of the same area years ago to become known to the world as the Brown Bomber. Joe wants to see Thomas, too, and when Thomas tells of their meetings, he sounds nothing like a guy tough enough to lay you out and plant you with one slug of his fist.

"I really have a strong feeling about what's happened to him," Hearns says. He says it haltingly, emotion clipping his voice.

"Actually, I've made three trips to see him this week. The first time he was in bed. The other times he was in a wheelchair.

"I talk to him a little while. He could not talk that much. He doesn't realize so much."

For whatever reason, nobody says Joe Louis is in such bad shape. Two years ago, the former heavyweight champion, now 65, had open-heart surgery. Later, he suffered a stroke and remains an invalid.

"I guess he looks OK for all of that," Hearns says. "But it's still sad to see him in that shape. It really downs you, because he meant so much to people."

Hearns is a day away from the fight of his professional life. He meets Harold Weston, who twice has fought (and lost) for versions of the welterweight title. Still, Weston is regarded as the toughest to date of Hearns' 18 opponents, all but the last of whom were knocked out.

Weston himself showed up at Louis' home to visit with the ex-champion while Hearns was there.

Oddly, perhaps, Hearns has a different perspective of Louis than others who almost revere the man.

"He was not really a special hero to me," Hearns says. "His time was before I was born. But I look up to the man for what he did for Detroit and people, and I would like do to that myself if I can.

"He shows a lot of interest in Detroit. He knew who I was and he kind of wished me luck. Like, he said, 'Luck,' and tried to wave his hand at me.

"He had this picture of himself when he was about 23. He's in a boxing pose, and he wants that picture to be used for the statue they will make for the new Joe Louis Arena in downtown Detroit.

"I really feel sorry for him, that a man like that should be hit so hard when he's old and after he did so much."

Emanuel Steward, Hearns' manager, accompanied him on the visits. More aware of history than his fighter, Steward sees Louis as more a national symbol than simply the most famous athlete to come out of Detroit.

"He was a symbol of a lot of things that helped bring people together in his time," Steward says. "He was not all Detroit — he was born in Alabama and lived most of his career in Chicago and became a man for the whole country.

"Everybody takes care of him. Even now there's a millionaire here who visits him every day just to see if he needs anything." ✦

1 9 7 9

Putting pedal to the metal is anything but a drag

You have the word of Mr. Jeb Allen, who seems trustworthy, that it is possible to ignite nitromethanol and a 2,000-horsepower engine at the seat of your pants and come away alive every time.

He has done it several thousand times and only once was he almost killed. Even then, it was an accident.

"The guy alongside me crossed over from his lane and ran right over me," he says. "We exploded in flames. From the pictures, you'd swear nobody was left."

Happily, Jeb was released from a hospital six months later with nothing worse than scars on his back and arms. The other guy had a broken arm.

Jeb is trying to convince us about racing top-fuel dragsters, those weird-looking creations whose thunder and flames at dragways around the United States are luring increasing millions.

It is not my favorite cup. We get enough noise in the neighborhood when kids tie balloons to their bicycle tires. But countless others are turning on to the dragsters, some for reasons that might surprise you.

"We had 40,000 at our race in New Jersey last week," Allen says. "Mostly it's a young crowd."

And Jeb is turned on worse than anybody else.

He is 23, easily the youngest of the hotshot top fuel dragsters, who tend to be middle-aged mechanic-driver whizzes, like Don Garlits, the Babe Ruth of the sport.

Jeb is a Californian, as are most of the top racers. His daddy and older brother raced, too, but all have moved into other pursuits, leaving Jeb to make his own noise.

"I got into it when I was 16," he says. "Then when I was 18, my father let me take my college money and invest it into building my own vehicle."

He designed and engineered his Praying Mantis. It looks like all the others, its huge rear tires sandwiching the engine, which nuzzles the driver's seat. A streamlined frame reaches 20 feet forward to hold the front wheels. They seem little more than cycle tires.

It's a $30,000 contraption, and Jeb has zapped it — or vice versa — over a quarter-mile racing strip in 5.85 seconds. The world record is 5.79.

It figures out to a top speed of roughly 250 miles an hour, or the kind of accelerating boost that could lift a guy into the clouds, if he were pointed that way.

"That's supposed to be the equivalent of three Gs, or the same kind of gravitational pressure astronauts get when they're blasted off in rockets," Jeb says.

Jeb and his kind do their thing, though, without aid of scientists and computers at Cape Canaveral and Houston. What they know is what they have learned in grease pits and garages, much of it by trial and error.

"Years ago there used to be lots of wrecks," he says. "That's when the motors were in front of the drivers. You'd have clutches blowing out of cars and other parts falling off. Everybody was sort of guessing at what they were doing.

"Now we've got it down to where motors run fairly safe and we have a lot of other safety equipment built in."

Like parachutes. They help bring these darting monsters to a stop, although as Jeb tells it, his car is such a dream he could get along without a chute.

"Stopping the car is almost as much fun as starting it," he says. "The chute is a safety factor. I've stopped several times without it, but you don't want to do that because every other run the brakes wear out and have to be changed."

To be safe, Jeb says, he makes sure he packs his own chute.

To be true, I was puzzled why a sturdy young Californian like Jeb Allen would not have adopted a cleaner, safer game, like, say, hang-gliding off a mountain, rather than pull the trigger on himself a dozen times every week in a dragster.

"A lot of competitors don't even consider this a real sport," he says. "But you have to get psyched up for it, and there's real teamwork and mechanical and racing skill involved."

Having beaten Don Garlits, the king, last week, he will try to do it again this weekend in Michigan at Milan Dragway.

"Sure my wife worries a lot. So do I," he finally admits. "But even when I had that accident, I never thought of quitting. I mean, the accident wasn't my fault. I didn't do anything wrong.

"It's scary, I'll admit that. We all get a little scared. Yeah, definitely it scares me. It scares the hell out of me."

I felt better when he said that. For a while, I thought it was me. ✦

1979

Talking tough is no joke until you add a punch line

Bar none and absolutely for sure, the very toughest punchers I have ever seen were not Joe Louis or Rocky Marciano or even Sonny Liston, but Bucky and Chuckie, who are brothers-in-law.

Maybe there are tougher, better one-shot take-out punchers somewhere, but the law should not permit contests to prove it.

One time, I swear, Bucky knocked a guy through a glass brick wall. It was like one of those Hollywood stunt scenes, the poor sucker running off into the fields holding his head with one hand, his bottom with the other, trying to pull himself back together before Bucky could get to him again.

Years ago Bucky and Chuckie operated old Detroit Recreation, the 88-lane bowling emporium that sat opposite the old Federal Building downtown. It's a parking lot now.

They had five bars operating in the building and any evening they would collect a weird assortment of patrons — politicians, judges, office girls, newspapermen, bookies, hustlers and bums off skid row. A moonlighting stripper occasionally mooned as she ran the elevators, to show you.

One evening, seeking a game of chess with Bucky, I stepped off the third-floor elevator just as a body came tumbling down the stairwell a few feet away. It hit the wall, bounced and ricocheted down another flight of stairs.

From above, you could hear Bucky, who had a hell of a short, corkscrew punch, hollering: "Here he comes!" and from below, Chuckie responding, "I'm waiting! I'm waiting!"

When the body reached the second floor, Chuckie belted it again. He used to pitch for the old St. Louis Browns and was especially proud of his straight overhand. The body tumbled and rolled down the last set of stairs, landing at the front door.

By then, Bucky had ridden the elevator down. He picked up the hulk, brushed it off and said, "Please don't come back."

Would I kid you? I could go on and on about Bucky and Chuckie, like the time six apes went after not only Bucky but me, too, and Bucky says to 'em: Do you want it one at a time or all together, for God's sake.

The brothers-in-law were at their best during that brief interlude when social disputes might be settled with bone and muscle, or that period before every other guy might be carrying a gun.

What brings us to such a topic is the invitation to any and all who think they are very tough indeed to join in the Toughman competition at the

Silverdome next month.

Mr. Art Dore, whose business is blowing down buildings in Bay City, Mich., and promoting an occasional boxing match, is putting up a $50,000 first prize to discover who is the toughest puncher in all of Michigan.

What he is seeking are genuine knockout guys, characters with fists bigger than their mouths. We've all seen a ton of the latter but not that many of the former, and Art Dore knows this is very true.

"An awful lot of guys walk around talking tough, but once they're challenged, they back right off," he says.

He knows because he has sponsored three similar contests around Michigan and has yet to find a big mouth advancing beyond preliminaries against a big fist.

At the moment, he has 175 entries, but only two dozen from the Detroit area, which is very tough, if you measure the noise.

One of the entries is Jim Trojanowski, who is 26, 5-feet-8, 230 pounds. He's an auto company stockman who grew up in Yale, a farming community in Michigan's Thumb. Even on the phone, he does not sound like a mouth.

"A guy who trains boxers told me about the contest," he says. "I guess I have a reputation. I've been in a few brawls."

The problem with being tough, so it seems, is that strangers demand proof. It happens to Trojanowski, who played football-basketball-track-baseball at Yale and briefly at Ferris State.

"You get in a bar and somebody hassles you," he says. "But I guess I was sort of the kingpin of Yale.

"One night a couple of farmers from Croswell came down looking for me. We went outside to the parking lot and I grabbed the one by the throat, flipped him up on a car and was ready to do him, and they begged off."

No knock against Croswell, mind you, but I do not notice an entry from the community on Art Dore's Toughman list.

Tommy Taylor, from Detroit's east side, is another entry. He is 19, stands 6-feet-10 and weighs 295 pounds. He was working at construction somewhere, but his brother Cortez tells about Tommy.

"I've seen him do things," he says. "He lifted the front end of a hi-lo truck with one hand. Other guys say they saw him actually stop a moving car. I mean, he just stepped in front of it, caught it and brought it to a stop."

C'mon now, Cortez. Did Tommy come out of a phone booth? Was he wearing a cape?

"Not all of us do," says Bucky, who basically is a har-de-har sort, when I tell him of Tommy Taylor.

What you should know is you never can be sure where you will find a guy who can knock your eyes out. When I interrupted Bucky, he was practicing a fox hunt.

He wants his pinks. ✦

**From
Louis'
death to
Hearns'
biggest
bouts to
titles by the
Panthers
and Tigers**

THE '80s

Detroit's Hit Man, Thomas Hearns, works out before his April 1985 bout with Marvin Hagler, one of the most thunderous, punishing fights in history.

1980

It was 'all in fun,'
Riggs says years later

What I remember most about Bobby Riggs, that ol' sonofagun, is wondering whether he would live when he seemed to be dying in the Houston Astrodome.

It was that awful night back in '73 when Billie Jean King almost killed him in a tennis match.

Poor Bobby sprawled on a chair at courtside as if in a vacuum. His legs ached so that they doubled up to his gut. His face was drawn, colorless. Guys hit by a train look better.

Few cared, or bothered with him. A brother. A son. A trainer.

They dipped into buckets full of chipped ice, rubbed his legs, his chest, his head. Somebody said call an ambulance, and from the rear of the circle came a shrill laugh: "Call the coroner."

There in the Astrodome, thousands of women whooped and hollered and at millions of parties around the country skirts swirled in celebration of B.J. King and her triumph.

The chauvinist pig, not the original and not the only but certainly the loudest, was dead.

Or so they thought.

Bobby Riggs still lives. That ol' joker is on display this weekend in the Boat and Camper Show at the Silverdome, ready to pitch pennies, toss cards into a hat, shoot basketball free throws, play gin rummy, backgammon or whatever.

Billie Jean King didn't teach him a thing. He hasn't changed much, if at all.

"She never would give me a rematch," says ol' Sugar Daddy, feeling only faintly responsible for what he says is the "nonsense" afflicting the men of the world today.

Even now he thinks he could beat her. Last year he became the first to win the national over-60 titles on almost any surface you could invent, and so he is willing to concede very little at all to women vs. men in competition.

A lot of things have changed since their match. Some people insist Riggs' loss hastened the changes, bringing about Title IX in the schools, putting girls on boys' teams, or at least giving girls the idea they could compete in sports.

What Bobby notices is the language has changed.

Checking into his hotel here, he called the desk for a bellboy, he says.

"They sent up a gal. They say she's a bellperson.

"We're not supposed to say bellwoman or bellgirl, or dame, broad, chick, doll, or anything like that. Person. It's nonsense. You're not going to get people to change to that.

"I don't expect them to change the way they talk when they refer to me or other men. Everywhere I go, people call me man, or guy or dude, or even a pig if they want.

"That doesn't bother me. What bothers me is once they called me stud. Now nobody calls me that anymore."

Well, he is 62. In his time he has been the world's greatest tennis player, sports hustler, put-on artist, etc.

He is a little guy, 5-feet-8 or so outside his cushioned sneakers. When he conjured up the showdown with B.J. King back in '73, spotting the queen of women athletes 22 years on court, it was "strictly all in fun."

Except a lot of women didn't take it that way, especially B.J. King and women tennis players, and when the queen beat the devil out of ol' Bobby, a lot of good things began happening for 'em in sports particularly.

"I'm happy for them," he says. "Certainly they deserve to make money in sports if they bring in the crowds like the men. I'm all for them."

His reputation as a true chauvinist, you should know, has been a bit phony from the very beginning.

He had some clever lines that shook women, like "they should keep their biscuits in the oven and their buns in bed," but he insists it was all a slick trick, a stunt and promotion, a way to perk interest and make a buck.

"Ever since I've had plenty of money in the bank drawing interest — at 12 percent — and I wander around the country doing things like this show and enjoying myself at whatever I choose," he says.

In that respect, he figures he has just had the women again. Fooled 'em, even as they thought they were trampling him.

"What's ERA? I'm not even sure I know what's it's about. I know they're still trying to get it passed. Maybe they will. I'm not for or against it. I think it's a dead issue. Who cares?

"I've got no problem with women, any of 'em. I've always been fair to my wives, to all our kids, to all the girls who come to me.

"Women are great. They come around and want to run their fingers through my hair. I've been the best thing for 'em. I gave their movement, whatever it is, impetus and credibility."

Still, he figures, it could have been different. He made a mistake the night before he played Billie Jean King in Houston.

"I played her husband Larry for a thousand bucks in a one-set exhibition match," Bobby says. "He was a very good player, a borderline pro, and I gave him a four-game lead and a 20-year edge, and he never won a game."

Bobby figures he never should have picked on B.J.'s old man. It cost him a war. ✦

No one knows the ropes like Freddie the promoter

P oor Freddie. His gut sears with pain, such dreadful pain that he disappears for days at a time, to a hospital in Los Angeles, a famous friend in Las Vegas, to some lonely motel room in Detroit.

His belly bends him in a stoop so he scarcely can walk and even with that he chokes constantly on those damnable cigarettes and any minute his head will pound and cry the folly of this world.

He woke up the other morning, to show you more, and heaved a huge breath just to determine whether he was still with us, and blew out one of his front teeth. Poor Freddie.

He's the guy who put together the big fight show coming up at Joe Louis Arena, the one sending Hilmer Kenty after the world lightweight championship and Thomas Hearns after a contrived bauble called the U.S. Boxing Association's world welterweight championship.

You wonder sometimes how and why some things get done in the sports world, how rival factions are pulled together, matches made, how athletes are paid, how promoters wind up with the big bucks.

Often they get done because of guys like Fred Sommer, who, where fights are concerned, knows anybody and everybody and deals in friendships and favors owed, and trust.

"Money has nothing to do with it," he says. "That's the old way, the best way. The money is there, but money is everywhere, so good deals are made on mutual respect and friendship."

He's an Old World guy. Guys from the Old World talk like that, although, in truth, a lot of them have been known to carve a gizzard out of their dear godfather. But some do have uncompromising loyalties.

Freddie's one undying loyalty is intriguing. It is to Joe Louis, the old Brown Bomber. You will see in a moment.

Freddie goes back about as far as you want to remember. He is 71, a silver-haired shrewdie who talks endlessly of the fight game and the ignorance-innocence of some and the intrigue of others.

He's a dandy. It is his habit to call all around the hemisphere daily, checking in with anybody, so that Ma Bell can count on maybe $20,000 a year from him. He calls me sometimes six, eight times a day, for as long as an hour when I can afford the time. Once I fell asleep on the kitchen floor listening to Freddie calling from Las Vegas.

I might be the only guy who really likes him. Everybody else seems merely to tolerate him. He drives Emanuel Steward, who manages the local fighters, to distraction, because Freddie has a very definite idea about how everything should be done where a fight promotion is concerned, and he advises, insistently. When people don't listen, he might even call 'em names.

"I'm Chher-man — you know how Chher-mans are," he says, as if that explains everything.

He drives John Yopp nuts. Yopp is the real estate broker who is promoter of the big show. To hear Freddie tell it, Yopp has not done one thing right yet.

"They're a bunch of amateurs," Freddie says. "This program should be sold out already. I come to Detroit and hardly anybody knows we're having these fights. What the hell dees amacheurs been doing?"

Well, it shouldn't be his concern in the first place. Freddie did his bit arranging for Kenty to get a shot at lightweight champion Ernesto Espana and for Hearns to beat Angel Espada.

These matches didn't "just happen." As Hearns has found, when you near title caliber, everybody ducks, nobody wants to fight you. Freddie says he put it all together because of an old friendship with Pepi Cordero, an attorney in San Juan, who handles the Latin fighters.

Cordero and Freddie dealt when no others could. For that, Freddie is due a slice of maybe $15,000 out of the big show, so he worries constantly over how it is progressing, money-wise and at the box office.

So you will know, it's a cinch. They sold $200,000 worth to network television and already have pulled $100,000 through the ticket wickets. Within the next week, they should do at least another $100,000 worth, so it's a locked-in promoter's dream.

You should know something more about Freddie. In the 1920s, while still a kid in Cologne, Germany, he promoted an exhibition match between touring heavyweight champion Jack Dempsey and a promising German fighter named Max Schmeling.

"Dempsey liked me," Freddie says. "He talked me into coming to this country, and when Choe Louis fought Schmeling in 1936, I was part of the Louis camp."

He still is. He is No. 1 believer and chief promoter of the Joe Louis legend. He has been Louis' sidekick and image watchdog for 40-odd years. That's how it happened that Hilmer Kenty and Thomas Hearns and Emanuel Steward and John Yopp wound up in the big show at Joe Louis Arena, and why Joe Louis will be coming to Detroit under Freddie's umbrella next week.

"I met them when they came to Las Vegas last May," Freddie says, "and in December I arranged with my friend Pepi Cordero, because I liked Emanuel and Tommy Hearns.

"Hearns looked to me like the best-hitting welterweight in the history of boxing. Not that he's perfect; he has problems — he spreads his legs too far and is off-balance; he drops his left the same way Choe Louis did against Schmeling the first time. And I'm worried whether Tommy can take it in the gut like a good fighter should."

It bothers him so much he frowns and grasps his belt, and it's like the fight people say. If Freddie isn't bellyachin', his belly is. ✦

If tennis has a queen, it's Billie Jean King

I n a moment of sad introspection, Billie Jean King, the sports revolutionary, looked back on the tragedies that had befallen her friends in recent weeks, and she figured there's only one way to approach life anymore.

Three of them had died — her grandmother, the daughter of a friend, the doctor who last year performed surgery on her injured ankle and saved her career.

Billie Jean decided to be happy. What else was there to do?

"You should have seen me last week," she said after walloping luckless Evonne Goolagong, 6-3, 6-0, in a surprising title-round rout in the Avon tennis championships at Cobo Arena. "I was terrible, impossible.

"But I made a commitment to myself that when I came to Detroit I would try to forget about everything and maintain a positive attitude every day, every moment. I'm basically a happy person, but the last month has been tough."

Once here, she was tough. Happy and tough. It helped, of course, that Martina Navtratilova, the dominant one in women's tennis today, and Chris Evert Lloyd, who was that of yesterday, and Tracy Austin, who will be that of tomorrow, all passed up the Detroit tournament.

The $35,000 first prize was sitting there, waiting for someone to reach out and grab it, if not by default, then by taking charge in the absence of the tour's best players.

Who better to recognize that, and do it, than the person who started women's tennis on its way in the first place?

Billie Jean King, 36 and supposedly in the twilight of the finest sports career of anyone who ever wore skirts, never played better than in her week's work at the downtown hall.

She had not, in fact, won a regular tour tournament since beating Rosie Casals here in the 1974 final. Injuries and other activities had interrupted her, and younger, more ambitious players had passed her by.

At one time she thought she was finished. But two years ago she decided she still loved the game that helped carve a significant place in all sports for women.

A six-time singles champion at Wimbledon (the last, 1975), she managed last year despite her ankle problem to wind up No. 4 in the world rankings. She even thinks she can be No. 1 again.

"Sure, I'm thinking of winning Wimbledon again — why not?" she asked.

She obviously tires of her recent role at the mecca of fuzzball, which is playing and winning in doubles, and as long as she is playing "better than ever," why not go for all that is available?

"What I want to prove," she said with a laugh, "is that life isn't finished after 30."

She said her husband, Larry, calls her the renaissance woman, but in truth she was a revolutionary, the one who started and inspired women tennis players to strike out on their own, if need be, until promoters paid the women decently, the same as men.

It all began in 1968, when women were getting merely $10,000 (vs. triple that for men) in major tournaments. Today, a half-dozen women, including B.J. King, have topped the million-dollar mark in prize winnings alone.

In no sport is there anyone quite like her, man or woman. She is far more than a mere player. She is counselor to other players, sometimes coach, almost always a friend. Because she leads so many of them, she has become the one most influential athlete around.

Billy Jean King. The lady is a champ. ✦

1 9 8 0

What about due process? Bo's actions indefensible

I f the court will come to order, we will open the trial of Mr. Bo Schembechler, who in one swoop the other day became prosecutor, judge and hangman for five of his athletes, and now he finds himself in mud.

In a way, his is a trial of all brethren, for the ability of coaches to rule imperially over their athletes comes into question.

As you recall, the five were dumped from the University of Michigan football team for violating rules. That sort of thing happens from time to time in all sports on our college campuses.

The problem here, though, was that the players had been accused of using drugs, particularly marijuana.

The public was shocked, and from what I gathered, understood and sympathized with Schembechler's outrage.

The pleasant village of Ann Arbor was shocked, too, but for a different reason. It is generally conceded that maybe 80 percent of the students there puff the sweet weed, and it is assumed that number probably includes some athletes.

Marijuana so prevails there, in fact, that the penalty for possessing it is little more than the assessment for illegally parking a bicycle.

That being the case, you are led to wonder why the penalty against football players for doing what so many others in their environment do regularly should be so severe, or why it would cause such a stir.

There are reasons. You know, of course, that undergraduate sports is the last bastion of personal discipline in civilian life. Or so those who govern athletes believe.

Coaches talk that way all the time. The church might have failed with some of us, and fathers couldn't do it for others. But coaches get it done. When rules are flaunted, coaches stand at the ramparts of righteousness flailing the miscreants.

It sounds mighty noble of 'em, and I have no great objection to it, having submitted three sons and a daughter to the hands of various coaches. They came away with a scar or two but considerably smarter and apparently better for it.

None of 'em, though, ran into the kind of condemnation and public embarrassment that befell the Michigan quintet when the reason for their banishment from the football team was revealed.

If Schembechler was outraged by what he considered a gross violation of his team rules, so was the father of one of the players, who claimed he learned of it on a radio report that said his son was a "pusher." When he sent the kid to Ann Arbor a few years ago, nobody could tell him how the kid would turn out; at the same time, he never expected assassination.

During the weekend, I talked with a judge and a lawyer about the Michigan episode, and both thought Bo Schembechler was in mighty deep water, no matter what sort of rules he had set up for his team.

"To begin with, there is the problem of due process," the judge said. "You simply can't accuse someone and dismiss him without furnishing proof and offering him opportunity to defend himself. From what I gather, the coach told the players they were finished — that's it. You can't do that."

The lawyer said any lawyer would love to have such a case working, especially with the players insisting on their innocence, because our laws do not permit anybody to play god, or even prosecutor-jury-hangman.

"If there was a legal challenge here," he said, "it could establish some clear restrictions on coaches. Whether on scholarship or not, an athlete cannot be dismissed on a coach's whim or for unsubstantiated breaking of rules."

It is curious, you notice, that within 48 hours of Schembechler's blast-off, U-M and all concerned were backing down and saying the players would be allowed to return to the team, after a year's suspension.

I suspect somebody overruled the coach on this one because his dictatorial dismissal of the players could not hold up, and especially because the athletes, not allowed to defend themselves, could claim to have been damaged personally by the school.

Lest you construe all this as a defense of marijuana or a minimizing of its dangers, be assured that is not the case at all. A doctor friend, in fact, was wondering recently where the hell is the government, and the newspapers, too, because recent studies show the weed can indeed cause permanent damage to habitual users.

You see from all this that unrestrained coaches, too, can cause permanent damage. ✦

1 9 8 0

Connors' mom molded Jimmy into a tennis champion

Y ou are aware, of course, that dealing with women in sports today is a matter as delicate as defusing a bomb.

If you can't be careful, you had better be lucky.

Which I was — careful and lucky — when Gloria Connors sat on the sofa to talk about her life and love and her creation of Jimmy Connors, the tennis player.

Until a year or so ago, or until Bjorn Borg, the Swede, began knocking the socks off Connors, Jimmy was headed toward all-time greatness. Now there is a question whether he merits that, having been topped in his own time.

Anyway, Gloria Connors came to town to hype the forthcoming tennis match between son Jimmy and Ilie Nastase, the nasty Romanian, at Cobo Arena.

Ilie was an elder brother of Jimmy when the kid began making the tennis stops at Cairo, Buenos Aires, Rome, Paris, London, Tokyo, Melbourne and assorted tennis spas, including Indianapolis. It is unclear whether Jimmy learned to love mamalega but, then, even Romanians hate the national dish.

Ilie is 34 and Jimmy 26, which is getting up there on the tennis scale, and they are putting together a tour of their own, and Detroit finally will get a live view of them.

"We picked Ilie because I wouldn't let Jimmy play with just anybody," says Gloria Connors. "Too many of the other tennis players are just deadheads. Nastase has color and gives good tennis and a good show."

If you are unfamiliar with tennis, Connors-Nastase and the new phenom, John McEnroe, are the most colorful characters in the game, one or the other inclined to drop his pants in protest during a match, or otherwise insult the audience and game officials.

By and large, nastiness is largely tolerated today even in a mannered game like tennis, maybe because the athletes are multi-millionaires, or perhaps because it is viewed as simply great fun.

No doubt you have seen Gloria Connors. She is an unusual star of television. Whenever Jimmy, the biggest moneymaker in sports aside from Muhammad Ali, is playing a match, cameras seek her out.

They know she will be at courtside wearing a heavy frown, a mean and ugly scowl, which gives the viewer a very definite idea about Mrs. Connors. The picture is one of a tough ol' mother, which of course she is.

What the picture does not show is a surprisingly attractive woman. Nor does it ever let her explain about her son, who was molded from the cradle by the mother to be precisely what he is.

You begin with Gloria Connors herself, whose father once fought Joe Louis in an exhibition in St. Louis.

"My whole life has been sports," she says. "My mother was a tennis player and swimmer, and when I was a teenager, I was ranked among the top 20 players in the world. I played Forest Hills, usually making third round, and I reached the semifinals in doubles with Pancho Segura as my partner."

That was back in the 1940s. Gloria Connors dropped tennis for a while to get married and produce two sons, Johnny and Jimmy. Johnny was going to be a tennis star, too — she says he could be among the top 10 players today — but he preferred football and racing cars. Today, 18 months older than his brother and looking like a football type, Johnny helps manage Jimmy's affairs.

"I started Jimmy at tennis when he was 3 years old," the mother says.

She did more than that; she invented a power style of play that revolutionized the game. It sprang from the two-fisted backhand, which is rather like teaching a Little Leaguer to bat cross-handed.

Deplored by purists, the two-handed shot nonetheless has been adopted by most of the dominant players in the game today — Connors, Borg, McEnroe particularly among the men, Tracy Austin, Chris Evert Lloyd with the women.

"I was really criticized for that," the mother says. "I knew it limited a player's reach, but I knew it could also be an extra weapon."

She will not tell us how the Connors' two-hander is different and special from all the others. ("It's a secret I can't give out.") She says she might have to write a book someday. But assuming you're curious, notice that Jimmy always takes a ball on the backside on the rise, stepping forward and into it, so that his return stays low, crisp and awesomely accurate.

"I've taught all over the country, but Jimmy is really an extension of myself. Nobody else taught him and I won't let anybody alter his strokes."

Since the rise of topspin swatters such as Borg and McEnroe, Connors, who rarely loops a return, has been advised to copy their strokes. His own style demands such precision there is little margin for error.

The mother says this is absurd; she will never allow anyone to change whatever Jimmy does on the tennis court. Nor would Jimmy be inclined. In the last two years Borg has supplanted him as the king of the court, but Connors relentlessly persists with a game of thunder strokes, which are magnificent, to be sure, but not as steady as Borg's splatter.

"He is an extension of me," says Gloria Connors. "He was 17 before he was able to beat me on the court. When he was finally able to do that, it became my greatest thrill, beyond all the championships that came later.

"Don't underestimate me. I am his mother, his coach, his manager, agent, chief bottle-washer and baby-sitter."

If you say, "My gosh, is this how great champions are made?" you would not be much wrong. ✦

1 9 8 0

Clubhouse confidential: The players behind the uniforms

S ome in the audience will be surprised to learn that as the baseball game progresses and the crowd's anxiety mounts, the bench is not filled with players applauding and encouraging their teammates.

It depends on the team, of course. Some are sharply disciplined and attentive to every wiggle and bounce. But others are loose and indifferent, oblivious to events on the field.

The players could be back in the clubhouse chomping ice cream bars, swigging pop or even watching a golf match on television. Imagine that.

"The Yankees ... they're always back in the clubhouse, and Oakland, those guys are the wildest. They'll be back here with 12 tape recorders going full blast, all of 'em playing different music."

You have it on the word of Mr. Rip Collins, who has labored in Tiger Stadium locker rooms and similar strip joints for nearly 30 years, or since shortly after he completed his 141st combat mission as a Marine fighter pilot in Korea.

He manages the visiting team's clubhouse, tending the laundry and needs of the touring players, be it socks and jocks, or gum, tobacco or playing cards.

His view of the players is unusual. He sees them in all their moods — intense and boiling, relaxed and clowning, or just plain goofing off.

"Some of the teams are very strict — like Boston, Minnesota, Baltimore, Toronto and Seattle," he says. "Their players stay out on the bench and watch the game. They're out here to play ball; that's the way I'm impressed. If the players drift to the clubhouse, the manager comes back and raises hell with 'em."

Aw, but that's only a few of the 13 teams that swing into town and alight in Collins' clubhouse.

"When Billy Martin handled the Yankees, he was tough about the players' staying on the bench, but the Yankees changed when he left," Collins says. "If a guy doesn't think he's coming up to bat that inning, he'll come back through the tunnel to the clubhouse.

"A lot of times they'll have coffee or ice cream or just stand around talking, or watching whatever's on television."

But the game, what of the game? Here the crowd is begging and praying and screaming, but underneath the stands, you mean the players are yawning?

"It will be interesting to see what Billy Martin has done with Oakland now," Collins says, "because the team was a zoo. They tell me they had a kid who if he wasn't in the lineup just got dressed and left."

He knows little of the Tigers' personal traits because the home team resides on the opposite corner of the stadium. But he sees all the visitors, and some of 'em are surprising.

"Reggie Jackson can be the nicest guy in the world, but he can be sitting there on his stool with nothing happening and then erupt and just blow you out. I think mostly he likes to test people.

"Remember George Scott?" (He's a former Red Sox first baseman.) "He was nasty. Just plain nasty. If a kid didn't do his shoes right, he'd throw 'em. I'd throw them back at him."

Rip has favorite teams, so you might expect, and generally they are the disciplined teams mentioned earlier. Generally, they are also the better teams, which should suggest something.

"I like a lot of the Kansas City guys," he says. "But you get a Marty Pattin, who's a very nice person until he gets knocked out of a game, and then you stand back because he kicks and throws things all over the place.

"Lou Piniella's another one like that. And George Brett. He's got a vicious, wild temper. He'll bust up the bat rack, throw helmets, kick things."

When that happens, Rip stands aside, minding his own business, mentally totaling up the damage so he can present the bill before the team leaves town.

"A funny one is Earl Weaver, the Baltimore manager. If he wins, we have strict orders not to touch his uniform, shoes, socks. We touch nothing. He's gonna wear the same stuff until he loses or it rots off him.

"The Orioles were on a winning streak last year and his uniform was really raunchy with tobacco juice all over the shirt, pants and socks. He really needed to lose a game before the board of health condemned him."

There have been delightful but scary moments in the visiting team's clubhouse.

"When Cleveland was here last year, we had a bomb scare. The cops brought in a dog to sniff out the bomb, and the players were in the whirlpool, or shaving or in the middle of getting dressed. They were ignoring the scare.

"We decided to turn on the heat. The blower hadn't been used since the previous year and when we flipped the switch, it went 'VoooooOOOOOM!' like an explosion, and dirt and soot flew all over the room and just scared the hell out of everybody."

The Indians haven't really relaxed in the clubhouse since. ✦

For bleacher creatures
the game's afoot

R ogie has Elaine down on her back in the centerfield bleachers at Tiger Stadium. She is laughing and screaming because Rogie is sitting there on his perch paying no mind to anything, including the ballgame, but he is tickling her bare feet.

"She loves it," says Rogie, smiling all around at his buddies.

"Rogie, I'm gonna kill you," Elaine says. She is giggling and thrashing on the concrete, but everybody figures Rogie is right, she loves it.

Lo and behold at the drug store a few minutes ago, there was the same Rogie, a big, bearded guy, maybe 28. He had in hand a roll of athletic tape and a flat pint of rum. He was preparing to go to the ballgame.

"If Elaine was going with me, it'd be no big deal," he says. "She'd just slip the bottle in her panties.

"But now I have to tape it to my belly. When the guards at the stadium frisk you, they never touch your belly below the belt. They'd better not."

To be sure. But that's how Rogie gets his booze into the park.

It is no big deal, as he says, except just before the Tigers left town on their recent road swing, the stadium erupted with drunks and fights all around. A dozen or so were arrested, some complaining that stadium guards were unnecessarily rough and, in fact, might have been the cause of the ruckus in the first place.

As the Tigers returned home, it was presumed the guards would be especially vigilant searching for booze being brought into the ballpark.

"To hell with 'em," Rogie says. "We don't cause the trouble. All we're looking for is a nice time. We mind our own business and don't bother anybody. You want the cause of the trouble, look to the guards."

Well, he says what many others in the bleachers at the stadium insist is true. He says this is not a coarse, unmannered and drunken segment of the audience at all, but maybe the best part of the whole crowd.

I tend to agree with him, because the bleachers crowd, so much maligned for rowdyism, is not that at all. It's where I watch my games.

Years ago I abandoned the press box because it is the lousiest seat in the stadium; that struck me when I left a gruesomely dull game early one evening only to discover on the way out of the park the fans down below were having a hell of a time. I joined the party.

I came by the bleachers accidentally, with a group who had been into track, football and the like but now that they were out of competition rediscovered baseball. One of 'em who sits on my hearth hasn't bothered with the Lions in eight years. I don't really understand it, either.

But for no reason I know, that sort comes back to baseball loving it like no other game around. They seem the type who fill the bleachers today. It is not a poor crowd. Bleacher seats are the cheapest at the stadium, but many are there because they prefer it.

They especially resent the slurs suggesting the crumbs of the baseball audience are in the exposed upper seats in centerfield.

"I don't give a damn what anybody thinks," Rogie says. "But we can sit here in the bleachers and see the drunks and fights around the box seats and in the grandstands and nothing's happening out in the bleachers, but everybody's having a nice time."

The view is unbelievably good and the atmosphere to their liking, so the game becomes their picnic every night — or until an ugly incident arises, as it did on the Tigers' last home stand.

"Hell, it's not the drinking," Rogie says. "The guards come in and try to remove one guy and he won't go, so they start beating the hell out of him. Nobody wants to see the guy get killed, so guys jump in and then you've got a riot.

"But hell, it's not a crowd of drunks. I'd prefer to have a beer or two. I don't even like rum and Coke. But in the bleachers it takes you an inning and a half to buy a beer, and then the beer is watered down. I mean, that's really lousy beer. I'll bet you there's never been anybody who got drunk on bleacher beer."

Careful there, Rogie. You're going to get us both in trouble with stuff like that. But it is lousy beer. ✦

1 9 8 0

'Raging Bull' LaMotta wears kid gloves now

R ecords are unclear, but not until 1958 or so had Fuller and Hoover and Colgate-Palmolive manufactured enough mops and brushes or created enough suction and soap to clean up a character like Jake LaMotta. Here is one of the world's greatest sports bums.

Alongside Jake, Sonny Liston was a sweetheart. Sonny, at least, never beat on anybody outside the boxing ring except cops..

But Jake LaMotta, a favored creature out of Detroit's past, was robber, thief, wife-beater, panderer, confessed boxing diver and more. He was as dirty, mean, rotten and vicious as any man ever to become the world middleweight boxing champion, or champion of any sort in any sport.

Why Jake LaMotta is walking around today is a mystery. By his own account, an awful lot of people owe him a shot.

But here he sits, back in the town where he says he "could have been elected mayor," and he is not the same Jake LaMotta of a score and more years ago.

He was New York City — the Bronx Bull, they called him — and he came here 21 times in the 1940s and '50s to fight, to beat Sugar Ray Robinson and Marcel Cerdan and Laurent Dauthuille, among others, in incredible fights, brutal bloody fights, in an era romanticized for reasons no one knows.

He is a very nice man today. He is 57, dapper in Hollywood-vested gray. Unscarred. Soft-spoken, patient, persuasive. Likable, even.

It happens that way with a lot of reformed bums. Ask the women who still love them. Usually, the metamorphosis has something to do with religion, or even kids. They see a light somewhere, somehow, from above or in a child's eyes, and they say omigod, what have I been doing? Not with Jake.

"My life changed in 1958 when they put me in a box," he says.

Operating a seedy nightclub on the Miami Beach strip, Jake became entangled with a 14-year-old blond. The cops nailed him for borderline pimping.

"They had me on a prison chain gang in Florida, and I did something and they threw me in this seven-by-seven-by-three-foot cell for a couple of days, and I began thinking."

Maybe for the first time in his life. He had been the world middleweight champion, the toast of the New York-Detroit-Chicago circuit. He had made and blown a fortune, and while doing it he had spat on anything and anybody, and then he found himself in hell's dungeon.

He changed. Dramatically. And almost overnight. Part of his meditation was rationalization — he was the way he was because he had to be that way to get what he wanted, he says now. It's a convenient excuse for anything, but Jake emerged determined to be nice and respectable.

He went to drama school to become an actor and he worked on a book called "The Raging Bull," his autobiography. It was published about 10 years ago — one of the best sports books I've read — and is being reissued now because the movie, "Raging Bull," starring Robert DeNiro, is going to be a smash hit. It will show around town this week. That's why Jake was here.

I remember him from before. He was never nasty with the press, though the record shows he'd beat on almost anybody else. The Bronx Bull was a 160-pound bully. We'd go to see him over at the old Book-Cadillac, and there to greet us in a flowing white robe deeply cut down the front was his astonishing, magnificently endowed blond wife, Vikki. Jake seemed deliberately to show her off, show off more of her than made any sense.

Which is why his movie "Raging Bull" does not quite fit. Much of the film revolves around Jake's insane jealousy where Vikki is concerned; he trusts not her nor anyone who lays eyes on her. It leads him to beat the hell out of friends, family and Vikki, too.

So you will know, Vikki — one of five former wives and still a stunner — came back to Detroit with Jake and Jake Jr., and they were delightful. Especially Jake, who always before had been guts and gutter. It makes you wonder.

Try the movie, if you like. DeNiro is superb, as are most of the others. But be aware the language is from the streets; at stages, every other word begins with an "f."

They're not shouting fight-team-fight, either. Jake LaMotta never did. ✦

1981

Cleveland coach suffers a mental Brownout

C LEVELAND — Down in the east end zone the cruel wind sweeping up over the bleachers from Lake Erie swirled in paralyzing circles. The screams of enthralled thousands crackled in the air on this dreadful Sunday as the Cleveland Browns, eyeing the dying clock, moved on toward the goal line and almost certain victory over the Oakland Raiders.

It had been a brutal football game, made so by incredible cold weather — zero degrees and a knifing, 30 mile-an-hour wind — that punished players and spectators alike. But now as it neared its end, the Browns, trailing, 14-12, were at the Oakland 13-yard line and 77,655 of their followers were on their feet stomping, shouting, already celebrating. In a moment, a decade of futility would end for the long-suffering Browns.

What happened then will live on as one of the strangest, most incomprehensible decisions in pro football history.

With only 41 seconds remaining to play and needing merely a field goal to beat the Raiders and continue their pursuit of the pro football championship, the Browns dared to pass.

Brian Sipe's throw was picked off in the end zone. The Browns never got a chance to kick the field goal. They didn't trust themselves to do it, and they lost.

It was astonishing. When it happened, I couldn't believe it. I was down on the Browns' sideline, the wind biting more severely on the field than the huddled spectators or TV viewers could imagine, as the Browns stormed into field-goal range on Sipe's passing.

Reaching the 13, they called time-out. It was second down, and coach Sam Rutigliano wanted to consult with coaches and with Sipe, his quarterback.

When Sipe returned to the field, you expected him to run one more play at least, maybe two, into the Raiders' line and inch the ball even closer for kicker Don Cockroft.

Instead, there was Sipe taking the ball and dropping back to pass. He whipped the ball into the end zone, but there in front of helpless Ozzie Newsome were the Raiders' Burgess Owens and Mike Davis. They closed him out and took the ball.

It was an awful moment at Municipal Stadium. It was as if a huge icicle had roared in off Lake Erie and pierced the hearts of the stunned thousands. An eerie scream, then a groan, fell from the stands, then instantly the crowd fell silent, incredulous that such a turn of events could finish the Browns.

The Browns themselves were unbelieving. Some were angry. Offensive tackle Henry Sheppard raged on the bench, as did receivers Reggie Rucker and McDonald Owen. They have been around. Nothing in their background could explain calling a pass in that situation.

Sheppard angrily flung his helmet to the ground, hollering profanely, "Who the —— called that play?"

If you recall, that is Alex Karras verbatim, circa 1962, Detroit vs. Green Bay, when Milt Plum's senseless last-minute pass into the flat was intercepted and deprived the Lions of a championship. Until now, the Lions were No. 1 for dumbness, but they were topped here.

This is the same Browns team, remember, that broke the hearts of the Lions a few weeks back, losing to the Vikings on a ricochet pass with no time left on the clock. It all but ended the Lions' playoff chances, so I don't suppose the Browns get much sympathy out at the Silverdome.

You can watch football a lifetime, you know, and never really understand what causes some teams to lose all awareness under stress. These Browns, for instance, were 11-5 this season, but in four of the losses they had yielded seven touchdowns in the final two minutes of play. Bent for disaster, they buckled.

They suggest great choke artists, and that surely seems to have been their final ruin this day.

Brian Sipe made no apologies: "I called the play I was given," he said. "It wasn't my choice to pass. I just do as I'm told."

Sam Rutigliano was being talked about as pro football's coach of the year before this game. But now he is the goat, or dope for all seasons.

"We just felt a field goal was no dead cinch," the coach said. "We'd had an extra point blocked and didn't get the ball down on another kick. I thought if we threw on second down, we could run on third down, and then kick."

Nuts. His explanation didn't cut the ice. He did what no reasonable football mind could imagine. He goofed as coaches seldom do with this much at stake. The field goal would have been a 30-yarder, not significantly more than an extra-point kick.

His Browns had rallied magnificently and on one of the bitterest of all football days, they had a frigid stadium panting in wild expectation and a watching nation holding its breath.

Sam, ol' fella, this time you made the pants too short. ✦

1 9 8 1

Button up your overcoat
for Silverdome Super Bowl

N EW ORLEANS — Dressed in their Sunday best, the Philadelphia Eagles and then the Oakland Raiders came onto the floor of the vast Superdome this Tuesday morning, into the swarm of hundreds of cameramen and news hawks awaiting them.

Ron Jaworski, the Eagles' quarterback, a guy who had been around but never around a Super Bowl, had never seen anything like it. The world's largest press conference startled him for a moment.

"For gosh sakes," he said, "all you guys caught the wrong train. Reagan isn't here — the inauguration's in Washington."

He wondered how a football team possibly could prepare for its biggest game under the glare of such lights and the probing of so many microphones and pencils.

John Madden stepped up to tell him.

"You've got to learn quick to relax with it, get it done, then forget all about it," said the man who had so much trouble doing it that he quit as coach of these same Raiders two years ago.

"But be careful, son," he warned. "If you sneeze, somebody's going to quote you."

It's true. That, and worse, has happened in the Super Bowl absurdity. I saw a player interviewed on a toilet once. Cross my heart.

Jaworski didn't sneeze — not within my hearing, although he might have, actually; I'll check it out, if you want.

I couldn't really stay with him this time because my ol' pal One-Eyed Jack, the poker wizard from Miami, kept pulling at my sleeve, dragging me away.

Jack wanted to know about the weather in Detroit because the Super Bowl will be played there in 1982. You have to understand Jack. He has been a sun-and-beach type all his life. He has worried about our weather for nearly three years, since the day the NFL owners knocked Miami out of the bowl rotation and awarded the game to the Silverdome.

"You got much snow? How cold is it?" he asked.

I tell him the January thaw is due in Detroit any day now.

"What the hell is the January thaw? Does it get so cold you have to pull the plug on the freezer for a few days?"

From the beginning, Jack has insisted the Detroits, led by Gov. Milliken, laid a snow job on the National Football League, and that's the only reason the football festival will go North for the first time.

And, of course, he's right. We told some little white lies, or stretched the truth a bit, and that's how we got the next Super Bowl.

For instance, the owners were assured there would be no snow at the Silverdome on Jan. 24, 1982, based on a review that showed no snow fell in the area on earlier Super Bowl dates.

We also told 'em we'd have plenty of hotel rooms to accommodate 70,000 out-of-state visitors.

Now that was a whopper — shame on us — and it's going to cause some problems.

A lot of doubling up — legitimate and otherwise — is done among visitors to Super Bowls. What that means, you see, is that even if everybody coming to our Super Bowl takes in a roommate, maybe 10,000 or more will be stranded on our streets getting their feet wet in the thaw.

I thought I could solve the problem, so I called Russ Thomas, the Lions' general manager who was largely responsible for bringing Super Bowl XVI to the Silverdome.

Why don't you just tell the NFL about the room shortage and let 'em increase the Detroit ticket allotment from 8,000 to 20,000, and then we won't have so many visitors without rooms?

Thomas laughed. He wouldn't go for it.

"I'd hate to excite our fans on that basis, or even suggest there's a possibility," he said. "The ticket formula has been set.

"A lot of people will fly in the morning of the game, so they won't need rooms. I know one group that's planning to spend that weekend in Toronto, then fly into Pontiac a few hours before the kickoff."

Of course, if we get 10,000 out-of-towners flitting in and flitting out, our local businessmen aren't going to make the $60-million-plus Super Bowl grab they expect, either.

They will get the notion that the Super Bowl is one big sneeze and not worth so much noise, and they might be right. ✦

1 9 8 1

City silenced one last time
by the passing of Joe Louis

The city hushed. An eerie silence gripped the neighborhoods, from the Black Bottom on the fringe of downtown Detroit to the Jewish sector out Dexter Avenue and into the enclaves of ethnics on the city's north and west sides.

It was as if a plague or deadly gas was slipping over the town, sending citizens fleeing for cover and leaving the streets deserted to the night.

Several times a year it happened — not only in Detroit, but in cities throughout the United States whenever Joe Louis fought on radio. The cities stopped and listened.

No single performer before or since ever captured the attention of the nation as did Louis, the legendary Brown Bomber of the deep, dark Depression years of the 1930s who has died at age 66 from cardiac arrest.

Strangely, biographies of the man many call the greatest heavyweight fighter ever either fail to mention the phenomenon of a nation stilled when he swung into action, or make little of it. Strange, because it remains one of the most peculiar mass reactions to any sports happening.

Joe Louis was special, a special man in a distinct period in history, and he has become a legend for that as much as his superb boxing skills.

Much of his life story has been distorted over the years, or at least is different from what was known of him in the 1930s and 1940s when his every fight captured the attention of millions and pulled them in huddles around radios to listen to the blow-by-blow descriptions.

He has been characterized, for instance, as a crusader for black America. He was not that at all; he was the first to deny it.

Rather, he was a simple young man with no discernible complaints or aggressions outside the boxing ring. Content with his role as prize fighter, he neither prodded nor offended anyone, either by manner or speech, and so he was universally popular and admired.

Race did play a significant part, however, in the building of the Joe Louis legend. Adolf Hitler created the circumstances in 1936 when he personally delegated Max Schmeling to prove the superiority of his white master race. When Schmeling beat Louis, Hitler danced, or so it was said.

Several years ago, before he fell ill, Louis recalled for me the circumstances of the first Schmeling bout and then the rematch two years later.

After the first bout, staged before Louis KO'd James Braddock to win the heavyweight championship in 1937, great controversy arose over Schmeling's victory. It was claimed the German had won with a foul blow, a shot to the kidneys.

Louis remembered only that it had been a rugged fight, that he had been hit hard and often, and that later his back did indeed hurt. But he never personally claimed foul.

As for the celebrated rematch in 1938, when the world was kindling a war, Louis insisted: "I never thought about any race thing. The papers were filled with stuff about Hitler talking and I met once with President Roosevelt, who said he hoped I would win.

"But I had nothing personally against Max. I liked him, and we're friends even now. In my mind, I wasn't champion until I beat him.

"The rest of it — black against white — was somebody's talk. I had nothing against the man, except I had to beat him for myself."

He destroyed Schmeling in the first round. The story goes that Hitler shuddered and cursed, just as he had when Jesse Owens, another black American, ruled the 1936 Olympics in Berlin.

In Detroit, the streets exploded with Louis' victory. It was perhaps the most joyous celebration the city has seen for one man, one athlete. We had plenty of practice from his earlier fights, for the Bomber already was a hero in a period that knew few.

He had been stamped as a champion of all Americans at that time, and it was almost tradition that whenever he fought, the cities would fall silent, the populace listening to radios.

When he won, whether by knockout, as was mostly the case, or by decision, the neighborhoods erupted all around, everywhere, acclaiming him and their own triumph.

Not in our time has there been any other like him. If Muhammad Ali was beautiful and if, as some believe, Ali was a better fighter, Joe Louis was something significantly more: a cultural phenomenon.

The celebrations were wild and joyous, street dancing developing spontaneously, the partying often carrying into the early morning hours with old men and tired ladies, with toddlers and house pets romping and raising hell in the streets over, of all things, a man who won a prize fight.

Reports of similar demonstrations came from around the country, but Detroit's own outpouring seemed more significant. Joe Louis had, after all, sprung from our midst, out of the old Brewster gym behind the Stroh's Brewery downtown. He was a kid who had discarded his violin and skipped his lessons to excel at a less delicate art.

He had gained his first recognition here in the Free Press Golden Gloves tournament when an economically battered town was proclaiming itself City of Champions, what with the Tigers, the Lions, the Red Wings and the basketball Eagles all claiming world titles in 1935.

His title finally came two years later, but it is not odd at all that he is best remembered from the era of champions. ✦

Louis remembered: 'He was a credit to the human race'

They say Joe Louis is dead. Do not believe it. Legends do not die.

In a black-draped boxing ring at a gambling casino in Las Vegas, the body of Joe Louis is on display. Mourners will cry and eventually the casket will be carried away. But Joe Louis, the Brown Bomber, will live on.

Legends do not die, nor do myths fade so quickly. The legend and myth of Joe Louis, perhaps the greatest sports figure in our history, will endure beyond our time.

So far as the public knows, he was above reproach. Some would attempt to deify Joe Louis. It would be wrong. He was no saint.

What he was, beyond his achievements in the ring, was a good man who frequently succumbed to temptation, but a kind and generous man with all he could give to any who needed and many who did not.

He was a paradox in many ways.

One of the highest wage earners in sports, he spent his final years on the dole of gambling men who understood and loved him, and also used him in their own strange way.

A fearsome man in the ring, he suffered in his later years from severe paranoia, fearing mobsters were gunning for him.

No one ever conceded him great wisdom, but he is credited with several of the most poignant observations of our time.

"God is on our side," he told a vast New York audience in the heat of World War II. Millions rejoiced; it was as if nobody had considered the possibility before.

"He can run, but he can't hide," he said of Billy Conn. Even today, that admonition is applied to bad guys and enemies everywhere.

He was a simple man with simple tastes, but he was an extravagant spender. By his 40th birthday, he had earned more than $4 million, unheard of in sports at the time. But he was broke; he was almost always broke, or nearly so.

"He was the most generous man God ever created," said Freddie Sommer, a fight agent who since the 1930s had been closer to Louis than any other man. "If he had only 10 bucks to his name and thought you might need it, he would give it to you."

I was with Louis at Caesars Palace in Las Vegas one night in 1976. He was employed there as a shill at the blackjack tables. He played with house money, attracting visitors to the casino and to his table.

"I need another $5,000 to play," Louis told Bill Weinberger, then president of Caesars. Weinberger, who had made his fortune selling hot dogs and beer at Cleveland's Municipal Stadium, had a genuine fondness for Louis.

"You've had a good night and won plenty," Weinberger said. "What did you do with that money?"

"Somebody needed what I won," Louis said, "and somebody needed what you gave me. Now I need some more."

Weinberger laughed. He ordered up more chips for Joe. He had kept Louis on the Caesars payroll (at $100,000 per) for years. Thousands of players each week would stop at Louis' table, some simply to gawk at this friendly legend from their youth, others seeking to touch him or talk to him. Nothing else slowed the play at the tables.

Frank Sinatra, they say, paid more than $100,000 toward the hospital bills of the ailing Joe Louis these last few years. Few knew he had a debt of gratitude.

Thirty years ago, Sinatra tried promoting fights in Los Angeles. Louis was to receive $25,000 to box a four-round exhibition, but the program bombed and Sinatra stood to lose a fortune. Hearing that, Louis declined his fee. Sinatra made him a lifelong friend.

"Back in '38, he had a pro softball team called the Brown Bombers," Sommer said. "People have forgotten Joe was a tremendous hitter, a first baseman.

"We are playing this game on Chicago's south side. He knows people do not have money, so he sends me to the bank to get a thousand $1 bills to pass out to people so they could come to the game. I told him these poor people will keep the dollar, and he said that's OK, let 'em keep it and let 'em into the game anyway.

"He was a wonderful, wonderful man," said Freddie, a 72-year-old German immigrant who once promoted Max Schmeling's fights in Hamburg. He left Max to join Joe in 1935. He was weeping over the phone from Vegas as he prepared to receive the mourners at Joe's funeral.

"A big-hearted guy," Freddie said, "so many good things he did. The people loved him, but they don't really know how really great a man he was.

"His people say he was a credit to his race," he said, echoing the famous line of the late sports writer Jimmy Cannon. "They sell him short.

"He was a credit to the human race." ✦

1981

Tiger Stadium vendor deals in scorecards and history

"Programs! Programs! They're a dollar, folks, and you get a freeee PEN-cil!"

The warm evening sun glistens off the chubby cheeks of Bob Benson. He nudges his ample belly up against the stand holding his supply of Tigers books, and he shimmies a bit, as if to relieve an itch without emptying his hands.

Eyeing the people coming through the gate at Tiger Stadium, he seems to know instantly who will buy a scorecard with a free pencil and who will turn aside. A lifetime of selling makes the peddler wise.

Most ignore him. Not that it really matters to Bob Benson, who has hustled around Tiger Stadium doing this and that for a half-century or more. He is 70, long and happily retired, and you suspect he does not really need his cut — a dandy $220 on Opening Day, $40 to $50 most days — from the program sales, anyway.

More than anything, he is simply a baseball nut. Always has been. He makes his bucks, but the game's the thing. He gets to watch them all. Free. Maybe 60 games a year and never enough.

He is one of the most delightful characters around the ball yard, or anywhere. A non-stop, relentless talker, funny and enthusiastic, he can get hyped by a cloud overhead, if only because each is different. As he is.

I first met him 20 years or so ago when he was managing the old Fairview Lanes out on East Jefferson. Bob showed up at a meeting of the Bowling Proprietors Association to tell the owners how they should be running their businesses.

One of the proprietors operated 11 establishments in the metro area. "I own 488 lanes, Mr. Benson," he said. "You know so much about this business: Tell me, how many lanes do you manage at … where? … Fairview?"

"Eight," Bob Benson said. It might have been his shortest reply to anything.

But baseball always was his game anyway. He does not know a one-word response to anything dealing with baseball. The history, the players, the good guys and bad have filled his life from the beginning, and will to the end.

"When I was a kid I used to shag balls for the players, Johnny Stone," he said. "You never heard of Johnny Stone? That's in the late 1920s. When Hank Greenberg came in the 1930s, he always had a lot of extra kids shagging. Charlie Gehringer — he made more spectacular plays than anybody ever. I remember Harry Heilmann, a great hitter, bouncing into four double plays in the same game. Goose Goslin, who had the winning hit for us in the 1935 Series, did it one day, too.

"Oh, I remember a lot. Hoot Evers was one of my favorites. Some players just appealed to me personally. Like Ben Oglivie. They never gave him a chance here. The day they traded him, I cried. Honestly, I cried." Benson was 66 at the time.

The current players, he says, are more distant, and it's a shame.

"You don't have a chance to talk to them or get friendly. Except maybe Dave Rozema. He's one of my favorites. When he comes into the parking lot here, I holler to him, 'Keep the ball low! Keep it low!' And he'll always holler back, 'I'm trying! I'm trying!' He's a nice guy who might develop, but might not. I hope he does."

Sure, he remembers Babe Ruth and how the Yankees always put him in leftfield here, rather than right. ("They wouldn't risk great players in that rightfield sun.") And he recalls Ty Cobb, the best of his time and maybe all time. He never liked Cobb, who was mean on the field and off.

"Few people liked him," Benson said. "A woman from Jackson or somewhere stopped at my stand the other day. She said she was related to Cobb. She said nobody in the family liked Cobb, either. He'd say hello once in a while, but mostly he'd just walk right past, paying no attention.

"I see Jim Bunning was put in the Michigan Hall of Fame. Great young guy. He and Harvey Kuenn used to come to all our Tiger fan club meetings. Young girls are crazy about ballplayers, you know. Kuenn never missed. I cried when they traded Kuenn for that hot dog (Rocky Colavito) from Cleveland.

"I've seen 'em all — Cobb, Ruth, Cochrane, Gehringer — but the greatest was Al Kaline. I liked him as a man. I liked the way he hit and fielded and never blew his top or complained about anything. He played as well as anybody could play this game. What more can you want from anybody?"

With Bob Benson, you get much more than a scorecard and pencil for $1.

"Free pencil, folks! Tell your friends about it!" ✦

1 9 8 1

You'll usually find Futch in the champion's corner

A s shepherd of Larry Holmes, the fistic millionaire, Eddie Futch has the delicate task of convincing him a world heavyweight boxing champion does not necessarily know everything worth knowing.

To do this requires exceptional skill. For instance, you do not put a dunce cap on a heavyweight champion and stand him in a corner until he accepts his lesson. Nor do you whack his knuckles with a ruler, or send a note home to his momma.

"I coax and reason with him," says Eddie, who had tutored a dozen world champions, including Joe Frazier, Bob Foster, Bobby Chacon, Harold Johnson, Don Jordan and a few near misses like Ken Norton (who later was awarded a title), until Larry Holmes summoned him six weeks ago.

In his 50 years in the fight business, Eddie Futch understands only two people can legitimately threaten a heavyweight champion, one being the guy who is prepared to fight him. The other would be his wife.

Eddie Futch is 69. As a kid lightweight, he dared to spar with Joe Louis at the old Brewster Center gym back in the 1930s. He became the Brewster coach in 1939 — forerunner of Emanuel Steward and his Kronk team of today.

He is one of the most respected names in the fight business, which is why Larry Holmes hired him in the first place.

"Sometimes I get on Larry," says Eddie, who is preparing Holmes for his WBC title defense against Leon Spinks at Joe Louis Arena. "I tell him I'm going to keep bugging him because we're after the same thing, which is to win. He responds. The big thing is you can coax and persuade, but you can't force."

If some others had listened, boxing history might be different.

"I had built Lester Felton (a stylish postwar Detroit welterweight) up to a title fight in 1951," Eddie says, "but his wife misunderstood. She thought Lester would have to fight Ray Robinson and it scared her. She wouldn't believe that Robinson had decided to become a middleweight."

Eddie quit in disgust. He quit decisively, moving his family to California and taking work as a riveter in an airplane factory. Within a few years, he was back in boxing in a new crowd.

If Charlie Powell, onetime 49ers footballer, had listened to Eddie, the world might have heard less from a kid named Cassius Clay.

Understand that a trainer in boxing is responsible for far more than a fighter's conditioning. The trainer teaches technique, studies the opponent's style and plots strategy.

"We had a trap set for Cassius Clay when Powell met him in 1963," Eddie says. "I'd noticed Clay always moved to his left after jabbing. So we had Powell feint a move to the right and come back with a hook. He did that in the first and second rounds and buckled Clay's knees."

In the third, Charlie thought he could knock out this fresh kid any time he wanted.

"It's too bad he thought that," Eddie says. "Clay hit him a jab and 18 more punches, and there went Charlie."

His fighters fought Clay — now Muhammad Ali — seven times and won twice. Ken Norton broke Ali's jaw and beat him one out of three; Joe Frazier batted .333 against Ali.

It's interesting that Futch does not consider Ali "The Greatest." He reserves that without question for Joe Louis, and insists old friendship with the Bomber has nothing to do with it.

"I don't look for charisma or popularity," he says. "I look at the basic fighter. All fighters have weaknesses, and Louis had his. There are some things I'd like Larry Holmes to do, but obviously I can't go into them.

"With Ali, the trick was to break his rhythm and counter his speed. For instance, Ken Norton was a very coachable fighter, so whenever Ali jabbed, we had him catch the jab and go right back with his own. He was smacking Ali right in the middle of the face. I thought Norton won all three of their fights."

Norton won only the first but, then, coaches, trainers and teachers of all sorts see a lot of things differently.

It's why a lot of us don't always listen. ✦

They took him for a chump,
but Spinks was also a champ

ADILLAC, Mich. — Up on the stage of New Orleans' old Memorial Auditorium, a strange tableau was being enacted. Leon Spinks, ex-Marine, Olympic gold medalist, stunning winner over the finest fighter in recent years, was trying desperately to mimic the movements of his new coach.

Two days later, Spinks would have to defend the world heavyweight boxing championship against Muhammad Ali, but here were his handlers anxiously trying to implant the rudiments of fighting in their champion.

It was as if Reggie Jackson on the morning of a World Series game needed instruction on how to hold a bat. Or picture Jack Nicklaus, teeing up in the Masters, inquiring which club was the driver.

Leon Spinks has changed, but not all that much, in the 3½ years since returning the heavyweight title to its rightful owner. Deep in the Manistee forest, the raw, rugged Spinks still is struggling to learn how to box.

Rather than learning how to hit, which he does very well, he is struggling to avoid being hit, and he is not doing so well.

Del Williams, his wise old trainer, is showing Spinks how to duck and slip down, then up and under the jabbing left hand of Vonzell Johnson. Time and again, Spinks can't get down. Vonzell peppers Spinks' head, which is masked by protective headgear.

Seeing that, a visitor wonders whether Spinks really can be much of a test for Larry Holmes, the champion, the best jabber going, when they meet at Joe Louis Arena a week hence.

"Remember one thing about Leon," says manager Jerry Sawyer. "He has an extraordinary career. This will be only his 15th professional fight. But it will be his third championship fight and fifth with a title possibility."

It's true. In the long and often sordid history of boxing, no one ever fought so quickly and often for the richest prize in sports. A creation of network television after his 1976 Olympic triumph — much like welterweight Sugar Ray Leonard — Leon has remained crude and unrefined in many ways.

Still, he stands among the best in his game. There is that to understand about Leon Spinks.

Lacking technique and artistry, he thrives in the ring with an unwavering courage, a seeming indifference for punishment of any sort. To beat him, you literally and thoroughly must beat him.

In the fight crowd, they say Spinks is "too dumb to know any better." It's a cruel assessment, although it is true that Spinks, having come out of nowhere socially or athletically, has seemed at times destined to return there.

He is 27. The bitterness of his youth seems to have left him. During those six months in 1978 when he held the title, he spoke often of his childhood in a St. Louis ghetto and how his father would string him up with rope and whip him.

But if those childhood wounds have healed, the scars and twists remain, leaving Spinks as one of the most puzzling personalities on the sports scene. He is recognized on dance floors, in barrooms and police precincts as undisciplined, a fun-loving, hell-raising free spirit.

Larry Holmes calls him a "freaky deaky," which is a favored Spinks dance movement, one in which his slim hips writhe in sensuous rhythm. Don King, the fight promoter, tells often of "digging Leon out" of a wild party scene only hours before Spinks was due in the ring.

"We had him locked in a hotel room with two cops outside the door the night before one fight," King says. "We found him the next morning in a town 100 miles away."

All of it has left the ex-Marine with a reputation perhaps fully deserved, but misunderstood, too. He is no bully. Outside the boxing ring he is even-tempered, almost placid. The only victim in his extensive list of escapades — as when he was "mugged" in a Detroit motel and lost his dental plate and clothes to a late-night companion last winter — has been Spinks himself.

That incident apparently ended Leon's marriage. He and his wife, Nova, who lived in a $150,000 home on Detroit's northwest side, have filed for divorce.

Whether because of his early privation — he was one of seven children in a family always in need — or whether the Marines let him stray, even the matured Spinks always seems bent toward fun and frolic, toward good times and delicious moments.

He is no fool. Not really. It takes some proving, especially with a man who at one time had signed himself away to four different managers. But Spinks knows where it's at when it comes to money.

He made $4 million in his fights with Ali, and he retains most of what the government left for him. His manager, Jerry Sawyer, is a former bank trust officer hired by Spinks to look after the money. He would trust no other and, in fact, he runs his own business.

"I got rid of all the leeches," he says. "That's what I learned after I lost the title. The leeches were there. They all wanted the money. When I saw that, I got rid of them."

It is a gorgeous spring day at the Caberfae ski resort where Spinks is preparing for Larry Holmes. He has been here for six weeks, secluded deep in the woods. He knows this might be his last shot at the heavyweight championship and he is doing everything he knows to be ready.

The daily routine of running, sleeping, exercising, sleeping, sparring, sleeping, seems tortuous. The only night lights Spinks sees are in the dark sky. It's a 2½-mile walk to the nearest highway. Spinks has not tried to escape, not that anyone here knows, or will admit.

"When I defended the title against Ali," he says, "I had all these people around. I was having a good time. I wasn't ready mentally for him. I was looking out for my money.

"I'm not a womanizer. But all these women were around. They kept telling me how cute I was."

Spinks even believed some of 'em. If they turned his head, it was away from a mirror.

"But then I noticed the women always were saying they needed a new dress or this and that, and other friends were trying to get me into a business deal. I finally realized what was going on. They got away with a little bit of my money — but not much."

The afternoon at the training camp drags on. There is no set schedule. Spinks runs when he decides to run; he comes to the makeshift gym at the ski lodge when he is tired of resting. He does his work when he wants to do it. But he does it, without fail.

The results are there. He says his weight is "under 200 pounds," surprisingly light. He will have to add five in the next week.

"It's boring, really boring here," Spinks says. "But I love it," he adds, unconvincingly. "I haven't seen a woman in months."

Can he beat Larry Holmes and regain the championship?

It's disturbing that Vonzell Johnson repeatedly raps him with that left, hooking, stabbing, cruel, painful jolts.

"Remember, some guys just don't look good in the gym," says Del Williams. "They are different people when the fight begins. That's Leon."

And Spinks?

"I don't say I can or can't beat Larry Holmes. But he knows and I know, I'm gonna give him a real shot. Everybody's gonna know I was there."

They usually do.

(Larry Holmes kept his WBC title with a third-round technical knockout of Leon Spinks in Detroit's first heavyweight title bout since 1970.) ✦

1 9 8 1

Sunshine, girls, beach blankets, hydroplanes — who needs baseball?

I know I hadn't told you, but this was the day I figured the Tigers would take over first place in the American League East. Milt Wilcox would shut up the Boston Red Sox, winning with Steve Kemp's grand slam. The town would go nuts.

Sparky Anderson would tell us the hard work on fundamentals during spring training finally had paid off. Gentleman Jim Campbell would say, gosh, fellas, what can I tell 'em on Broadway now that they've seen our farm.

Several million people around the state would have watched this game televised from Boston.

But, of course, the baseball strike not only destroyed the Tigers' timetable, it killed whatever interest most people might have in anything at all. So it is said.

For instance, only a half-million of them showed up on the riverfront yesterday.

There's no way of knowing what the others were doing, but the estimated 625,000 who jammed the shorelines on and across from Belle Isle were distinguished for one reason. Few of them carried baseball bats. Or gloves. Or balls.

They carried Frisbees and kites and volleyballs and soccer balls and horseshoes. They had golf sticks and fishing poles and beer and charcoal stoves and coolers loaded with ice and whatnot. There were babies and grandmas, and young lovers and old, and just plain pals.

I wouldn't want to upset Jim Campbell, or even Milt Wilcox, who is a pitcher first and union man foremost, but the people seemed to be having a hell of a good time.

I wandered on the beach at Belle Isle, stepping carefully between spread blankets where the girls were catching some rays. I had not been there for maybe 30 years, so I can tell you that, as a class, girls today are much healthier than they were in 1950. Amazingly so.

I don't intend to dwell on it, but I notice a phenomenon I had not heard mentioned. A lot of them are tattooed. I'd seen a tattooed lady only once before, at a sideshow, but this day I saw 20, at least. When did all that begin?

I also saw them in the men's room. I know it happens all the time in, say, France, and especially Yugoslavia, which I will tell you about someday. But it is a shock in the ol' hometown, to be sure, to be standing in a men's room minding your own business and have a soft voice whisper, "Excuse me, can you help me please?"

They never did build enough facilities for the lady visitors at Belle Isle. A hundred ladies and more were waiting rather desperately outside the door, and then four tough-looking characters in leather jackets and carrying chains moved in and declared, "All you guys get the hell out of here. The ladies have a problem."

You know that couldn't happen at the ball yard, where everybody is expected to await his or her turn at bat, regardless.

Over at the Bath House I met Fred Geigle, a mailman from Grand Rapids, and his son, Gary, and their friend, Martin Gingrich. They said they come to Detroit this time of year.

To take in a ballgame, no doubt?

"You kidding?" Fred said. "I wouldn't walk across the street to see a ballgame. We've been coming to the powerboat races for 15 years. I wouldn't miss 'em. It's just the greatest sports event going."

"Fred and I belong to the same American Legion post," Martin said. "Yesterday we took a hundred retarded kids on a bus trip to a trout farm, and then early Sunday morning we were back on the road to make these races."

Martin is a truck mechanic. In the first heat of the unlimited racing, the jet turbine-powered, super-smooth Pay 'N' Pak died in the water at the starting line. "He's finished," Martin said. "The only way he can restart that turbine is to haul it back to the docks."

Which is what happened. Even Martin wondered why anybody would build a boat that can't be restarted in the water.

We looked off to the west, at the Belle Isle bridge, and tried to guess how many thousands of baseball bleacher fans were lined up there. The gawkers stretched from shore to shore, five rows or more deep, and you could see them through the binoculars screaming and waving as the huge, thundering water-monsters roared up the river at them, then bounced and skidded to turn and pound the ears of the bathers at the beach.

"God, it's beautiful, just an absolutely beautiful sight, with all these hundreds of thousands of people," Fred said.

They'd better get that baseball strike settled soon. ◆

1 9 8 1

Flash fire at MIS singes racing's sense of security

B
ROOKLYN, Mich. — I looked disaster in the face yesterday, turned away, then looked back and watched helplessly as fire and smoke swallowed the north end pits at Michigan International Speedway.

I was within 20 feet of Herm Johnson's pit when suddenly I noticed his crewmen vaulting over the pit wall. A flash of fire leaped up. A huge cloud of smoke belched from the car.

Dozens of officials, semi-officials and reporters leaped back in terror, then turned, fleeing in panic toward the opposite end of the pits.

A moment of horror gripped a small knot of us watching from a hundred feet away. We clearly could see a silhouetted figure leaping in obvious agony in a cloud of smoke enveloping Johnson's car.

Long moments seemed to pass before he was noticed by firemen rushing to the pit. Then they quickly doused him and pulled him to safety. It was Graig Nelson, a Johnson crew member, whose feet, we learned later, were afire.

Johnson, dazed and hurting, was being led away. He wanted to return to help his crew.

"I don't know what happened," he told me. "I don't know. I saw the fuel spill, then everything flared up over me."

Johnson, who escaped a fire in his pit in a Milwaukee race last month, suffered minor facial burns this time. He was one of 14 people injured in the scariest moment in the track's 10-year racing history.

As Johnson was being led away, the pit area suddenly erupted again.

An explosion — more like a crack of lightning — tore the air. Flames and smoke belched from the pits beyond Johnson's, and horror gripped the grandstands across the track.

You could hear the distant spectators' screams and shouts as hundreds along pit row turned and fled.

Security guards raced through the area strong-arming everyone, ordering them to "get the hell out of here, the whole place is going up."

It looked like it. Smoke and flames leaped into the air, then danced farther down the pits, swallowing one station after another, apparently 11 in all.

The ill-fated Michigan 500 was stopped, the cars and drivers resting on the track apron.

The drivers think they have adequate safeguards, but just last Memorial Day weekend Rick Mears suffered severe facial burns in another pit fire at the Indianapolis 500. Obviously, they do not have adequate safeguards.

One fire here led to another, it turned out, and the consequences multiplied as the flames and intense heat leaped from one pit to another.

Firemen Ron McWilliams and Russ Smith were stationed at the fourth turn, at the head of the track stretch, leading into the pits. They rushed to the scene of the trouble.

"What happened was that the original fire melted hoses — air hoses and fuel hoses — and exploded spare tires," McWilliams said. The fuel from the tanks — each pit has a fuel tank containing 249 gallons of methanol — began running through the adjoining pits, and fire spread as the leaking fuel poured down the pit area.

"The problem with methanol," Smith said, "is that you can't see it burning. You see it destroying what it burns, but you don't often see the flame. So it can creep up on you."

Many hundreds of us who were down in the fire area owe a thanks, or more, to the fire fighters at MIS. They were remarkably quick and fearless when anything less could have brought instant tragedy to many.

There are those, of course, who will say auto racing is the dumbest of all sports, since its history is filled with horrible accidents, and those who bother with it are sadists, at best.

It has its dangers, to be sure, but the protests will go unheeded, as usual.

You are reminded of a condemnation of auto racing issued by the Vatican some years ago, following a particularly gruesome series of accidents.

The Indianapolis Speedway, admonishing the Vatican, issued a statement declaring that more people are killed going to church every Sunday.

It's also true, though, that a few more than usual will be in their pews Sunday. ✦

The one that got away wasn't Thomas Hearns

LELAND, Mich. — It is a glorious morning on Lake Michigan. The water is calm, the sun glistens through the haze and dances on the ripples around our boat.

Suddenly, a cry comes from captain Jim Munoz.

Five of us leap for the fishing rod. In a few minutes, Lake Michigan contains one less chinook salmon. Before we are done, nine of 'em, weighing nearly 150 pounds, will be safe in the cooler, and Tommy Hearns will have proved himself a superb hook artist outside the boxing ring, too.

This is how Hearns, the biggest striker in boxing today, spends his day off from the gym where he is preparing for his welterweight showdown with Sugar Ray Leonard.

Hearns, his brother Billy; camp aide Ernie Hamilton; Jim Ingram, sports editor of the Michigan Chronicle; and I were aboard Capt. Munoz's charter.

"We'll get salmon," the captain promises. "It has been a good season."

Tommy Hearns is a devoted fisherman. On a boxing trip to Phoenix several months ago, he pulled a giant catfish from a small lake outside his hotel room. He was fishing from a second-floor window.

"I caught a huge shark — maybe 20 feet — down in Florida once," he says. "But I've never been after the salmon before."

He sits quietly and detached, as if preoccupied with some matter, while we wait for hits on the lines trailing behind the boat.

We never mention Sugar Ray or boxing, or anything to do with it, aside from the fact that Hearns' road work this morning consisted of running straight up the steep, 200-foot hill that rises behind his training quarters at Sugar Loaf Ski Resort — because "it was there."

Brother Billy feels a jolt on his line: "Omigod, if feels like a really big one!"

"Keep the line tight, but play with him," Hearns says. "This isn't a strength contest."

The salmon breaks the water's surface, thrashing, struggling to shake free of the hook. Billy, who is 20 and considerably smaller than his older brother, is working mightily reeling in the fish. Finally, the 20-pounder is aboard.

"Whew! My wrists are sore," Billy says.

"You're gonna wind up with salmon elbow," Ingram says, laughing.

Tommy Hearns calls Ingram aside and whispers something to him. He was concerned for Ingram, it turned out, urging the writer, who suffered a heart attack two months ago, not to tire himself foolishly if a large fish happened to hit his line.

Soon enough, one does. When it breaks water, Hearns finally is excited.

"Whooie! Wooo! Look at that!" he hollers. He moves to Ingram's side, quietly instructing him how to play the fish so it could not escape. It was a 22-pounder.

"My left arm almost gave out on me," Ingram says. "But I don't need anything else; this one makes my day. Who's got a camera?"

A ferryboat loaded with youngsters rolls past us several hundred yards away. A cheer comes across the water, then a voice: "Be a big winner, champ!"

Hearns smiles and waves. In just a few days, everyone in the Traverse City area seems to know he is here and what he is doing at almost any hour. Even the fishing is no real escape.

Munoz, a school athletic director who moonlights as a charter boat operator, is studying his depth finder, searching for another school of fish. He finds one. In a few minutes, there is a strike on Hearns' line.

He plays the fish expertly. The captain never bothers to tell Hearns how to handle the rod. He has another big one hooked, and the fish wants to run a bit.

"He's going farther out, man," Hearns says. "Look at him. He's getting tired now. Man, he looks like a shark with all that tail fin riding in the water."

This one is not giving up easily.

"He's not gonna get away," Hearns vows. "I'll jump in and grab him around the throat if I have to."

He doesn't have to. When the chinook is aboard, it turns out to be another 20-pounder.

"We're ready to go, captain," Hearns says. "Leave some fish for another day."

Somehow, word was out that Hearns was fishing in Leland. When the boat arrived back at its well, the dock was jammed with people eager to get a look at the Hit Man from Detroit.

The fish were strung on Capt. Munoz's trophy board, pictures were taken, and Hearns patiently signed autographs for spectators.

"We'll freeze the fish and take 'em home," he says. "I don't eat out much anymore. I've been at Joe Muer's only once because I never did get to eat my meal. People kept coming over to talk to me."

Once, the water and fish were his certain escape from the world's clamor. Now he sees there really is no escape, anywhere. ✦

1981

Cornerman Dundee can jab
with boxing's best champs

L AS VEGAS, Nev. — Sitting back-to-back with Emanuel Steward and engaging in separate conversations, Angelo Dundee, the celebrated handler of Sugar Ray Leonard and a great collection of world boxing champions before him, was in a playful mood.

"Emanuel Steward is going to have a heart attack," he said loudly, intending for Steward to hear and respond. "Yes, sir, Emanuel's going to have a heart attack when he sees Sugar Ray Leonard knock out the great Hit Man from Deetroit. He won't believe what he's seeing, and his heart will break."

Dundee, a sly ol' cat who masterminded the careers of Muhammad Ali, Willie Pep, Willie Pastrano and a dozen other champions, laughed heartily. Steward ignored him.

No one questions the cleverness of Dundee, and now that he has arrived to take charge of Leonard's preparations for the fight with Tommy Hearns, he has people listening.

Dundee exudes confidence and, as he prattles on about Leonard's vast superiority over Hearns, his audience begins to wonder whether Hearns really belongs in this fight.

"Ray will outbox, outmaneuver and outpunch Hearns at every turn," Dundee said. "There's no comparison between the two, so I figure Ray will knock him out within 10 rounds."

Of course you have to know Dundee and sprinkle a bit of salt on what he says. At 62, he is not only the most widely known manager in boxing but also probably the most respected and loved.

Even so, he has been wrong before, as recently as Ali's pitiful fight against Larry Holmes last October. Dundee was convinced Ali was in great shape, when, in fact, the fighter had been taking appetite suppressants for several months and showed weakness even in his sparring sessions.

Just 14 months ago, in fact, Angelo was saying that Hearns, because of his height and reach, his strength and punching power, would be too much for Ray Leonard, and that Leonard should dare not fight him.

Somehow his opinion has changed. It's not because his job is to guide Leonard through his fights. In the last year he has studied Hearns, he said, and he sees holes in Detroit's champion.

"Hearns has never contended with anybody like Ray," he said. "Ray has captured the lost art of being able to feint you right out of your shoes. He's a master at it. He reminds me of Pep that way, and he has a knack of sliding from side to side on an opponent, like Pastrano.

"Tommy Hearns is going to be confounded by all that. Ray can't punch for power with him, but he can hurt him, and he'll finish him. I'm convinced."

There has been talk that Dundee really doesn't have much to say about how Leonard fights anymore, that Sugar Ray ignores him, as he did in Montreal in June 1980 when he chose to fight Roberto Duran toe-to-toe and lost his WBC welterweight title for a few months.

"I think Emanuel Steward started that talk trying to create a situation," Dundee said. "I'm doing my thing with Ray. There has been no change in our relationship since it began in 1976, when he won the Olympics in Montreal.

"Ray respects me, and we have great rapport, as I have with Janks Morton, who handles Ray's conditioning. I know one thing: We're together on getting our guy ready to lick the other guy — and that's what's gonna happen."

Early in the Dundee-Leonard association, Sugar Ray needed Dundee's expertise in carefully selecting opponents as he progressed in the professional ring. Now his opponents are automatic — as with the Hearns match — and so Dundee's value is in devising techniques to be applied during a fight.

He will close Leonard's Friday workout to outsiders, and supposedly in that hour will implant the tricks Leonard will use against Hearns.

Among other things, Angelo Dundee, for all his charm and friendliness, is one of boxing's great dirty trick practitioners.

It was Angelo, foe instance, who sneaked into the stadium at Zaire seven years ago and loosened the turnbuckles on the ring ropes. Ali later leaned back over the sagging ropes, his head easily out of reach of flailing champion George Foreman. Ali won on a KO in the eighth. Thus was created rope-a-dope.

Early in his career, Ali was floored by England's Henry Cooper. When the round ended, Ali was still in a dangerous daze. Dundee sliced open the stitching on one glove and complained to the referee about the tear. During the search for new gloves, Ali regained his senses and went on to finish Cooper.

Angelo confesses to these tricks, although he denies he has applied astringents to his fighters' gloves to irritate opponents' eyes. In any case, he usually has more than arms up his sleeves.

Despite Dundee's reputation, Leonard does not always heed the words of his famed cornerman, as in his first match with Duran.

"Sure, he ignored me then and tried to go toe-to-toe with Duran," Dundee admitted. "It's understandable. What created that was Duran's actions outside the ring.

"Duran is an ugly animal. He has deliberately insulted Ray's wife with obscene gestures, and it infuriated Ray so that he was determined to thrash the guy. It cost him, and he learned a lesson."

Just remember: When Tommy Hearns meets Ray Leonard in the middle of the ring, he will need to keep one eye on Dundee in the corner. ✦

1981

Leonard tips his cap to Hearns after taking crown in slugfest

L AS VEGAS, Nev. — Sugar Ray Leonard, in a strange role reversal, turned slugger last night and battered Detroit's Thomas Hit Man Hearns into a 14-round technical knockout in a raging struggle for the undisputed world welterweight boxing championship.

A sellout throng of 24,083 at the Caesars Palace Sports Pavilion, and millions more at television outlets around the world, saw Hearns suffer his first defeat even as he led significantly on all three judges' cards.

"I definitely knew I was ahead," Hearns said, "but there was just one problem. I got hit with a good shot. I thought I was in pretty good control, but the ref didn't, and there's nothing I can do."

Asked whether Leonard hurt him, Hearns said, "Of course he hurt me. I admit it. One thing I never did is underestimate Ray Leonard as a fighter. He's a hell of a man."

Hearns and Leonard sat together at a post-fight press conference, exchanging compliments and hoisting each other's arms. Leonard wore dark glasses over his puffy left eye.

"In my book, we are both champions," Leonard said.

Hearns told the Las Vegas crowd, "If you never see another show, you saw one tonight." He also had a message for the fight fans back home. "Detroit," Hearns said, "I shall return."

The end came moments after Leonard caught Hearns flush on the jaw with a looping right, sending Hearns staggering and falling along the ropes.

Leonard, sensing his chance, leaped after Hearns as the Detroiter sagged, stunned, on the ropes, and hammered him with heavy blows to the body.

A stunning left sent Hearns, desperately trying to cover up, along the left ropes leading away from his corner.

He was plainly in deep trouble. Referee Davey Pearl leaped forward to signal an end to the fight at 1:45 of the round.

Hearns, the undefeated WBA welterweight champion entering the bout, said he did not think Pearl should have stopped the fight.

"No, I didn't think the fight should have been stopped," he said. "But those are the breaks. The referee saw differently."

"He didn't say anything to me," Pearl said. "He seemed like he knew it was over. He put his head down and headed back to his corner."

Hearns said he never doubted Leonard's ability.

"I have nothing against Ray," Hearns said. "He's a hell of a person. There were just two champions and one had to be eliminated."

Hearns, 22, said Leonard, the 25-year-old WBC welterweight champion, hurt him in the sixth round, but he thought he had recovered. He apparently was right, as he began to win rounds on the judges' cards.

But Hearns made an error in the 13th round, and Leonard capitalized on it. Leonard connected with a left hook and then a combination to the head, and it was the beginning of the end for Hearns. He went down in the 13th and it was ruled a push, although he seemed helpless draped on the ropes. The second time he went through in almost exactly the same spot, and Pearl went to a nine count before Hearns struggled back to the ring.

"I made a mistake by leaving my right hand low and letting Ray counterpunch with good left hooks," said Hearns, whose record dropped to 32-1. "He hit me with some good body shots. My body was in perfect shape, but not my head.

"Of course I want a rematch. I think I deserve one."

It was a remarkable performance by Leonard, who proved he is the finest craftsman in the ring today. He had survived his own moments of peril, changed his style and changed again to wither Hearns.

"I was afraid of the right hand of his until the very end," Leonard said. "He dropped some real bombs on me, and I knew he had another one left.

"I pulled this one out by reaching down into my guts, into my heart. I knew I had to pull out the reserve, and I did."

Leonard said his left eye, which began closing in the fifth round after numerous Hearns left jabs and overhand rights, was rapidly getting worse.

"I had lost half to three-quarters of my vision in the eye by the 12th round," he said. "Everything was blurry, and I knew the longer it went the more chance he had of catching me with one of those right hands. So I knew I had to put him out. I was afraid to let it go another round. I might not have been able to see at all by then."

Leonard had criticized Hearns throughout the pre-fight buildup, saying his opponent had "no brains" and telling the WBA champion he was in over his head. But as Leonard sat before two dozen microphones, his face swollen and bruised, he knew Hearns had been a worthy opponent.

"My hat is off to Thomas Hearns," Leonard said. "I may have said some things before the fight that I didn't really mean. He was everything he was supposed to be. He hurt me several times. He's a good man."

When the end came, neither Hearns nor Emanuel Steward offered any protest. Hearns grimaced and shook his head as if to say, "Well, I tried."

Indeed, he had. ✦

1 9 8 2

49ers stop the Bengals cold in Super Bowl at Silverdome

F orget Bill Walsh, the coach. Never mind Joe Montana, the quarterback. It took no genius on the sidelines to make the San Francisco 49ers champions of the pro football world. No artist on the playing field was needed to beat the Cincinnati Bengals in Super Bowl XVI.

All that was required was the presence of the Bengals themselves.

In what could have been their greatest hour — certainly the finest hour of the long season — they were one of the great flops in the history of the football extravaganza. San Francisco won, 26-21.

All week long the Detroit area — indeed, the entire country — had built toward a fever pitch for the Cincinnati-San Francisco confrontation. The Super Bowl came off beautifully, out-of-towners reveling at their pregame parties and tolerating the sting of our winter. Nothing says the Silverdome can't be a regular site for future Super Bowls.

There was a monumental traffic tie-up surrounding the stadium before the game, but once the fans arrived, they roared in anticipation — and kept roaring.

Only the Bengals seemed to lack enthusiasm. They were as cold and sloppy as the weather. They arrived in a deep freeze and played with a perplexing numbness. Maybe a dumbness, too.

It's difficult to say why a team that has come through as much as the Bengals have this season suddenly should lose touch and poise, especially with so much at stake. Often, there is no logical explanation. The Bengals had none.

It was true, though, that from the opening moments they were a cold team prone to errors that belied their standing as champions of the American Football Conference. You would guess any team would be up and ready for its only Super Bowl appearance, but the Bengals were amazingly flat.

Nor could they explain it. Forrest Gregg, their tough-minded coach, would not admit to raising hell with them in the halftime locker room, after they had fallen behind, 20-0. But he did have a talk with them.

They were headed for shameful embarrassment before the largest football crowd ever assembled — 100 million watching television screens around the world, and a record 81,270 screaming over the ruin of the Bengals at the Silverdome.

"I just told 'em it was about time we played a little football," Gregg said. "And we did for a while in the second half."

In his heart, though, he knew it was too late — the Bengals already had blown the game.

"We have come back in similar situations and won the game," he said, but then conceded. "You just don't spot a team as fine as the 49ers a 20-0 lead. You can't get away with that."

To the Bengals' credit, they tried. They took the play away from the 49ers in the third quarter, flashing to one touchdown to cut the 49ers' lead to 20-7, then storming toward another.

The game's pivotal moment followed. It challenges the wisdom of the Bengals' bench and the muscle of the 49ers' defense. The Bengals banged four times at the 49ers' line from the 3-yard line. The 49ers won. The final try of the Bengals' huge fullback, Pete Johnson, was the one that raised questions about bench strategy. Johnson was battered down, short of the goal, and the Cincinnati rally was broken.

Quarterback Ken Anderson wondered about the play call, as did many others. He seemed to prefer a play that would have taken the ball carrier wide, away from the surge of the 49ers' line.

"They decided to run," he said of the coaches, "and then it was just a question of which play to run and which side we'd run it to."

Having tried the left side — where 49ers linebacker Jack Reynolds had dropped Johnson — the Bengals decided to go to the right.

"We've scored on that play every time this season," Gregg said. Except this time, when it counted most, they didn't.

If the Bengals did not lose all their zip with that failure, they lost a lot of time. Only 10 minutes remained in the game before they closed within striking distance, 20-14, but that proved their last gasp.

They had given up too much too early, and because they did, they never really got into the game plan; it was not recognizable, once they had tossed away their opportunities.

"In a nutshell," said Paul Brown, the founder of the Bengals and a coaching genius in his old day, "we made too many errors, and they destroyed us. It was that simple."

At the heart of it all was the basic fact that the 49ers were cracking the Bengals heavily, punishing them physically. They are a bold, aggressive team with a heavy portion of young players mixed with veterans. From the outset, they came at Cincinnati with an eagerness that shook the Bengals. Nor did they ever relent.

That usually is what happens when a victim complains of being flat in its performance.

Chances are, it had been flattened. ✦

1 9 8 2

Lions coach Buddy Parker
saved the best for last

ven now, nearly 30 years after his greatest success and hours after his death, Raymond (Buddy) Parker remains a sad enigma, a man nobody understood or really knew.

A handful of his former players, all prosperous if not wealthy beyond their dreams, will assemble today in Kemp, Texas, 40 miles southwest of Dallas, to bury their old coach, and they will be shocked. The man who led them in their grandest years and for nearly a decade dominated our richest game died nearly destitute at age 68. He had been ailing the last few years with kidney disease and an ulcer that ruptured. It was not the sort of farewell anyone ever figured for Buddy Parker.

A lot of football coaches are strange characters, as you might have noticed. Some worship military heroes; others fancy themselves as creative geniuses. Historically, they have been labeled neurotic, paranoid, egomaniac and cruel. They also are known, with some notable exceptions, as brilliant.

Nobody ever determined where Parker, the finest football coach the Lions ever had, fit in his trade. He climbed to the top of the football mountain, then ran down the other side. Personally and professionally, he was not really like the rest. He was strangely different — friendly but distant, as if he were constantly preoccupied. He was properly intense, as coaches are, but always he seemed lonely, rather sad and humorless.

"I never figured him out," says Nick Kerbawy, then the Lions' general manager and about as close a confidant as Parker would allow. "He was tough to know. He was the kind of guy who might say hello on the first day of the season and good-bye on the last — except some years, he might forget to say good-bye. He was outrageously superstitious, and he had a temper. But nobody ever said he was cruel."

What everybody always said was that he knew how to win. The acknowledged genius of pro football then was Cleveland's Paul Brown, who now operates the Cincinnati Bengals. Parker and the Lions beat him seven out of eight, losing the 1954 disaster that broke Parker's string of two world championships.

The Lions back then were amazingly deceptive. They rarely performed well in the first half; crowds often called for Parker to replace quarterback Bobby Layne. What no one accepted was that Parker was not all that concerned about the first half, so long as the Lions remained close.

"I don't suppose there's ever been anyone who could remake a game plan at halftime as quickly with such results as Parker managed," Kerbawy says.

"In the second half, the Lions always seemed to be a different team. It was almost as if Parker deliberately had them hiding in the bushes in the first half, waiting to spring on somebody when it was too late for them to do anything about it."

That was the mark of his coaching genius, if genius it was. In later years, Parker admitted to saving special plays for months on end, never exposing them until the critical moment when they really were needed and were sure to work. Most often, they did; the Lions soon were known as the most dramatic team in sports.

Rival coaches credited him with an uncanny eye for talent and an ability to weave that talent into the framework of his team. Layne, for instance, is the most celebrated of all Lions players, but he had been shunted aside by two other teams when Parker entrusted the Lions to his erratic touch. Together, they made the Lions a sellout fixture in Detroit.

Parker might have been the most tolerant coach pro football has seen. At least, he was recognized as such at the time. For much of the 1950s, the Lions were known as the hell-raisingest outfit in sports, much like the recent Oakland Raiders. If there were training rules to be broken, they broke them.

The coach's strongest protests came when his assistants tried to curtail the frolickers.

"Once at training camp," Kerbawy says, "an assistant coach came to Parker with a list of players who had missed bed check the night before. Parker was really upset. He told the coach to mind his own business: 'When I want a bed check, I'll take it.' "

His tolerance of player mischief probably sprang from his own habits. The coach loved to get blitzed after a game — win or lose, and especially after winning. The Lions did a lot of winning in those days. Always, the bourbon was waiting.

"That was one of the remarkable things about Buddy," Kerbawy says. "He had such strict personal discipline. He loved his bourbon, but the only time he ever touched it was after a game."

Parker's astonishing walkout as head coach of the Lions during a preseason banquet is well known, even though it happened 25 years ago. What is not generally known is it was not the first time he walked out on a team, or the last.

All three incidents followed what he considered interference by club owners. He had quit the Chicago Cardinals in 1949, when the owner questioned him about plans for the following year. With Pittsburgh, after leaving the Lions, he walked out when a son of the owner suggested Parker use a different quarterback.

He never returned to pro football. He never really tried. We are left to wonder why. ✦

1982

Bonehead management moves send Detroit players elsewhere

W hen the proclamation was read the other evening elevating a half-dozen former Pistons to honored status as the best who ever played for the team, the audience applauded wildly. The names were revered, even for a team with a history not worth recounting.

No one could seriously challenge the selection of Dave Bing, Bob Lanier, Dave DeBusschere, George Yardley, Bailey Howell and Gene Shue, so outstanding were they in the first several decades of the Pistons.

Left unsaid, however, was that not one of these stalwarts, having played so superbly, was permitted to finish out his career with the Pistons. All, in fact, had been bounced while still in their prime and with much still to contribute — which they later did with other teams.

Newcomers to town often wonder whatever became of the City of Champions. They suspect, reasonably so, that for a long period of years this town that once fought among the best on all sports fronts suddenly became stuck with generations of bum basketball, hockey, baseball and football players.

It is not the case, of course — not wholly or mostly. What has been the case is that Detroit teams from time to time all have suffered from incredibly bad management judgment. For one reason or another, players of worth have been cast away to satisfy a front-office objective.

That was particularly true of the old Pistons, several of them becoming victims of the peevishness of former owner Fred Zollner, a generous man in all respects, except when he felt personally slighted.

George Yardley, the first 2,000-point scorer in the NBA, often had been cited by Zollner as one of his very favorite people, and not simply because of his basketball ability. The studious Yardley was a math-aerospace whiz headed toward the moon.

Following the 1959 season, however, Yardley was quoted in a sports magazine, criticizing some league matters, but nothing related to the Pistons. Zollner, one of the NBA's founding fathers, took offense at the remarks and never talked to Yardley again. Before a new season could begin, Yardley was traded.

Pistons history is filled with such episodes, and, in fact, each member of their all-time team was run out of town not because of failure on the basketball floor but usually because of some dispute with hardheaded management.

That was particularly true of Bob Lanier, the giant center now with Milwaukee. In the midst of a hot argument, he asked to be traded. Later, he relented, but he was shipped out anyway. The Pistons still suffer for it, while Lanier thrives with a title-bound team.

The Red Wings are an even greater tragedy, because they fell from greatness as a Stanley Cup champion in the mid-1950s in what could be interpreted as a deliberate dismantling of that team to help another, and they never fully recovered.

The Chicago-based Norris family owned the Red Wings and had a large interest in the fortunes of the Chicago Black Hawks. It was a conflict that curiously never was seriously challenged by the National Hockey League. The Black Hawks of those years suffered on the ice and at the gate in spacious Chicago Stadium, so, one by one, Red Wings (including Ted Lindsay and goalie Glenn Hall) gradually became Black Hawks.

The Red Wings seldom have been legitimate contenders in the years since, though until recent seasons one could find enough of their alumni doing well with other teams — enough of them to make the Wings successful, if they had been permitted to do so.

Nobody hung the "cheap" label on the Lions during the early 1960s when the NFL was involved in a talent war with the fledgling AFL. Perhaps the word had not been invented. But the fact was, the Lions lost their 1-2-3 draft choices (in addition to lesser choices) to the AFL for two successive years, because management, though selling out its park regularly, would not pay the price. The might-have-been Lions included Fred Biletnikoff and Johnny Robinson, both now headed for the Hall of Fame.

Is it any wonder the Lions have been in the NFL playoffs only once since? It takes years to build a contending team. Like the Red Wings and Pistons, they suffered years afterward for all-but-forgotten failures.

You are left to wonder whether the same will be true of the Tigers. Management could not tolerate Billy Martin, considered by many the best field manager in the game. He was a winner, though obviously there is a limit to how much abuse management must endure.

The Tigers turned out Rusty Staub, Ron LeFlore, Ben Oglivie, Jim Slaton and Steve Kemp, among others, with the expressed view that none of these was worth the price or the trouble anymore for their ballclub. They are worth the price to others.

If you say that is a strange attitude, indeed, for a team that has not finished higher than third in nine years, well, there you are.

The chances have been there, you see, and it cannot be said the players alone flubbed them. ✦

1 9 8 2

Too many cooks spoil
the broth for Caveman

Who threw the overalls in Mistress Murphy's chowder?
Nobody spoke, so he shouted all the louder.
It's an Irish trick it's true; I will lick the Mick that threw
The overalls in Mistress Murphy's chowder.
— **Irish ballad**

W illiam Lee, a quiet, gentle young man known rather inappropriately as "Caveman," is not acquainted with the legend of Mistress Murphy, nor is he quite sure of the proper ingredients of chowder.

But he would sympathize with the lady, for he, too, has become victim of someone's folly. Or so he insists.

Somebody else — a surrogate, no less — put a urine specimen in his bottle.

The saga of Caveman Lee and his bottle is fast becoming one of the most bizarre tales in a sports world newly rife with charges of illegal drug use.

Back on March 7, shortly after Caveman had been knocked cold by middleweight champion Marvin Hagler in Atlantic City, N.J., he was led down a hallway to a room to recuperate. I found him there, still woozy, but mostly embarrassed for having fallen in 67 seconds.

We were talking about it when Dr. Paul T. Williams of the New Jersey State Athletic Commission interrupted.

"We've got to have a urine specimen," the doctor said. With that, Lee, accompanied by several others, adjourned to the bathroom. He does not remember who they were, or whether the doctor was among them.

Eventually, Lee returned to resume our conversation. The doctor reappeared with a bottle, writing on its label. He tossed it in his bag, and he left. A most unlikely suspect.

What happened since not only threatens to destroy Caveman Lee in boxing but puts others under suspicion and questions the validity of sports safeguards. The bottle and its contents were delivered to a lab and, lo and behold, the tests showed the specimen had come from somebody who might have been using heroin. Naturally, Caveman Lee stands accused.

The New Jersey commission delayed nearly three months before revealing the test results publicly; it blames the World Boxing Association and the World Boxing Council, which were notified some time ago. When the charge was made public, nobody who knows Caveman — who neither drinks, smokes, cusses nor messes with people who do — would believe it.

"They've made an awful mistake," said Emanuel Steward, who handles Lee. "They had to get the specimen bottles mixed up."

"A lab error of this sort is only a remote possibility," said Dr. Stuart Kirschenbaum, Michigan's new boxing commissioner. "But I've handled a lot of people on drugs, and Lee certainly is not the type. There could be shenanigans."

"A guy can't fight on drugs," said Thomas Hearns. "Going into a fight, it would tell right away. It makes it look bad for Cave, but I can't believe any of it. Man, he had a police officer with him all the time he was in Atlantic City."

The officer was Allen (Jocko) Hughes, who worked narcotics in the Detroit police department for four years and occasionally in his free time joins the touring Kronk troupe as a bodyguard.

"I don't believe it," Hughes said. "I was with him all the time for more than a week and slept in his room with him. You spend a half-hour with somebody on heroin and you know it."

Still, the New Jersey commission insists there was no mixup of specimen bottles in the lab.

Faced with all that, Lee, who had stayed silent, finally felt compelled to explain how illegal drugs were found in the specimen bottle bearing his name. He insists he never did produce a urine specimen for the doctor. How he'll convince anybody is a problem.

"Somebody else did it," he said. "I tried once, and then the doctor sent me to the bathroom to try again, and I just couldn't and I left the bathroom. It was somebody else's."

Well, if not Lee's sample causing this damning fuss, whose? From what I remember, only other Kronk associates were in the room.

"I don't know," Caveman said. "I didn't pay any attention to who was there in the bathroom with me."

Of course, the New Jersey commission is accepting all this with a ho-ho, tell-us-another-story attitude. Robert Lee, the deputy commissioner there, was skeptical but insists "it will all come out when we have Caveman here for a hearing."

Caveman, ranked No. 6 among middleweights until his loss to Hagler, obtained a lawyer and got the hearing delayed until Aug. 24. It's not clear if a suspension by New Jersey would be honored elsewhere.

I've always said one of the great challenges of pursuing the fight crowd is that truth and fiction mingle. Often people are damaged more outside the ring than in; that is the case here.

I'm not sure what to believe, except that I'd always thought of Lee as maybe the least sinful man I know. But, of course, he also might be one of the dumbest.

When a doctor hands you a bottle, for instance, you are not expected to share it with anybody.

(Caveman Lee was suspended despite Kronk's protests. Lee quit boxing and held up a bank in what many interpreted as a suicide attempt.) ✦

1 9 8 2

Athletes learn to live
with the prospect of death

I n a fit of remorse, Mr. Bob Arum, the celebrated New York boxing
promoter, has called for a two-month suspension of all activity in his
sport. His latest promotion has left a fighter near death, and Arum, who
is not a heartless man, is saddened.

Yet knowing what you do about the sports business, you are allowed
to guess Arum is not distraught enough to abandon boxing. You would
be right. His fighters will be back in action this weekend on CBS-TV from
Nashville, Tenn.

"I'm sick about it," he said, referring to Duk Koo Kim, the South Korean
who suffered brain damage in a fight against Ray (Boom Boom) Mancini in
Las Vegas last weekend. "I'd always believed when a guy died in the ring,
something was wrong — that he took too many punches, the fight should
have been stopped or the guy was overmatched. All correctable things that
could be helped by closer supervision. I never believed a guy could get killed
by one punch."

For a smart guy out of Yale's law school, Arum obviously knows little
about the human head, although he knows a lot about human mentality. He
will continue promoting, he says, because "fighters will fight, and if I didn't
do it, they'd find some other promoter."

It's the way in all manner of sports. Life, and death, go on, whether it's
boxing or football or racing or mountain climbing. Eventually, somebody gets
hurt, fatally so, and though millions might mourn and then condemn the
vehicle of death, we play on.

Why we do is unclear. Explanations are offered as diverse as "sexual
gratification" and "death wish." But all that's really known is that while
thoughts of peril frighten many of us, they lure many others to the brink.

It was mere coincidence that Chip Hanauer, the handsome blond who won
the Gold Cup unlimited hydroplane race on the Detroit River last summer,
appeared here last week shortly after Sugar Ray Leonard announced he was
retiring from boxing at age 26, still in his prime.

Like Leonard, Hanauer has risen to the top of his game during the last
year. And Hanauer understood Leonard's decision. He always had promised
himself that once he reached all his goals — the Gold Cup, the national
championship, speed records — he would quit racing hydroplanes, a sport
that regularly kills its finest competitors. It occurs to him that he cannot quit.
Confronting death, tempting the devil, is a way of life, and though friends and
rivals die as they chase each other toward eternity, Hanauer is not dissuaded.

"When the five climbers died on Mt. Everest recently, people generally ignored it," he said. "Our sports here are more visible; the competitors are better known, and when it happens to one of us, people are distressed. They ought to know none of these activities can be made totally safe.

"Bill Muncey and Dean Chenowith died at their own hands, so to speak. Both made errors pressing for more speed, more than they needed."

Both were killed within the last 13 months.

It almost happened to Hanauer on the Detroit River last summer. Looking back on his incredible run on the final lap against Chenowith, he realizes he was mighty lucky he did not flip and disintegrate with his boat. Yet he would chance it again. He would do it because there never has been anything in his life before or since quite like those 10 or 15 seconds when he had Miss Atlas Van Lines skittering on the edge of one sponson at 180 m.p.h.-plus, inviting the ultimate disaster.

"The hardest thing to deal with is people who think we're crazy," he said. "I don't think I'm a crazy man. But, yeah, I took that boat to the limit and beyond. It was the Gold Cup and the Detroit River and Muncey's hometown, and I did it, and it was absolutely the finest moment of my life.

"You have to do it, you know?" he said, searching for understanding. "It's the intensity, the challenge. There are times I don't want to do it, but then there are times when you put your life on the edge of a cliff, and then you come away with a tremendous exhilaration, and all life seems so much richer."

He has seen men die chasing him and his records — as Chenowith did July 31 on the Columbia River in Pasco, Wash., in what should have been a meaningless practice run — and he knows the horror of such waste. But he knows, too, what happens to those of his kind who give up the chase, and that seems to scare him more than racing.

"Guys who quit," he said, "say they get a lump in their stomach all the time. They want to compete. They want to race. They never find anything to equal it. Whatever they do afterward, life is never the same again."

No one, of course, ever has attached much ecstasy to the boxing ring, which generally is regarded as sport's cruelest battleground. To many, there is something offensive about men challenging and pummeling each other.

What we must recognize is that the world is full of rings, and whether with car or boat, with football in hand and spikes on their shoes, or simply with gloves, always there are men driven to prove they are the best at what they do.

It's a fact of life, and death. ✦

1 9 8 3

Dempsey lacked size but added stature to boxing

W as Jack Dempsey the greatest heavyweight fighter who ever lived? Or was he just a man of his own time, a character romanticized during a period in sports history when everything was regarded as the best ever?

The Manassa Mauler might well have been the meanest man who ever stepped into a boxing ring. His passing will renew the debate over his place in fistic history.

There are a lot of Dempsey doubters today. Fifty-six years have gone since his last title fight. Other champions have emerged and passed. At least two — Joe Louis and Muhammad Ali — accomplished as much, or more, than Dempsey.

Those three generally are regarded as the finest of all heavyweight fighters. For sake of debate, a couple more could be included — Jack Johnson, the first of the great black champions, and Rocky Marciano.

In what order do they belong?

Jack Dempsey never joined the debate. He would smile politely and say it was not for him to judge. That was his answer when he last visited Detroit about 20 years ago to promote a book he had written.

He was a large man then, maybe 30 pounds over his 185 fighting weight, but still firm and graceful.

He had heavy, gnarled hands, the knuckles bulging and misshapen, remnants of his years in the ring.

His reputation was that of a fearless, reckless vagabond, which indeed he had been in his youth. But the years had changed him remarkably. No one would have guessed he had been a prize fighter, one of the most controversial figures in American sports lore.

He seemed then, in the 1960s, like any other quiet old gentleman. His eyes were soft and smiling and he appeared grateful for whatever attention anyone would give him.

"Louis is a great fighter, perhaps the greatest," he said at the time. "But there have been a lot of great fighters. I leave it for others to decide."

Dempsey reigned as heavyweight champion in the 1920s, a period the sports poets called the Golden Age. It was the time of Babe Ruth and Lou Gehrig and the Yankees, and all that emanated from New York was endorsed as the best anywhere. Dempsey, no doubt, benefited from that.

He was, however, considerably more than a product of Eastern media hype. His fights with Luis Firpo and Gene Tunney remain among the classics of his sport. Tales of his raging battles fill the fight history books. If Joe Louis opened the way for blacks to dominate boxing, it was Dempsey who brought the game big money — million-dollar purses and crowds of 100,000 and more.

It's odd that many in boxing today recall Jack Dempsey as a much beloved figure. He was not that, not until age softened him in body and manner. Through much of his early life, he was widely disliked. He had been a crude, illiterate youth, a hobo who wandered through Western tank towns fighting hastily arranged carnival exhibitions for whatever purse was offered.

When he finally rose to title contention during World War I, he was embraced by an adoring public, then quickly rejected. He had spurned the military draft, as would Muhammad Ali a half-century later, and took a job building ships when public wrath landed on him. It was his contribution to the war effort, he said, but the public was unforgiving. Nearly a decade would pass before he regained favor of the masses, and by then he was nearing the end of his reign as heavyweight champion.

Few men who saw Dempsey fight at his prime survive in boxing today. The measure of Dempsey as a fighter largely is gleaned from stories of his durability and his fierceness, and from old films. His merits as a fighter are not doubted.

But was he the greatest who ever lived? Naturally, Dempsey never would win an all-time greatest election in Detroit, which spawned Joe Louis, nor would Louis win such a test in Louisville, which produced Ali.

The doubt about Dempsey springs not from his ability as a fighter but from the evolution of the heavyweight class itself.

People are larger today. If it's true in other sports that a good big man is better than a good little man, shouldn't it also be true in boxing?

Dempsey, a murderous puncher, was smaller than Joe Louis, who also held thunder in his fists.

In turn, Louis was smaller — and slower — than Muhammad Ali, whose forte was not knockout power but classic fighting skills.

Ergo, the greatest heavyweight of all was not Jack Dempsey, nor Joe Louis, who died two years ago, but Muhammad Ali, who always said he was.

Now that's the way to start a fight. ✦

1 9 8 3

Panthers players a mile high after winning USFL title

ENVER — Down on the bench, the Panthers were frantic. The lead that seemed so secure was vanishing. So was the championship they already had celebrated.

"I don't like this at all," John Corker said. Sweat poured off the linebacker's head. He stamped his feet, then jumped up and down, imploring his teammates on the field to do something, anything, to break the storm of the Philadelphia Stars.

Line coach Kent Stephenson called his players together. The next time they went on the field, he said, they simply had to move Philadelphia linemen and make running room for their ball carriers.

"We're gonna move 'em. We're gonna move 'em," yelled guard Tyrone McGriff. "Oh, God almighty, please let us move 'em."

It was that desperate among the Panthers. Then Anthony Carter caught a 52-yard pass that finished the Stars, 24-14, and made the Panthers champions in the first year of the United States Football League.

What followed was almost incomprehensible pandemonium on the bench, then on the field of Mile High Stadium. The Panthers rushed onto the field, grabbed Carter, hugged him, embraced each other in unrestrained celebration. Three minutes remained in the game, but they knew there was no way they could lose.

Fans stormed the field fences, broke through them and delayed the playing of the final seconds. They mobbed the Panthers and threatened to trample them.

It took a gallant charge of the Panthers to reach their locker room, where champagne shot through the air, showering the ceilings and walls and everyone.

The players were delirious. They had expected to beat the Stars, but now that they had done so, they couldn't quite believe it.

"It doesn't get any better than this," yelled Cleo Miller, who filled in for injured fullback John Williams. He stumbled through the champagne shower, repeating over and over again, "It just can't get no better than this."

A moment later, he paused. "Nah, we weren't worried at all," he said. Then he confessed that, yeah, man, he really was worried for a long while.

"We didn't play well," he said. "We knew we were in for a fight, and we just had to stop making mistakes."

The Panthers did, long enough to win. This was no classic performance. It was probably their shabbiest offensive showing in recent weeks.

They dropped a half-dozen passes, fumbled a couple of kicks, saw a field goal blocked and drew more careless penalties than usual. But their defense, staunch through most of the game, saved them, and when it began to wilt and the Panthers needed one more scoring push, they had the man to do it.

Quarterback Bobby Hebert, voted the game's most valuable player, explained the pass to Carter that clinched the championship:

"Actually, it wasn't a play designed for Carter. We called an out-pattern to Derek Holloway, then when they came up with a blitz, I called the deep-out to Carter."

Carter caught Hebert's pass, faked out defender Antonio Gibson and raced free down the sideline and all but into the laps of an end zone filled with ecstatic Panthers fans.

Coach Jim Stanley was as overcome as his players.

"I can fly back to Detroit without an airplane," he said. "I feel three miles above sea level. It's a great tribute to the city of Detroit."

A full hour after the game, the Panthers still were congratulating each other in the locker room. It was an hour and a night they did not want to end.

(The Panthers, despite large crowds, played only one more season. They merged with the Oakland Invaders before the 1985 season, the USFL's last.) ✦

1 9 8 4

He laundered money …
now he launders clothes

rom the office of Mr. Harold Smith, the celebrated sportsman-bank
embezzler, came an unexpected phone call.

"I hate to call collect like this," he said, "but that's all they will allow."
He was phoning from the laundry of the federal penitentiary at Danbury,
Conn., where he is the resident clerk.

Harold sounds lonely. He never says he misses his private jet, or
yacht, or the dancing girls and shoot-outs in Las Vegas. But a guy not long
removed from the fast lanes of life is bound to have pangs of some sort when
his tires blow.

This is the same Harold Smith, a.k.a. Ross Fields, who three years ago was
accused of looting the Wells Fargo bank of California of $21 million. It shook
and embarrassed the banking industry, which quickly realized bulletproof
teller windows do nothing to thwart slickers at work on the company
computers.

Harold used the money, or some portion of it, in an attempt to become the
world's biggest promoter in boxing and track and field. He almost made it. But
six months ago, having exhausted all appeals of his conviction, Harold
surrendered to begin serving a basic 230-year sentence, compressed to 10
years of concurrent terms.

"I've got a good job," he says cheerily. "At least I get clean clothes every
day. I'm hanging in there."

Always one of the world's smoothest talkers, Harold has occasional
vernacular lapses. Guys in jail, for instance, do not say "hanging in there." But
no matter.

He is calling for no reason that is apparent, except to gossip about boxing
and talk of a book he is writing. It's called "How High the Fence?" and it will
explain, he says, how $21 million can be lifted from a bank without benefit of a
shotgun.

A lot of people, especially the FBI and Wells Fargo stockholders, are still
wondering what happened to the $21 million. Harold squandered millions
buying up champions and promoting others. He's the guy, remember, who
bankrolled Thomas Hearns' WBA welterweight title victory over Mexico's
Pipino Cuevas in August 1980.

The suspicion is that Harold has a good bit of money stashed somewhere,
waiting for the day he departs famous ol' Danbury.

He denies it.

"No, I don't have anything left, not really," he says. "But being honest, even if I did, I wouldn't answer that question. The most important thing is, I've always had the knowledge of how to get money again."

Queasy bank officers might take that as a warning, but, of course, to this day Harold Smith — who in his youth in Alabama was a nationally ranked track star named Ross Fields — protests his innocence in the looting of Wells Fargo. He doesn't deny he received a lot of money. He insists the bank simply gave it to him.

The jury didn't believe him, nor, chances are, would many who ever have had paper held by a bank.

No doubt a few in the audience are hanging on every word, wondering how it is possible to acquire millions of dollars from a bank without so much as a "Stick 'em up."

"What happened was the president of the bank came to my office and had me sign some blank sheets of paper," Harold says. "I believed it was for an unlimited line of credit."

You understand that more than a few people sign papers blindly these days. It's Harold's story that the bank president did him this great favor, and millions flowed to him freely and easily.

He simply kept drawing on the line of credit, buying up one fighter and another and paying them extravagant wages, until one day the transfer of funds between branch bank offices in Santa Monica, Calif., revealed a monumental shortage.

Poor Harold. He tells such a marvelous story it's a shame hardly anybody believes it. When lawmen asked Harold to present his copy of the line-of-credit documents, he presented blank sheets of paper. They didn't believe him, either.

Several bank officers who were his pals later confessed to a scheme to defraud the bank.

Harold figures he's got about 30 months to do at Danbury, and then he will be up for parole. Meanwhile, he's writing. Before long, his book will grace the market.

"How High the Fence?" No doubt some will say not high enough. ✦

1 9 8 4

Monday nights won't be the same without Howard

When summer begins to wane each year and millions come home from the shore, the nation quickly settles into a weekly ritual known as "Monday Night Football."

Preparing for its 15th year of excitement, "MNF" has earned a place at America's hearth, proof of which is the fact that secretaries of state, war and whatnot, and even presidents, have visited the broadcast booth.

From the beginning, there was a magnetism about "Monday Night Football," and it wasn't always the games, many of which were late-night horror shows.

The attraction was Howard Cosell, the most famous broadcaster in the business, sports or otherwise.

I'm going to miss Howard, who has tired of what he calls the "football mentality" that pervades television in the fall. At 64, he is headed for retirement, meaning he will do a lot of radio.

There was a time some years ago when Howard, pal to our nobles, considered running for the U.S. Senate. He is an Eastern-educated lawyer, which is a preferred beginning.

Why he didn't run is not a matter of record, but you understand even the Senate can be confining to a man accustomed to talking down to 20 million viewers weekly.

Howard stuck with what he does best. He loves to talk, or pontificate, for real or practice.

We were watching Howard tape his introduction for a major fight in New York some years ago. Always, this was his strength — the great unabashed hype, setting the scene for drama that might or might not develop.

He was effluvient, mellifluous, and all in all magnitudinous. Even as technicians repeatedly screwed up the taping, Howard never lost a beat.

He'd do it all over again and again without script or prompting, the coming event growing in magnificence with each retake. No river ever ran deeper with the superfluous.

"Howard's a dream," said director Chet Forte. "If you have five minutes or an hour of air to fill, you can always count on Howard."

There's a natural consequence of that. You find it with a lot of people who won't shut up. They end up speaking a lot of nonsense.

It was Cosell who popularized the phrase "telling it like it is." What few understood was that Howard was telling it like Howard, the way he perceived a situation.

He could be as cockeyed as the next guy, but he got away with it because how many knew otherwise?

Public relations people in pro football often scoff at Howard's fabled memory. His ability to rattle off statistics and the career trails of countless athletes was intriguing but not always accurate. Usually, only those concerned knew the difference.

He divorced himself from professional boxing in 1982 after nearly a quarter-century of fashioning the legends, or myths, of Muhammad Ali and Sugar Ray Leonard.

He called boxing a cruel, sordid business, which it often is. But he had spent much of his air life enriching the game and himself, and when he withdrew, his own credibility suffered more than boxing.

A lot of people learned to hate Howard Cosell, which is unfair. The world never has been exposed to his off-air charm.

What the public has seen is an often pompous character who lured them to "Monday Night Football" not to follow the ball but to marvel over his cerebral processes. Besides, he just might say something controversial, or even outrageous.

Last season, you recall, Howard slipped. Referring to the swiftness of a Redskin, he said look "at that little monkey" run. The player was black.

I happened to be watching the game in Las Vegas with a room full of blacks.

"Oh, oh," said Prentiss Byrd, who squires Thomas Hearns. "Now you've done it, Howard."

Ridiculous, I said. It's a common expression. Howard didn't mean anything by it.

"Maybe so," Byrd said. "But you're not black. There's gonna be a lot of hell raised about that."

A few days later, there was. It might have been Cosell's unhappiest time in the broadcast trade.

For years every autumn, he was reason to stay awake. Now he has had his gastrointestinal fill of it. Larynxicologically, he is spent. "Monday night Football" never will be the same without him.

It might be the most lamentatious thing that ever happened to us. ✦

1 9 8 4

Party hearty, Tigers fans, but you can't match 1968

T here's no intention here, understand, of putting a knock, a damper, a kibosh on anybody's celebration.

It's OK by me if the town goes nutty over the Tigers' American League East championship. The new generation of baseball fans can whoop and holler down the avenues and raise hell in the bars.

Everybody has my permission.

The thing is, once you've been to a real party, anything that follows seems like imitation.

Winning in 1984 can't match winning in 1968. In no way. I can get as goofy as the next guy, but I just don't feel the same about '84.

You might say this is another case of some joker insisting the old days were better. They were — 1968 was.

The last time the Tigers won the American League pennant and the World Series was extraordinary for a lot of reasons, and it touched off the wildest civic celebrations this city — or any city — had seen in years.

Many mistakenly think the largest party came with the winning of the Series. It didn't, if only because the Tigers were in St. Louis when they claimed the championship.

By far, the goofiest hours followed the clinching of the pennant at Tiger Stadium. Soon avenues stretching from downtown were filled with cars and people on a crazy romp that lasted through the evening and into the morning.

Downtown streets were so jammed with people rushing to join a party, or start one of their own, that cars couldn't move. Within a few hours, it was almost impossible to leave the area.

Nor did anyone want to leave. It was a once-in-a-lifetime bang and binge that developed for a lot of reasons often overlooked.

Today, many people say it happened because the Tigers hadn't won a championship for 23 years. The fans were restless; they had been frustrated so long that when the team finally won, their joy was unrestrained.

But more than the long wait between 1945 and 1968 was involved.

All of our teams — the Lions, Red Wings and fairly new Pistons — had taken a nosedive. We had more than our share of champions through the 1950s, but the 1960s were barren until the '68 Tigers.

The city had been through a terrible riot the year before, and thousands of suburbanites had forsaken Detroit. The Tigers brought them home.

There were other reasons, too. Strangely, many native Detroiters never were a part of earlier Tigers celebrations.

When the Tigers beat the Chicago Cubs in the '45 Series, World War II had ended only weeks before. Thousands of Detroiters still were in military service. Many had only skimpy knowledge of the team's progression through the season. Besides, the city recently had flipped its lid over the end of the war in Europe, then Japan.

Winning a championship in that era was not all that unusual for the Tigers, or any of our teams. Detroit still was clinging to its City of Champions label, and winning was accepted as our due.

The Tigers won the American League pennant in 1940, and there were no great rallies in the streets. They lost the Series to the Reds, and if anyone wept, it wasn't noticed.

Old-timers say only the celebration that followed the Tigers' World Series triumph over the Chicago Cubs in 1935 might match the extravagance of 1968.

Again, there was good reason. The victory over the Cubs produced the first world championship, although the Tigers had won the pennant — then lost the Series to St. Louis — in 1934.

Streetcars were lifted off their tracks by rampaging crowds hailing the Tigers' victory. The city hadn't seen a celebration like that since Armistice Day, ending World War I.

It touched off a year that was to bring championships from the football Lions, the hockey Red Wings and the basketball Eagles.

The Tigers of 1968 were not a great team, but they were that year, and they came at a time when the city badly needed something, or somebody, to help restore its image and faith in itself.

So you see, there was a lot more than baseball involved when we all went bonkers 16 years ago.

It's nice to do it again. But somehow, the verve is missing. ✦

1 9 8 4

Fetzer dripping with delight
after Tigers win World Series

Ol' John Fetzer, soaked again in the wine of champions, had a confession to make: He knew it would happen. He knew it all the time.

If others had doubts months ago about the 1984 Tigers, the man who had owned them and sold them had none.

As long ago as last spring, at the start of his 28th season with the Tigers, Fetzer, 83, was convinced he would be standing again amid the players and celebrating another World Series championship.

He stood off to the side of the Tigers' locker room, away from the tumult, quietly watching the celebration. His champagne-soaked shirt clung to his body, but he didn't mind.

He got off easy. When the Tigers won the World Series in 1968, the players dumped him in the whirlpool. He didn't mind it then, either.

"I think we're getting used to scenes like this," he said, laughing. "We had a pennant-clinching celebration and then the pennant. The boys are a little more restrained now."

From Fetzer's view, and that of others in the Tigers' hierarchy — general manager Bill Lajoie, president Jim Campbell, new owner Tom Monaghan — the Tigers' championship in 1984 might well be a harbinger of more to come.

"I think that's right," Fetzer said. "There's no such thing as a dynasty in baseball — Baltimore is proof of that. But this certainly should be a top contending team for some years to come. We won't stand pat."

Several moves the Tigers made last spring had convinced Fetzer they had enough to go the distance — right through the World Series.

"After we made a couple of deals" — acquiring relief pitcher Willie Hernandez and first baseman Dave Bergman — "I kept saying this team looked like 1968. It had what it needed to go all the way. I knew Sparky (Anderson) would hold it together."

The others on the Tigers' management team, the men who acquire the talent, might not have been so certain, but they say they thought all along no team in baseball was better.

Monaghan, protecting an injured back, escaped the torrents of locker room champagne that splashed over everyone within reach.

"I'm on a cloud," he said. "I can't believe it. I'm totally numb. That was so much fun watching Kirk Gibson jumping and clapping after his second home run."

And the joy went on. Outside the stadium, thousands were celebrating into the night, singing, chanting, hailing the Tigers' finest hour.

Old-timers might still insist this was not the greatest team in the Tigers' history — but none accomplished more.

The 1935 Tigers with Hall of Famers Mickey Cochrane, Charlie Gehringer, Hank Greenberg and Goose Goslin might well have been the best.

The 1945 champions were a cherished memory from a dreadful war, but not a great team.

And the 1968 Tigers of Al Kaline, Denny McLain, Mickey Lolich, Jim Northrup, Bill Freehan et al, might have been more spectacular, more dramatic with its power.

None of them ever won like the 1984 Tigers. None was so dominant. None won as many games in flashes and in streaks. None was more convincing. And none ever captivated the town as did the 1984 Tigers.

"Our 1968 team had a style all its own," said Al Kaline, the best of them. "This one had a style, too."

Perhaps Terry Kennedy, the catcher of the beaten San Diego Padres, described them best:

"They're not flashy, just very professional," he said. "There's no bull—— about them. They just go out and kick your ass. I like that. I like them."

Maybe, despite all, it was not the all-time best Tigers team. No matter. It was the team of its time. ✦

1 9 8 5

Parents have little to fear
from the likes of Babe, Gibby

One of these days we will pause in our romp through the flowers to conduct a scientific survey among America's young people, and use it to rid the world of one of its great fallacies.

If the survey turns out as I suspect it will, we'll also relieve a tremendous burden from a select group of citizens known as sports heroes.

For as long as we can remember, for instance, it has been assumed that sports heroes exert tremendous influence on the nation's youth. It is said they are role models and idols whose example helps guide the young.

It is a myth, thank God.

Nobody ever seriously asked the kids about it, although I did once, on a rather informal basis, after a woeful day at the office.

We had run a story about Denny McLain, then in the midst of his 31-victory season. The story mentioned that McLain relaxed in the clubhouse with a can of beer in hand.

I don't recall anything we've ever done that so offended the public. Mothers were outraged that McLain should be so pictured in the family newspaper.

I asked one mother whether her husband drank beer when their son was around, and, of course, he did. The difference, she said, was that McLain was the kid's hero, and we were destroying Denny's image and thus damaging the kid.

I couldn't quite believe it. That evening I polled several Little League teams in the neighborhood, and the results were enlightening. Not one kid mentioned an athlete as his idol, or someone who might have significant impact on him.

They mentioned uncles and coaches, older brothers, fathers, grandfathers and the like. Many, of course, wanted to be ballplayers, but none said they wanted to be just like Denny McLain — or any other star, for that matter.

I haven't worried about the young, and the country's future, since. They're smarter than we think.

You begin to suspect the athlete's assignment as a model for the young is thrust upon him by people groping for a symbol to lay on their kids.

We'd better find another way, for the years have shown athletics is not an activity where saints are created. There are far more good men than bad in the games we play, but there are enough bad to break a million hearts daily, if athletes are to model for our young.

It always has been so. No athlete ever was more popular, for instance, than Babe Ruth, the baseball immortal, who dearly loved dogs and kids. They gave him a false image.

We know today that, in many respects, Babe Ruth was a bum. In his time, baseball might have benefited if countless kids had mimicked his swing, but fortunately few copied his lifestyle.

Sports history is filled with illusions like Ruth. At least the athletes are honest about it; they are uncomfortable being examples for others to copy.

Many athletes openly disown the role. Some polish and use it, as in the case of Olympic hurdles champion Edwin Moses, who tumbled hard last week when, falsely or otherwise, Los Angeles cops tagged him for soliciting a cop playing prostitute.

Just the other day, the Los Angeles cops caught Texas Rangers pitcher Dave Stewart in the act. Only then did he discover his partner was a man, proving, I suppose, that some athletes really are stupid.

At least, from what we suspect, the athlete as a role model is fiction; the kids aren't paying attention anyway. We have that going for us.

So you will know, an interesting change in sports hero worship — such as it is — seems to be developing. Kirk Gibson, the Tigers' brash outfielder, is a case in point.

Gibson might well be the rising new slugging sensation of the American League. But his severest critics are men, old and young, who view his manner so crude as to taint his value as a ballplayer.

It is men, you see, who perpetuate the notion that sports is a great calling, and damn the unworthy. If you doubt it, ask a few what they think of Kirk Gibson.

There is little beyond his hitting they find admirable. A kid inclined to use Gibson as a role model is going to have soap for supper regularly.

Conversely, Gibson's strongest following — at least the mail suggests it is so — consists of women and girls who not only tend to be more forgiving but find an appeal in Gibson not easily understood by others.

They always were smarter that way. They might dream of a shining knight, but they will settle for less. ✦

1 9 8 5

Hearns goes down swinging in brutal bout with Hagler

L AS VEGAS, Nev. — Thomas Hearns' quest for boxing greatness ended in shattering defeat last night, with Marvin Hagler hammering him into a technical knockout after eight minutes and one second of the most incredible fighting of modern times.

The end came at 2:01 of the third round with Hearns, who had been floored by two rights from Hagler, locked in the embrace of referee Richard Steele.

Steele gazed into the eyes of the shaken Detroiter, saw that Hearns was hurt and dazed, and waved an end to the battle for Hagler's undisputed middleweight boxing championship.

After the bout, Hearns was taken to Valley Hospital for X-rays of his right hand, which Kronk boxing team officials speculated had been broken in the first round. Prentiss Byrd, one of the Kronk corner men, said that when Hearns' glove was removed after the fight, his hand was so sore they couldn't touch it.

A screaming throng of 15,128 roared from opening bell to the finish as Hearns and Hagler traded awesome, crushing blows. First Hearns, then Hagler, then Hearns again was rocked backward in a fistic duel that raged on, unrelenting, until Hearns fell.

Hagler was bleeding profusely from two cuts, one alongside his nose, the other over his right eye, as he pursued Hearns. He never wavered despite a series of awesome right hands landed by the challenger.

"I was afraid the referee might stop the fight (after the second round)," Hagler said. "But I showed I could take Tommy's right hand, and the rest is history."

Hearns had to be carried to his corner, then helped from the ring to his dressing room, where he remained long after the crowd had departed.

Before leaving for the hospital, Hearns said he had no excuses for his loss.

"Hagler is a great fighter," he said, adding that he would like to fight him again.

Said Hagler: "I would like a rematch, but I need time to heal, time to recover."

It was another cruel defeat — the second of his career — for Hearns, a 26-year-old fighter known as Hit Man. And it was the second time Hearns' mighty right hand could not save him from a reigning champion.

In September 1981, in the same backyard stadium at the Caesars Palace gambling casino, Hearns lost on a 14th-round TKO to Sugar Ray Leonard.

In the four years since, he had groomed himself to challenge Hagler for the middleweight title. But his vaunted power, which had smashed 34 of 41 rivals into knockouts, could not take out Hagler.

"He fought the way he had to," said Hagler, 30. "He came after me. He's a good fighter, very courageous. But he's very cocky, and I had something for him."

Without a doubt, this fight — which Hagler had predicted would be a war — will be remembered, despite its brevity, as one of the great ring classics.

"I haven't seen that much action in three rounds ever," said Steele, who has officiated bouts for 15 years.

Hearns had said it would end in a third-round knockout, but he never figured he would be the victim.

From the opening bell, he and Hagler began to tear at each other as if each blow, each breath, might be their last.

Hagler came right across the ring at the outset to meet Hearns' challenge, and within a moment he had reason to regret it.

Hearns rapped a stiff left to Hagler's body, then shot a right uppercut that snapped back Hagler's head. Midway in the round, he slammed a hard right that rocked Hagler back on his heels. A moment later, another right opened a cut alongside Hagler's nose.

While all that was going on, Hagler was slamming Hearns, first with lefts from his southpaw stance, then with several ripping rights.

In the final minute of the round, the champion showed Hearns had not convinced him of anything. He caught Hearns with his stiff right and shook him, then a right uppercut, a left and another stiff right knocked Hearns back on his heels as the round ended. It was enough to win the round for Hagler.

The crowd was gasping in amazement at the fury of the fighting. It was quickly apparent that the fight would not go the 12-round distance to a decision, that one or the other would have to fall.

In Hearns' corner, manager Emanuel Steward — hoping to keep Hagler at a distance — urged his fighter to change tactics, to begin boxing rather than attacking Hagler directly.

For a while, that plan succeeded. Hearns began dancing away from Hagler, then reaching in with his long left, then lead rights, to stab and hurt the champion.

Just then, as it seemed Hearns' scheme was working, Hagler lashed out with a right that stung Hearns. Hagler followed with a left, another right, then a left-right that sent Hearns into retreat.

Hearns escaped that assault, came back to slam Hagler with a left-right combination, then a left and another lead right.

Hagler, blood flowing down his nose, kept coming, and soon Hearns could not escape. He ripped Hearns with a left-right to the head, then another right, and still another.

Hearns danced away. He came back to slam another right to Hagler's head, then a left to the body and another right. It was the last great moment for Hearns.

Before the second round ended, Hagler rapped Hearns with two lefts, then chased him to slam home three more rights. Hagler won the round.

The third began with Hearns dancing away from Hagler, hoping to frustrate the champion while his own long jab stabbed at Hagler's wounds.

For the opening minute of the round, he got away with it. But then, as he danced away from Hagler, Hearns made a fatal mistake.

He bounced away, but not quite far enough to be out of danger. Hagler leaped forward and slammed a right hand alongside Hearns' head. It shook Hearns, who stumbled awkwardly toward Hagler's corner, his back half-turned to Hagler.

Hagler, sensing that he had hurt Hearns, leaped in, smashed him with another right that drove Hearns into the ropes, then two more rights that sent Hearns tumbling to the floor.

Hearns rolled onto his back. It seemed he might never get up. But he slowly struggled to his knees, then stood up, just before Steele would have counted him out.

Hagler came forward, but Steele stepped in front of Hearns, protecting him. He looked at Hearns and quickly sensed that it would be merciless to let the fight continue.

And so it ended, and so ended the dream of Hearns to etch his name alongside the great fighters in history. He had hoped to defeat Hagler, claim his third world title — he is the WBC super-welterweight champion — and then move on to claim the light-heavyweight title.

Those hopes disappeared as he found one man — Marvin Hagler — who was more than he could handle. ✦

1 9 8 6

Before Billy Sims, Doak Walker was the Lions' All-Everything

C ANTON, Ohio — Some might have noticed with dismay the retirement last week of the Lions' Billy Sims, and the accolade accorded him.

In a description that overlooked all who had gone before, Sims was called "the greatest runner in Lions history."

Was he really?

Here we are at the shrine of pro football, standing with a man forgotten by modern football fans but remembered by others as the ultimate player. Doak Walker, a Lion from the best of times.

In his time, and for years before and after, there was no one like him, none his equal.

All the honors available came his way — the Heisman Trophy, the Maxwell, three-time All-America at Southern Methodist University, a player-of-the-half-century, a four-time All-Pro in the Lions' great 1950s championship era. He ran, he passed, he caught passes, he punted and kicked, returned kicks and intercepted passes. Sure, he played defense, too.

Buddy Parker, who coached him, said Doak Walker, the consummate halfback, would have been All-Pro on defense. He weighed 167 pounds.

Dozens of pro football Hall of Famers and thousands of fans are in Canton to witness the enshrinement of another group of former players into the hall. Finally, Doak Walker's turn has come.

"After all these years," he said, "it came as a total surprise to me."

He looks terrific — a bit heavier — but hard and sturdy and sparkling bright. He's 59, born on Jan. 1, 1927, the golden year of the golden age of sports.

The long delay in his selection to the hall was not the result of anything Walker failed to accomplish. His shortcoming was that he had played only six pro seasons.

"I was told that once the electors understood I played both ways (offense and defense), they treated it like 12 seasons," Walker said, laughing.

Men who were his contemporaries say his play in college and pro football was uncanny, unforgettable.

"Billy Sims couldn't match him," said Nick Kerbawy, the Lions' general manager through Walker's pro career (1950-55). "That's no knock against Sims. Doak was so versatile, nobody matched him."

Bobby Layne was the Lions' quarterback then. He and Walker grew up in Dallas and were high school teammates. They went separate ways in college, joined the Merchant Marines together, then by an odd twist of trades, wound up teammates on the Lions.

"He was the greatest clutch player I ever saw," Layne said of Walker. Elected to the Hall of Fame in 1967, Layne will present Walker for induction in the ceremonies.

"There was nobody else I would have," Walker said. "We've been closest friends since I was in grade school. I live in Denver and he lives in Lubbock, Texas, but we still phone each other at least once a week."

It figures that Layne, who dreads speeches, would gut-out one more.

"Well, I'll tell ya," Layne said, "if we were ahead, 28-0, or somethin', you might not notice Doak on the field. But if it was a close game, everybody knew he was there, and he would be the difference."

Russ Thomas, the Lions' general manager, was a scout during Walker's career in Detroit. He has vivid memories of the time.

"There was that championship game in Cleveland in 1952," Thomas said, "and Doak literally ran 67 yards through the whole Cleveland team. I don't know how 11 guys missed him, but he was like that.

"He made things happen. He had uncanny field vision, but I was always amazed how he survived. He wasn't particularly big."

Walker remembers 1952, too. He was All-Pro and the NFL's leading scorer in his rookie season (1950) and again in 1951. But 1952, when he didn't make All-Pro, was his most gratifying season, even though he missed 10 games with a hamstring injury.

"That Cleveland game was my biggest thrill in football because it was a great climax to a great Lions season," Walker said of the Lions' 17-7 victory.

A week earlier, he had thrown a 24-yard touchdown pass to Leon Hart as the Lions beat the Rams, 31-21, in the division playoff.

"To take the championship back to Detroit, which hadn't won one since 1935," Walker said, "to have the kind of year we had, and the way we were treated by the fans, well, nothing could match it."

In the 1953 championship game, again with Cleveland the victim, Walker produced 11 points in a 17-16 victory, scoring one touchdown and kicking a field goal and two conversions.

The Browns mauled the Lions, 56-10, in the '54 title game, Walker kicking a field goal, catching two passes for 39 yards and returning a kickoff for 20.

"We had Hunchy (Bob Hoernschemeyer), Pat Harder and Gene Gedman as runners during Doak's time," Layne said, "and they shared the work load so that they all had about the same yardage. We got so we were using Doak as a receiver a lot."

Walker ended his career prematurely after the 1955 season, Kerbawy said, in an attempt to save his first marriage. His wife was a former cheerleader and Cotton Bowl queen.

"They had to get out of Texas," Kerbawy said. "Doak was so worshipped there, nobody gave him time for business or even regarded him as a businessman in the off-season."

Walker, unfailingly gracious and widely admired for his clean living ("He didn't do the things I did," Layne said) was known as the "last of the great

American glamour athletes." He graced the covers of every major magazine and countless others.

When the Lions played an exhibition game in Dallas, the promoters insisted that the team give Walker 10 percent of its game receipts.

"That's how much he meant to them," Kerbawy said. "They loved him so much he got an extra $4,100 from the Lions just for that game. He was only making about $15,000 for the season."

Walker and his wife shortly moved to Denver, but he was being pressured to quit football. He sat out one season, then came back.

"He came to training camp for three days in 1957, and Buddy Parker told me to sign him," Kerbawy said. "But Doak said he had to make the most important phone call of his life. It was to his wife, and when they were finished talking, he left camp. That was the end."

The marriage ended two years later. Walker later married Skeeter Werner, a former Olympic Alpine skier whose family owns a ski resort in Steamboat Springs, Colo.

Walker soon became an avid skier. It almost cost him his life in 1970. He was buried in a snow avalanche in the Canadian Rockies in a near-tragedy that haunts the Werner family. Buddy Werner, his wife's brother and a world ski hero, had died six years earlier in an avalanche near St. Moritz, Switzerland.

"No, I don't have any regrets about quitting football when I did," Walker said. "I'm not sorry because I've got all my teeth, both knees — and most of my faculties."

Old Lions have rallied in Canton to salute Walker's entry into the Hall of Fame. There's Layne, Yale Lary, Joe Schmidt, and Dick (Night Train) Lane, already in the hall, and Cloyce Box, Jimmy David and Gil Mains.

"We were together just a few weeks ago in California," Kerbaway said, "for the funeral of Jack Christiansen."

Four others will be enshrined with Walker. They are Paul Hornung of the Green Bay Packers, Ken Houston of the Washington Redskins, Willie Lanier of the Kansas City Chiefs and Fran Tarkenton of the Minnesota Vikings.

Walker had given up any hope of making it into the hall. His election came as an old-timer, a player from the deep past overlooked or not properly evaluated. All the other honors bestowed on him seem shallow by comparison.

"This is the greatest honor any pro player can receive," he said. "It's the climax to the closing of a career, and I just thank goodness that I'm able to enjoy it while I'm still alive."

At his side on the steps on the Hall of Fame will be his wife, Skeeter, his two daughters and two sons, his sister, and his father, Ewell Doak Walker Sr.

"My dad has been waiting for this," he said. "He's 88. He was a high school football coach. When I was 2, 3 years old, he started shoveling passes to me."

Did Doak Jr. become the greatest Lions runner? Maybe.

There was Sims, from a new era, a different style of football. And there were Bullet Bill Dudley and Frankie Sinkwich in the 1940s, and Earl (Dutch) Clark in the '30s. They had their time, which is all anybody can claim. ✦

1 9 8 6

Greenberg the standard-bearer for City of Champions

I t's strange how descriptions from long ago, nearly a half-century and another baseball age ago, suddenly pop into mind today.

"Hankus Pankus," radio announcer Ty Tyson called him.

The name reflected the city's affectionate embrace of one of the greatest of baseball sluggers.

Hank Greenberg is dead. His grace and power at the plate were rewarded with unmatched popularity in a city of baseball worshipers.

For thousands of aging lovers of the game, the memory of Greenberg, the tall, shuffling first baseman who powered the Tigers to four pennants and two world championships, 1935 and 1945, cannot die.

The record books will show others have hit more home runs, but the numbers are misleading. Without a doubt, he was the greatest home run hitter the Tigers ever had.

He was, in fact, one of the great home run hitters in baseball history, though the record shows him with what seems today only a respectable 331.

The numbers were magic in his time. He ignited the town:

"Going ... going ... gone!" Tyson would say, and on porch after porch down the city blocks men and women, relaxing with the afternoon radio broadcast, suddenly would leap off their swings and wave and shout to their neighbors.

There was not much else to shout about in the 1930s. But Hank Greenberg had a huge grip that spanned the neighborhoods, reached into the markets, the factories, and the schools.

Few players are so blessed. Greenberg found everybody had a grip on his bat. They all swung with him, and when he connected, Detroit scored.

These were years when City of Champions had real meaning, when the best was our standard in all respects.

Babe Ruth was nearing the end of his career in 1933 when Greenberg arrived in Detroit for his first full major league season. He had hoped to play with his hometown Yankees, but they had no need for him, not then.

It was an era when not everyone could reach the outfield seats with a fly ball. Many players were delighted to have a half-dozen home runs a season.

Soon, the great bangers of the game were Jimmie Foxx, Lou Gehrig, Hack Wilson and Hank Greenberg.

In Greenberg's second full season, the Tigers won the American League pennant, and in his third, 1935, they won the World Series. That season, Greenberg led the American League with 36 home runs.

This might have been the best of all Tigers teams — catcher Mickey Cochrane and second baseman Charlie Gehringer are rated among baseball's best-ever at their positions.

In 1937, Greenberg's reputation as a slugger began to crest. He hit 40 home runs. The next year, he had the nation following his every swing as the season wound down. He hit 58, a tantalizing two short of the incredible 60 Ruth had set as the major league record 11 years earlier.

When he visited Detroit last year, Greenberg, 74, fit and happy, spoke modestly of his pursuit of Ruth's record.

"I suppose I had a chance to break it," he said, "but I was delighted to come that close. The truth is, I was disappointed I never came that close again."

He talked, too, of how lonely he had been in his early bachelor years in Detroit.

"I really didn't know many people," he said, "but I managed to enjoy myself. Often, I'd go over to Belle Isle in the mornings and play ball.

"I had a great time, just pickup games with some guys around. For a long time, they had no idea who I was, but when they found out, it didn't matter. We still had a great time — especially when I struck out."

In 1940, the Tigers won the pennant again, and this time Greenberg was in leftfield, leaving first base so Rudy York, another slugger, could be inserted in the lineup.

Greenberg was an ordinary outfielder, but the Tigers could not do without his bat. He knocked in 150 runs that year — and that wasn't his high. He had driven in 170 in 1935 and an astounding 183 in 1937.

Soon after the Tigers lost the 1940 World Series to Cincinnati, Greenberg, then 29, was drafted into the U.S. Army.

He was out of baseball, except for 19 games in 1941, until the summer of 1945, rejoining the Tigers in time to help them to another pennant — he hit a grand slam to clinch it — and a World Series triumph over the Chicago Cubs.

The next year, Greenberg was sold after the season to the Pittsburgh Pirates in a deal that outraged Tigers followers and brought public condemnation upon team owner Walter O. Briggs Sr.

Briggs, a wealthy industrialist known for pinch-penny operations, never really explained what prompted his move. But word soon leaked out that Greenberg dared demand a pay raise. Some fans never forgave the owner.

Nor, apparently, did Greenberg. He seldom returned to Detroit, although he was active in baseball as part-owner of the Cleveland Indians from 1948-58 and vice president of the Chicago White Sox from 1959-63.

After his retirement from baseball, Greenberg became active in recreational tennis in Los Angeles and achieved national ranking. He was a slugger there, too. ✦

1 9 8 6

Cash raised the roof
on and off the field

GREEN BAY, Wis. — Another of our great baseball heroes is gone.

The call announcing his tragic end came to the press box here and cast a pall over what had been one of the Lions' few delightful Sunday afternoons on old Lambeau Field.

Norm Cash, the friendliest, most likable of the old Tigers.

Stormin' Norman, the fun-loving jokester, always ready with a quip, always ready to play. On the field, or off.

Good ol' Norman, everybody's pal — and one of the Tigers' greatest sluggers of the last quarter-century.

The year has been unkind. Only a few months ago, we lost Hank Greenberg, the Tigers' great slugger of an earlier era. And now Cash.

He was the one who made the rightfield roof at Tiger Stadium a special attraction. Others before him, and more since, had used that 94-foot-high roof as a target and a symbol of hitting power, and cleared it with magnificent home run blasts.

Ted Williams did it; Mickey Mantle, too. But nobody did it with the flair of the left-handed Cash, the Tigers' first baseman of the 1960s and early 1970s.

It seemed that every time he came to the plate, the roof was his aim. And those four times he did clear it with Ruthian swings — once in 1961 and three times in 1962 — it was as if he had conquered a world of his own.

In a way, he had. Power was his game. He believed it. He believed it so strongly it changed him as a hitter. His strikeouts often seemed as mighty as his home runs.

For years he was my favorite baseball enigma. Never had I been able to understand how a guy could hit .361 and win the American League batting championship, as Cash did in 1961, and then never come anywhere near that average again.

It could not have been a fluke year. No one hits .361 by accident or luck over a 162-game season.

Only later, when Cash explained, did it seem to make some sense. After that phenomenal year, when he also hit 41 home runs, Cash began thinking of himself more as a power hitter than a consistent stroker.

"The world is full of guys who can hit singles," he said. "But you always have to make room for somebody who can hit home runs."

Certainly, he could do that. He was attracted to power games, anyway. He was a former football halfback drafted by the Chicago Bears. He also was a versatile athlete with speed, agility and a sturdy body.

Cash made a choice on the type of hitter he would be, and paid a price, of sorts. He hit .283 in 1971 — the closest he ever got to his league-leading .361.

We are left to wonder how consistent or dominant he might have been at the plate, had he not committed himself to power.

When he did, however, Cash clearly established himself as the leader of a home run-banging collection of Tigers — Jim Northrup, Al Kaline, Bill Freehan among them — who powered Detroit to the 1968 World Series championship over the St. Louis Cardinals in seven thrilling games.

Those were the unforgettable days for a generation of Tigers fans approaching middle age. Current Tigers followers marveled over the team's breeze through the 1984 season and its romp through the World Series against the San Diego Padres.

But that team lacked the drama of Cash's champions, who rattled late-inning home runs with such frequency that a recording of broadcasts of their game-winning blows became a popular hit itself.

Norm Cash was 51, and his sudden death in Lake Michigan was a shock, though he was not in the best of health. Five years ago, he suffered a serious stroke. He had an extended recovery period, and his speech remained affected.

It was that episode that rekindled the public's affection for Cash, a native Texan who had spent 15 seasons with the Tigers before retiring at the end of the 1974 season. For weeks, readers called inquiring about his health. Many curiously remembered him not for his bat but for the fun he brought to his game.

It was in his bouncy gait, in his face and manner. He liked to laugh, and he would, anytime, anywhere. He was no clown, but he was not above occasional clowning.

He was a marvelously uncomplicated man who loved his world, and his world loved him back. He was lucky that way. ✦

1 9 8 6

Layne lived life
like a two-minute drill

T ime ran out on Bobby Layne, the former great quarterback of the Lions.
He was, in his time, bigger than life, certainly bigger than the game
he played. The Lions, and perhaps the NFL, never have known anyone
quite like him. He was the leader of the Lions in the 1950s, the brightest
era in Lions history, a decade in which they claimed four division and
three world championships.

"There's no question," said Lions general manager Russ Thomas, a scout
and assistant coach then, "that he was a legendary figure. No one ever led a
team as he did."

More than anyone else, the 1950s belonged to Layne, a swaggering,
ruddy-faced Texan who left his personal mark on every game he played, and
on the hours that followed it. He was 59.

Weakened by a three-year battle with throat cancer and cirrhosis of the
liver, he died in Lubbock, Texas. Three weeks earlier he had collapsed
following a reunion of Lions in Detroit, but he seemed to be recovering.

Last August, we had met again in Canton, Ohio, where Layne had come to
present his childhood friend and former teammate, Doak Walker, for
induction into the Pro Football Hall of Fame.

"I'm shakin'," he said in his Texas drawl. He was wan and weak. "I don't
make speeches. But I'm gonna tell 'em what kind of player ol' Doak was, and
they'll be stompin' in the streets."

Stompin' was his style. It's difficult to separate the off-field Layne from the
man who made the multi-talented Lions the dominant force of his time.
Stories abound of Layne's adventures about town. He was not shy about
them. He neither hid nor alibied.

On the chill, dreary afternoons immediately following practices at old
Briggs Stadium, Layne's day would begin when he would lead his troops to a
nearby bar. The Lions were known as roustabouts in the NFL. If not older,
they were more distinguished, loaded with All-Pro players such as Walker,
Leon Hart, Les Bingaman, Lou Creekmur, Thurm McGraw, Jack
Christiansen, Jimmy David, Dorne Dibble, Cloyce Box and Dick Stanfel.

At the bars, they would gossip and carouse, eventually to go their way.

"You can call it cornball," Layne said, "but it's effective. Football is a team
game and the guys have to belong. This is a feeling you can get just in one
day on the field."

Except Layne, so the stories go, seldom retired early.

He was a nightlife regular who not only thrived on it but seemed to require late-hour drinking and entertainment for refueling.

"I don't know what it is," he explained in his late years. "But I've always been a guy who requires only four, five hours' sleep."

Alex Karras, only briefly a teammate, had another explanation. He said that years before, Layne's father had died in a car crash, and Bobby, then 7, was trapped inside with the body for two days before he was found.

"He hasn't been able to sleep right since," Karras said.

There are those who say Layne never played without a hangover, or never played sober, and wouldn't be effective otherwise. It's probably an exaggeration, but Layne never bothered to deny it back then.

Layne's epitaph was written years ago by his childhood friend, Walker, who declared, "Bobby never lost a game in his life. Time simply ran out him."

Layne's style was to hold the Lions in close contention — they seldom routed anyone, even in their best years — and then win dramatically in a race with the clock through the final two minutes.

Even a quarter-century after his last game, he is remembered as the master of the heart-pounding, clock-stopping drive to a winning score.

Bobby Layne, however, was far more than that.

"I don't know of anyone who made a larger contribution to football," Thomas said. "He brought great excitement to the game with a great bunch of players brought here by Bo McMillin. He put it all together. No one was a field general like him. Remember the 1953 title game?"

Having beaten Cleveland for the title in 1952, the Lions trailed the Browns, 16-10, with three minutes left in the 1953 championship game. The Lions had the ball at their 20.

"Aw right, fellas," Layne said in a nasal twang with a touch of whiskey on his lips. "Y'all block and ol' Bobby'll pass you raht to the championship."

It was a storybook line that rang around the NFL, for Layne was to do it one more time. The Browns expected him to pass to Walker or Dibble because Jim Doran, subbing for the injured Hart, had caught only six passes all season. Layne passed twice to Doran to work out of danger. Then, shortly, Doran suggested another pass. Layne floated the ball to Doran, Walker kicked the point, and the Lions won, 17-16.

"If I wanted a quarterback to handle my team in the final two minutes," said the Chicago Bears' George Halas, "I'd send for Layne." Ironically, Halas traded Layne after the 1948 season because he still had Sid Luckman and Johnny Lujack at quarterback.

Layne remained with the Lions from 1950 through the second game of 1958, when he was traded without explanation to the Pittsburgh Steelers. At the time, rumors of gambling (Layne was a frequent poker visitor in Las Vegas) and Layne's discontent circulated about town. But neither Layne nor the Lions' owners ever explained his sudden departure. He remained with the Steelers until 1962, when he retired.

He remained close to the Lions and was a frequent guest at the Michigan Sports Hall of Fame banquets. He led the parties there, too.

Always the leader. Always Bobby. ✦

Rozelle has Lions to thank for NFL commissioner's job

Perhaps Russ Thomas, never known for eloquence, said it best.

"When you sit in this seat," said the Lions' general manager, "it's the hottest seat in town."

Edwin J. Anderson had sat in the same seat through the best and bitterest days of the Lions.

Thomas is the man who succeeded Anderson as general manager. Thomas originally was named to help absorb some of the public heat directed at Anderson.

Anderson is dead at age 84. Good ol' Andy. Few really understood him; fewer bothered to try.

At one and the same time, he was the most successful and most criticized sports boss Detroit has produced.

He seemed to invite it. He had an aristocratic bearing in a blue-collar town, and it was his lot — his job — to be blamed for everything and credited for little, even as his team won three world championships in six years, in 1952, '53 and '57.

Fans loved to hate him. So did some of his players.

Once, the players, unhappy because the Lions had let their first three draft choices escape to a rival league, gathered in the locker room to protest.

They filled a uniform with dirty socks and underwear, painted a bushy-browed face on the effigy, and called the newspapers to come take pictures. Then they hanged the effigy of their boss from the goalposts at Briggs Stadium.

Anderson never winced, not publicly. He never mentioned that his board of directors had limited the money he could pay to compete with the new American Football League.

Besides, he had been hurt worse the year before. He was the reason Pete Rozelle became commissioner of the National Football League.

Anderson was president, head of a syndicate of businessmen-owners of the Lions through most of their glory years of the 1950s. But in 1960, the city became aware of a crack in its football dynasty.

In Miami Beach, Fla., NFL owners assembled to elect a new commissioner, Bert Bell having died several months earlier.

Soon, a division among the Detroit owners became evident. After several days of wrangling and more than a dozen ballots of hopeless deadlock, Anderson emerged as the leading candidate. But then... .

"When his own team didn't vote for him," said Art Rooney, owner of the

Pittsburgh Steelers, "he couldn't get the vote of some other teams."

It was a startling revelation, for it was the first public suggestion of a feud among the 144 Lions owners.

Out of it came two developments:

Wearying of the owners' fight, Tommy Devine, the former Free Press writer who was sports editor of the Miami News, and I in jest suggested to several owners that Pete Rozelle would be a dandy compromise.

Pittsburgh's Rooney, Chicago's George Halas, Baltimore's Carroll Rosenbloom and several others kibitzing in the press room laughed. Rozelle, a former sports writer, always had been close with the press; they knew that.

It was unlikely the owners would even consider Rozelle, then 34 and general manager of the LA Rams. But several days later, they picked him as a compromise. What began in folly ended with wisdom.

Of more immediate concern in Detroit was the proxy fight being waged among Lions owners to unseat Anderson, who had been president of the Goebel Brewing Co. Anderson returned home to win the battle, but he knew the dissidents could not be satisfied.

He persuaded William Clay Ford, a board member, to replace him as president, and he remained as general manager. With Anderson's help, Ford then began planning to buy out the other owners, and when a second proxy fight erupted, Ford was ready.

It long has been the conviction here that the Lions' failure to win after the 1950s stems from failure to restock their talent in those years of ownership squabble.

Because of it, they lost the 1960s to Green Bay, and then a succession of poor coaching selections and draft choices stymied them.

Anderson's work with the football team effectively ended in 1972, when Thomas was elevated to executive vice president. But Anderson had other contributions to make.

He spearheaded the Lions' move in 1975 from Tiger Stadium to the Silverdome. The Lions' practice field there is named for him.

Some have yet to forgive the Lions for that move. But it made them one of the most valuable franchises in football. It was Anderson's farewell. ✦

Duffy fought for MSU every step of the way

Nobody ever called him Hugh. Maybe his mother, occasionally his coal-miner father. To all others, he was Duffy.

Always Duffy.

Some people wear their nicknames well, but nobody ever wore one better than Hugh Daugherty, the former Michigan State football coach who died in Santa Barbara, Calif., yesterday.

There was little formality about him. He was publicly the Irish pixie, short and stocky, a man of endearing charm, with smiles and jokes that seemed constant.

For years he regaled banquet crowds around the country and made college football seem like a game filled always with fun for all.

It's an exaggeration, of course, to say that it was all fun and everybody loved Duffy Daugherty. There were notable exceptions. But he made it close.

On the football staff at MSU are two men who were Daugherty disciples when they were here with top Detroit high school teams.

One is George Perles, the head coach, out of Western High. The other is Ed Rutherford, from Denby, who is Perles' administrative assistant. They had been Daugherty's pipeline into the fertile city football fields, and both later were hired by him.

Daugherty could inspire a deep sense of loyalty, perhaps because he had one.

Several times in the midst of his long reign at MSU, he had opportunities to move to another school at far greater pay.

In 1962, we were at a Big Ten meeting in Chicago, and word came that Texas A&M, which had tried to hire him earlier, now was offering $75,000 a year — more than double his MSU pay — and other blandishments to come there and coach.

We sat at a hotel bar talking about it, and finally he said: "Thanks for drinking with me. I've decided not to take that job, you know."

It led to the line that Duffy Daugherty had joined health and happiness as things money cannot buy. But a day later, he called.

"That's not true," he said, laughing. "I can be had."

Nobody ever had him, not in the sense that they could take him away from Michigan State. When he left in 1972, the decision was his; the well had gone dry at MSU, and perhaps, at age 57, so had he.

Gone were assistant coaches who later made their own niche — Bob Devaney, Bill Yeoman, Dan Devine, Hank Bullough, Perles. The school hasn't done very well since.

In his time, Daugherty had the Spartans perking. He had become immensely popular nationally, and once was pictured on the cover of Time magazine.

Never was his team better than the 1966 version. He had put together a group that throughout the season rated 1-2 with Notre Dame in the national polls.

The MSU-Notre Dame duel culminated in a 10-10 tie that just might have been worthy of its billing as "Game of the Century."

As is usually the case, a team like the 1966 group is the result of recruiting success, and Duffy in his prime was a master salesman. He was able to reach into the Deep South in years when schools there refused to use black athletes, and bring valued players — Bubba Smith was the best — north to East Lansing.

He would have been a grand politician. People who met him usually came away feeling he was their instant friend.

That was his public image. But there was another side to Duffy. He was an unyielding in-fighter.

In the modern history of Michigan State football, dating back to the school's entry into the Big Ten in 1948, two men stand out.

They are Daugherty and Biggie Munn, the man who preceded him as football coach. Munn had hired Daugherty as his assistant at Syracuse, brought him to MSU, and Duffy would be his successor as Munn moved up to become athletic director.

If not from that day, then soon after, Daugherty and Munn quarreled and feuded. Their eruptions did not often become public, but frequently their disputes were carried into the office of John Hannah, the school's president.

Munn, hugely successful in MSU's early Big Ten years, had sought to maintain minute-by-minute control of the football team, and Daugherty, always the assistant, resisted. Soon the new coach was complaining about his limited budget, travel arrangements and a myriad of real or imagined slights.

How much their enmity affected the team is difficult to estimate, but it was ever-present and no laughing matter to the laughing coach. Ironically, Daugherty's coaching decline in the late 1960s developed as Munn, ailing from a stroke, stepped down as athletic director.

It was said that Duffy seemed then to lack interest, the fire had gone from his coaching. But it also was true that southern schools were beginning to play black athletes and MSU's recruiting program was collapsing on all fronts.

In Daugherty's final game at MSU in the 5-5-1 1972 season, the Spartans beat Northwestern, 24-14. His players carried Duffy from the field on their shoulders.

Those who loved him are left today with one last, sadder march. ✦

1 9 8 9

Wings' three-star selection:
Gordie, Stevie and Bruce

D uring a pause at the elevator in Joe Louis Arena the other night, a fan looked my way and uttered the ultimate compliment about Stevie Yzerman.

"Isn't he the greatest Red Wing of all time!" he gushed, not really expecting an answer.

"You ever heard of a guy named Gordie Howe?" I said, not expecting an answer, either.

Later, I mentioned this bit of hysteria to Bruce Martyn, the Red Wings radio announcer. He didn't think the fan was stupid at all.

"He was close, wasn't he?" Martyn said.

Well, yeah, maybe, but close to what?

Is Yzerman, who's still a kid, for gosh sakes, better than even Syd Howe? Remember him? Once at the old Olympia, before Gordie even arrived in town, Syd scored six goals in one game.

I remember our headline: "Howe, Howe, Howe, Howe, Howe and Howe!"

Is Yzerman better than Sid Abel or Ted Lindsay, those dashing demons of the 1950s who have their names etched on the Stanley Cup and emblazoned on the roster of the Hall of Fame?

Hey, is he better than Alex Delvecchio?

"Right now, I'd have to say yes to all of that," Martyn said. "He's better."

What a lot of nerve. Everybody knows the announcer is a close pal and buddy of Delvecchio. Friendship ought to count for a point or two in any debate, shouldn't it, Alex?

"Well, Alex was a fun guy to watch and all that," Martyn said. "He made the plays and was always doing the right thing. But there was nothing spectacular about him. He never had to carry a team the way Yzerman has."

So there you are. Bruce Martyn says Yzerman already is at least the second-best Red Wing ever — sorry about that Goodfellow, Aurie and Bruneteau.

You, too, Barry, Cooper, Grosso, Liscombe, Kelly and all the rest. All of you guys, move down a notch.

Normally, a microphone type can't convince me of much, because, as Martyn admits, at least half of his radio job is entertainment and what's left is reporting.

But then there are games, as the other night at Edmonton, when Yzerman was maybe 15 feet in front of the goal, facing the far end of the ice as a defender rode his back. The kid laid a backward pass on the stick of Paul

MacLean at the goal mouth. MacLean scored. Easily.

"Oh, my," Martyn said into his microphone. Sometimes he sounds like a guy melting right off his seat, like he can't quite believe what he has just seen.

Nobody, in fact, really believed what Yzerman had done, and in two words, Martyn said so.

"Oh, my," he said again.

We don't often hear the Canadian broadcasters who are supposed to be such hotshots on hockey, but I've never heard anybody better than Martyn.

I'm not the only one who thinks so. Some years ago, I offered a playoff ticket to a young fellow who seldom had a chance to attend games, his work confining him to a photo lab at night. He refused it.

"I don't need to go," he said. "I listen to the game on radio while I work, and it's just as good as being there."

He meant Martyn's broadcast. It might not be a favor to Martyn to let his hockey bosses know that some people don't buy game tickets because the broadcaster is so good, but the bosses should know.

Martyn, 58, hasn't broadcast a football game for years, but so you will know, he was the best radio play-by-play football announcer I've heard, bar none.

He was, at the time, a hit disc jockey in town, spinning pop tunes of the 1950s on WCAR. The station changed its format and he was fired.

Several years later, a sponsor of Red Wings broadcasts remembered Martyn's football work, and he was hired for hockey.

"I miss football every now and then," he said. "I think I'd like to do a game or two, but, then, I've found my niche; I know I have."

The niche has been there since childhood. Martyn grew up in Sault Ste. Marie, where the most popular magazine among kids of the day was, of all things, the Saturday Evening Post.

"It was just the right size," he said. "Larger than the news magazines but not as bulky as Esquire. We'd tape it around our legs and it served as shin guards against flying pucks."

It was the way kids of his day played their games, the world being short of sports equipment and such during the 1930s. They stuffed old socks to make baseballs, chiseled 2 x 4s to fashion bats and created a demand for the Post.

"I still feel the one issue," Martyn said. "They had very little advertising in it — and I've got a chip out of my shin bone because of it."

This weekend, before the Red Wings play Toronto on the riverfront, Martyn will be honored at the near-completion of his 25th season as the team's radio play-by-play announcer.

Yeah. He scoorrres! ✦

1 9 8 9

Sugar Ray brought sweetness and fight to boxing game

L OS ANGELES — Sugar Ray Robinson would have loved his last round.
He won going away, as they say.
His final hour was grand, the way he would have wanted it.
The house was full. Television cameras reached into every corner, and the crowd spilled out beyond the doors, into the courtyard and across the street. Millie, his widow, wondered whether many would remember and come to Sugar Ray's funeral. She need not have worried. They came.

Some who had fought him, hundreds who admired him and many others who seemed genuinely to have loved the former five-time middleweight champion gathered at the church on the west side of this pounding town.

One after another, they testified that here in the bronzed casket was a man who would live on in the minds of some still captivated by his craftsmanship, and in the hearts of thousands more who had felt his personal warmth.

Robinson, 67, a native Detroiter, died in nearby Culver City, Calif., a week ago. He had been in failing health for several years.

He was the fighter for whom no superlative seemed excessive. "Pound for pound the greatest fighter who ever lived" was a famous description that never belonged to anyone but him.

He was a man known for his style and grace, his charm and kindness, and, sure, his showmanship. Fittingly, his funeral had a touch of Hollywood about it.

A string of 25 limousines transported stars of sports, entertainment, politics, even religion. The limos all but circled the huge West Angeles Church of God in Christ complex. Someone watching from across Crenshaw Boulevard remarked: "It's like the Academy Awards have come to West Angeles."

Perhaps. Inside, in the jammed audience of more than 2,000, were Dodgers manager Tommy Lasorda, Raiders owner Al Davis, Motown Records founder Berry Gordy, singer Lou Rawls, boxing's Mike Tyson, Don King, Archie Moore, Bobo Olson, Hedgemon Lewis and a bevy of political hotshots.

The Rev. Jesse Jackson presided over what he called "an hour of sadness and celebration." It was sad, never more so than when Tyson, 23, the heavyweight champion, sought to eulogize Robinson and broke down repeatedly. Perhaps few know it, but Tyson, despite his youth, is an authentic boxing historian. He knows Robinson's record because he grew up studying the fight films and books — the largest known collection — of the late Jim Jacobs, his former manager.

"I had the pleasure of meeting Sugar Ray a few years ago," Tyson said, "and he had a great impact on me. He was a very special individual. When you think of the kind of man he was — style, class, dignity — well, some of us worry about where we'll go when we die. Sugar Ray had no reason to worry."

The kid champion said it almost as well as Don King, his would-be promoter-counselor-benefactor.

"He was a rhapsody in black," King said. "You only have to look around to see the legacy of this man, who touched black and white, the young and old."

King couldn't resist a promoter's jab into the famed Robinson tactic of twisting the highest possible pay out of promoters.

"He told me once," King said, "that the way to live is work hard, be good at what you do and make sure you get paid the most for it. I'm still trying hard to fulfill the profitcy."

Gordy, a native Detroiter and onetime prize fighter who moved to Los Angeles after launching Motown, had known Robinson for many years.

"The more time I spent with him," Gordy said, "the more he surpassed his image. He could show anybody what true perfection was all about."

Davis said: "I've known a lot of great stars, but none had the courage to ask for a pink Cadillac."

In a career that spanned 25 years and 201 fights, Robinson not only was a frequent winner of the middleweight title, he once held the welterweight championship and in 1952 narrowly missed winning the light-heavyweight title. The litany of his victims is lasting proof of his greatness: Sammy Angott, Fritzie Zivic, Jake LaMotta, Kid Gavilan, Henry Armstrong, Charley Fusari, Olson, Randy Turpin, Rocky Graziano, Carmen Basilio, Gene Fullmer.

He won 40 straight fights before losing to LaMotta in their classic slugfest at Detroit's old Olympia Stadium. But three weeks later he avenged that defeat at Olympia. Robinson's adventures as a middleweight champion were curious. Three times — in fights against Turpin, Fullmer and Basilio — he regained the title from men who had beaten him.

Robinson earned an estimated $4 million in boxing during years when that sum was more like $30 million today. His wealth disappeared in taxes, bad investments and free spending. He continued to box until he was 44, when repeated defeats finally convinced him his great physical gifts of speed, rhythm and power had deserted him.

In 1965, he and his wife moved from New York to Los Angeles, where he played bit parts in movies and television shows.

He founded and operated the Sugar Ray Robinson Youth Foundation and was its active leader until he was afflicted with Alzheimer's disease a few years ago. The foundation counsels youngsters, steering them into a variety of activities, not only sports.

Among its graduates are Olympic gold medal sprinter Florence Griffith Joyner and the NFL's Marcus Allen and Freeman McNeil.

"The foundation is looking for $5 million," Jackson told the crowd. "You and I know that you ain't gonna contribute a dime to the foundation once you leave here. So we're gonna do it right now."

It's the way Sugar Ray would have wanted it. So they said. ✦

1 9 8 9

Victory not in the cards as Hearns, Leonard draw

AS VEGAS, Nev. — Deep in Thomas Hearns' corner, the men who guide him during fights seethed in the aftermath of his latest.

They were not alone — Hearns, manager-trainer Emanuel Steward, cornermen Prentiss Byrd, Walter Smith and Ralph Citro.

The crowd of 15,400 in the Caesars Palace Stadium took up a thunderous chant: "Bull——! Bull——!" in the dark desert air.

All of it was in protest of the 12-round draw that deprived Hearns, in his finest hour in recent years, of a clear victory over Sugar Ray Leonard.

The judge who made it a draw is Dalby Shirley, a 55-year-old Las Vegas car salesman who once was a member of the Nevada Boxing Commission. He scored the last round 10-8 for Leonard, while the two other judges, Jerry Roth and Tommy Kaczmarek, gave the round to Leonard, 10-9.

The two-point edge was just enough to give Leonard a draw, enabling him to keep his World Boxing Council super-middleweight title.

"I had Hearns ahead going into the 11th round," Shirley said. "I didn't know how far I had him ahead, but after the 10-8 in the 12th I still thought that he won the fight. I was kind of surprised that it came out a draw, because I do not keep a running total. I just felt that my 12th round was consistent with previous rounds where I had scored it 10-8. I might have a tendency maybe to score 10-8s a little bit more liberal than other judges."

Despite their immediate disappointment at ringside, Hearns and Steward refused to protest. "Certainly I think I was ahead and should have won," Hearns said. "I thought I had put a few rounds in the bank. Maybe that judge saw a different fight and wasn't with us. He couldn't possibly have given Leonard a 10-8 in that round."

Hearns had banged Leonard smartly early in the round, but Leonard came back and appeared to batter Hearns in a closing rush.

"He hit me a couple of times," Hearns said, "but he didn't hurt me. I was just too exhausted to do much except try to avoid him."

Steward similarly refused to be drawn into a hot feud with the judges.

"My fighters never complain," Steward said, "no matter what happens with the judges. They learn that as amateurs. I thought Hearns was a clear winner, but we can't do anything about that, can we?"

Not really. Judging fights is subjective, so protests are frequent. Larry Holmes, the former heavyweight champion, took a protest to civil court when he was deprived of victory in his second bout with Michael Spinks, in 1986. He lost there, too.

One problem for the judges is that their instructions often are vague and inconsistent. Generally, a fighter wins a round 10-8 by knocking down his opponent. But it's also permissible, though not usual, for judges to score a round 10-8 when a fighter wins it by a wide margin. That apparently is the standard Shirley used.

"I thought the 10-8 in the last round was a bad score," Steward said. "I thought 10-8 was a method of saving Leonard for another day."

All three judges gave Leonard 10-8 margins in the fifth round, his best of the fight, when he had Hearns in serious trouble.

"What bothers me," Steward said, "is that when we look back in the books years from now, we'll see that Tommy didn't win. That's all people will know."

It was a great fight, better than their classic 1981 encounter — which Leonard won on a 14th-round knockout — because Hearns spent most of this one on a cannonading attack.

After a slow start, the fight raged a half-dozen times toward a sudden finish, turning one way and then the other as Hearns, then Leonard, took charge. Hearns' best rounds were the third and the 11th, when he knocked down Leonard, and the seventh and eighth, when his right hand wobbled Leonard. Nevertheless, Leonard won the seventh on two cards.

From Hearns' corner, Steward frequently exhorted his fighter to "Let it go! Let it go!" — meaning to use his powerful right to hammer Leonard.

"You'll notice," Steward said, "that Tommy's best rounds came when he used that right. It was our plan."

Leonard's best round was the fifth, when he staggered and dazed Hearns with a left hook. Hearns grabbed him, but Leonard broke away and bounced a sequence of blows off Hearns' head.

"When that round ended," Steward said, "I told Tommy everything he had done in boxing was on the line. It woke him up."

Leonard was gracious afterward, conceding that Hearns was far more effective than Leonard expected.

"I never got into the rhythm and flow of the fight," complained Leonard, his eyes still puffy from Hearns' pounding. "But I'm gonna have to study the films — I'm not sure my age (33) was to blame, or whether it was Tommy Hearns (30). He fought a damned good fight."

Immediately a question arose of another Hearns-Leonard rematch.

"There might not be a World War III between them," said Mike Trainer, Leonard's attorney. "Ray wants to take some time to study what happened here. A rematch depends on the answers he comes up with."

The Hearns camp would accept a rematch, but Hearns and Steward really have their eyes on former middleweight champion Marvin Hagler, who KO'd Hearns in the third round in a tremendous slugfest in 1985.

"I'd like to avenge that one," Hearns said, "but it's a matter of getting Marvin out of retirement."

The draw was the first in the long careers of Hearns (46-3-1) and Leonard (35-1-1), the only fighters to have won championships in five weight classes.

Hearns was paid $11 million-plus and Leonard $13 million-plus. ✦

THE '90s

Tigers pitcher Hal Newhouser, twice the American League's Most Valuable Player, with his wife, Beryl, and mother, Emilie, before his Hall of Fame induction in 1992.

Ol' No. 98: First in war, first in peace, first in yards gained

om Harmon, ol' 98, as he often called himself, was, perhaps, the greatest of the legendary football players who made the University of Michigan an enduring power in the collegiate game.

Name the great players in 111 years of U-M football — Willie Heston, Adolph Schulz, Benny Friedman, Bennie Oosterbaan, Ron Kramer — and leave room at the top for Harmon.

Never on old Ferry Field or in the huge stadium that became the home of Wolverines football has there ever been his all-around equal.

Death came to Harmon, 70, in Los Angeles, where he had lived since the late 1940s. He had been a nationally syndicated radio sportscaster until his retirement two years ago.

He was stricken with a heart attack shortly after picking up airplane tickets at a travel office there. The tickets were for a visit to former U-M star Forest Evashevski in Ft. Lauderdale, Fla.

Evashevski, from Detroit's Northwestern High, was Harmon's blocking back.

"I always felt Tom was the best football player of all time," Evashevski said. "He was a complete player. Maybe a lot of guys could run like him, but he could pass, kick, play defense, do anything that was needed to win a game. I just lost the best friend I ever had."

Harmon won the last sports competition he entered. Shortly before he died, he and a partner won a match in a golf tournament at Bel-Air Country Club.

In his time at U-M, Harmon was as widely applauded as young collegians ever get, not only in Michigan and among his own. Rival fans from California to Pennsylvania and in cities throughout the Big Ten marveled over his play.

Although his U-M teams of 1938-39-40 never won a championship, national magazines regularly featured stories on him. Harmon won the 1940 Heisman Trophy and was named the nation's outstanding male athlete.

Hollywood even made a movie — "Harmon of Michigan" — extolling the kid from Gary, Ind., and his football career.

All of this came to Harmon before television could create instant heroes of athletes. It happened because his exploits were followed by millions via network radio and the newspapers.

Fielding Yost, the fabled U-M coach and athletic director, once called Harmon football's best player since Heston, the Wolverines immortal from Yost's point-a-minute powerhouses opening the 20th Century.

Fritz Crisler, who with Harmon as his foil made the single-wing offense the most appealing and devastating attack of its day, said his star certainly was "better than Red Grange," the fabled Galloping Ghost from Illinois.

"Tom could do more things," Crisler told Will Perry, author of "The Wolverines," a history of U-M football. "He ran, passed, punted, blocked, kicked off and kicked extra points and field goals, and he was a superb defense player."

Harmon was a 60-minute player when that type was fading from the gridiron. His unusual uniform number — 98 — became as widely known as Grange's 77 had been in the 1920s. Harmon's number was retired when he graduated.

Some of my earliest football memories involve Harmon, Crisler and the Wolverines teams before the outbreak of World War II. I was a kid among reporters watching U-M's practices.

Even a novice could see Harmon was not a good practice player. When it didn't count, he didn't punt very well, or run so powerfully, or throw with such precision.

Often, Harmon exasperated Crisler, but the coach rarely chided him. Crisler knew, as he explained years later, that on game day, no one would play football better.

Harmon was an awesome runner, big, powerful, quick, with that peculiar instinct of all great runners to find the open field and reach it.

The Harmon cutback — drifting wide to his right, then turning sharply to his left and slicing back through tackle — was classic in his day.

He made the single wing so much a part of U-M football that for years after he departed, Michigan teams lined up in the formation and then shifted to whatever set they really intended to run.

Harmon's best game might have been his last at U-M, when Michigan beat Ohio State at Columbus, 40-0.

Harmon rushed for 139 yards, completed 11 of 22 passes for 151 yards, ran for two touchdowns, passed for two more, kicked four extra points, averaged 50 yards with his punts and intercepted three passes, returning one for a touchdown.

With 15 seconds left, Crisler pulled Harmon from the game. Ohio State fans gave him an unprecedented ovation and swarmed over him, tearing pieces from his jersey for souvenirs.

We overlooked that game a few years ago while recounting the great games in the Michigan-Ohio State series. When we acknowledged the oversight, Harmon called to thank us.

"I didn't think anybody would remember that game," he said, "because it wasn't a close one. We didn't even win a championship because we had lost earlier to Minnesota."

Actually, the Gophers claimed the national championship, and U-M, which never could beat Minnesota in Harmon's time, was runner-up.

Harmon scored a career total of 33 touchdowns, a Big Ten record then. In three years and 24 games, he gained 2,134 yards rushing, averaging 5.4

yards, and passed for 1,304 yards. He and Billy Sims (1978-79) were the only players in modern college football to win successive scoring titles.

The Chicago Bears made him the NFL's No. 1 draft pick in December 1940, but he never played for them. After graduation from U-M, Harmon and several of his teammates, including Evashevski, later head coach at Iowa, starred in his movie.

During the making of the movie in Hollywood, Harmon met starlet Elyse Knox. They married; their family includes actor Mark Harmon, daughters Kelly, former wife of John DeLorean, and daughter Christie, once married to the late singer Rick Nelson.

With the outbreak of World War II, Harmon enlisted in the Army Air Corps. Twice he parachuted from crashing planes. In 1943, his bomber crashed in the jungles of South America, and he was presumed dead. The nation mourned. Six days later, Harmon came marching out of the jungle.

Later that year, in a battle with Japanese Zero planes over China, he parachuted into a lake and spent a month returning to his base with the aid of Chinese guerrillas.

"If you didn't have religion before the war, you did then," Harmon said two years ago. He was awarded the Silver Star and Purple Heart.

He had a brief pro football career following the war, playing for the Los Angeles Rams in 1946-47, then turned to broadcasting. At one time, his nightly radio sports show was broadcast on more than 400 stations across the country.

"He kept in touch with his friends," said Don Canham, the former U-M athletic director. "He had a word processor and, geez, he'd write three-page letters. He'd do things for people no one ever knew about."

Harmon was a member of the National Football Foundation Hall of Fame, College Football Hall of Fame, Michigan Sports Hall of Fame and the University of Michigan's Hall of Honor. ✦

1 9 9 0

All's forgotten when fans gather for grand openings

I'm not sure when the craze over baseball's Opening Day began. But I know it wasn't always this way.

All around, people are gushing over the return of the Tigers, who will begin their home season at the stadium in a few hours.

It beats me how a team that lost 103 games one season can have thousands of fans in a tizzy when it returns home the next spring — already having lost its first three games in the new season. Yet there's no telling what turns people on when it comes to baseball.

"What we need," said the man at the gas pump, "is a 10-degree drop in the temperature, a cloudy sky and a good wind. Then we'll have perfect weather for the opener."

He means typical opener weather. Maybe it will snow. He would be delighted.

A young man who grew up at my table called to brag about the great seats he had for the opener. I reminded him of his vow last year, repeated just a few weeks ago, not to attend another Tigers game until significant improvement was evident.

"But it's the opener," he explained. "Nobody misses the opener."

Some people do.

Years ago, when this town made more sense, some people deliberately avoided the ballpark for the first month or six weeks of the season, at least.

We never sold out or even came close because fans understood that in early April it could be awfully cold at the stadium.

Back when the Tigers were at their all-time best — in the mid-1930s, when they had such greats as Mickey Cochrane, Charlie Gehringer, Hank Greenberg and Schoolboy Rowe — even then, people didn't gush over 'em the way we do now.

True, the town fell in love with Schoolboy and the lady he loved after he asked during a radio interview one day in 1934, "How'm ah doin', Edna?" But they were exceptions.

We've had a lot of players who were great on the field, not so great off, beginning with Ty Cobb, who was a lout, at best. We didn't make excuses for them or worship their stats.

Not a season arrives that I don't hear from poets writing about the romance of baseball and stuffing your face with hot dogs at the ballpark on Opening Day.

It's like nobody ever has a hot dog and a beer from October, when one season ends, until April, when another begins.

Maybe I've lost a beat somewhere. I probably wasted the first third of my life playing baseball and whatnot, but I don't recall attending a season opener until years later.

When I finally went, it was to work, not to cheer.

I haven't missed many openers since, but I don't recall much about any of them. One year, I remember, it snowed so hard the game was halted; another time, the Tigers let Frank Lary pitch too long in the cold, and he ruined his arm forever.

But we've never had anything like Bob Feller pitching a no-hitter on Opening Day. Nobody ever hit a home run over the roof. We never had a triple play or anything fancy in one of our openers.

So you wonder why the season's first game is so important, why it commands the appearance of every Loyal Fan.

Going to openers, best I can tell, became the thing some people absolutely had to do about the time television began playing footsies with the baseball business.

Say about 1960 or so. It took a few years, but, then, major league openers became civic events in most places. The ballpark was the place to go, to see and be seen.

Watch TV news today and right about dinner hour the anchors will show you more compassion for the losing Tigers than the latest crime victims.

It's their way of letting the town know what's really important, and whose side they're on.

Marvin Miller, former boss of the players' union, said recently that "baseball fans take themselves too seriously. They're merely consumers, and sports consumers are no more important than any other consumer."

It was dumb of Miller to insult baseball's customers, but nothing shows more clearly what he meant about fans' involvement in baseball than our situation right here in Detroit.

We have a group of fans who love Tiger Stadium so much they have spent who knows how much money drawing up dandy plans to remodel and save it. The drawings look great and seem to make sense.

Problem is, neither the mayor nor the Tigers' owner wants the plans or the old stadium anymore. They want the fans to mind their own business.

Or open their own. ✦

1991

Elusive as a ghost, Illini's Grange galloped to greatness

One by one, the greats of our football century leave us with only memories.

In recent months, we have lost Tom Harmon, the Michigan legend, and then Bennie Oosterbaan, perhaps the best of all Wolverines.

And now Red Grange, a legend from another campus, another time, is gone.

Illinois' great Galloping Ghost, one of the most historic figures of football — college and pro — died at a hospital in Lake Wales, Fla. He was 87.

Grange was from the Golden Age of sports — the 1920s, when Ruth and Gehrig, Dempsey, Tunney, Rockne and the Four Horsemen, Hagen, Tilden, Weissmuller and more enthralled the nation.

If Grange wasn't the greatest of all college football runners, then and now, he was close. He was electric on the gridiron, incredibly fast, strong and elusive. He quickly became the most celebrated college player of his time.

So popular was Grange that when he left school to barnstorm with the Chicago Bears in 1925, tens of thousands turned out in eight cities across the nation to see him perform.

Bookmaker Tim Mara and boxing manager Billy Gibson had founded the New York Giants earlier that season, and they were losing big money — until the Grange Tour arrived.

A crowd of more than 70,000 watched Grange and the Bears play the Giants. That turnout assured the future of the Giants — much to the regret today, perhaps, of the Buffalo Bills.

That tour also is largely credited with gaining public acceptance of pro football, which had been frowned upon as a rogue's game and generally ignored by fans, who much preferred campus play.

Grange had gained his greatest collegiate acclaim a year earlier. It came at the expense of the University of Michigan, which had been eagerly accepting stadium dedication games.

Fielding Yost, the U-M athletic director, had taken his team to Nashville, Tenn., for Vanderbilt's stadium dedication in 1922, and escaped with an 0-0 tie.

Later that season, the Wolverines dedicated Ohio State's horseshoe with a 19-0 victory. Then, early in the 1924 season, the Wolverines slipped away with a 7-0 victory at Michigan State.

Yost confidently agreed to play the dedication game of Illinois' stadium on Oct. 18, 1924. What resulted was one of the most astounding individual performances college football has seen.

Grange, flashing his No. 77, took the opening kickoff, stepped to his right, cut back up center, broke through a wave of charging Wolverines and ran 95 yards for a touchdown.

It was only the beginning of a magical day for Grange, a junior. He scored the next three times he handled the ball — on runs of 67, 56 and 44 yards — all in the first quarter. In the second half, he scored again on a 15-yard end run. Illinois won, 39-14.

Eleanor Steele of Greenville, Mich., daughter-in-law of Harold Steele, a former U-M player who died in 1984, said she and her husband have a great memento of the Illinois-Michigan game.

"It's a wonderful picture of Harold on the ground and Grange running by," she said. "He always liked that picture."

A neighbor, Syd Dewey, 86, of Greenville, a U-M sub guard in that game, well remembers Grange and the Wolverines' humiliation.

"At the time, the conference was known as Michigan, Illinois and the Other Eight," said Dewey, who as far as he knows is the last U-M survivor of the '24 team. "We went to Champaign feeling we were going to beat them badly."

Certainly, the Wolverines did not intend to let Grange surprise or damage them.

"We were told to meet Grange at the crossroads — in other words, don't approach him at an angle, go straight at him," Dewey said. "He always ran with his knees high, the way backs are told. Well, what can I say? He was terrific — very fast, a broken-field runner. He seemed to see a hole to run through before one was there."

Nobody ever mentions, Dewey lamented, that the following year U-M beat Grange and the Illini, 3-0.

By then, Grange was a national hero. The barnstorming tour that followed the 1925 college season was so successful that he demanded a five-figure salary and one-third ownership of the Bears to play in 1926.

After the Bears refused his demand, Grange and his manager, a Champaign, Ill., movie theater operator, went to New York and founded the first American Football League.

After one season the league folded, and Grange rejoined the Bears. But his New York Yankees team was accepted into the NFL.

Three games into the 1927 season, Grange suffered a knee injury that seriously hindered his running. He wasn't as effective thereafter, although he scored the first touchdown in an NFL championship game when the Bears beat Portsmouth, 9-0, in 1932. His playing career ended in 1934.

For years thereafter, however, Grange remained associated with the Bears. When television came to the NFL in the 1950s, Grange, with his raspy voice and friendly manner, became one of the tube's first analysts.

In recent years, he had lived quietly and in failing health in Florida. ✦

Russ Thomas' world
was 100 yards long

R uss Thomas is dead. Nobody in the long history of the Lions spent more years with the team or worked in so many roles as Thomas, the club's former general manager.

The retirement he hoped might never come ended a little more than a year after it was forced upon him.

Few men ever come to a major sports job, or any job for that matter, with such thorough training and education in the business that Thomas brought to the Lions.

A lineman at Ohio State, he played two years with the postwar Lions before his career ended because of knee injuries.

He turned to coaching and worked as an assistant to Buddy Parker, who masterminded the Lions' dominance of the NFL during the 1950s.

Thomas was also a Lions publicist, a radio analyst, scout, personnel director and, finally, general manager and executive vice president of the team that filled his life.

He was proud of that rich and varied background, and he was convinced he knew how every phase of a sports operation should be handled.

Though few were aware of it, Thomas' most significant role was as William Clay Ford's stand-in at NFL owners' meetings. He was in many ways Ford's football tutor and adviser, as well as his chief executive officer.

Thomas' duties in the heady gatherings gave him a power and influence available to few non-owners.

"Aside from business," Ford said, "he was a very dear personal friend. The thing that really stood out was he had such unyielding personal integrity and loyalty."

Most of all, Thomas, who during the 1950s also was a business partner of coach George Wilson, was the key operator of Ford's football enterprise.

Was he good at it? By all accounts, he was terrific.

We are not privy to the Lions' books, but it is said that during Thomas' long term as head of the club, Ford never had a losing year — financially.

Thomas helped build the Lions into a franchise worth an estimated $125 million.

In the process, however, he antagonized many and dismayed many more, for the Lions usually failed miserably on the field. Many blamed Thomas and wrote him off as an arrogant bungler.

He was far from that. To those he thought were genuinely interested in the Lions, he was usually friendly and helpful. He simply refused to answer or battle publicly with his many critics.

In his later years with the Lions, public and media abuse was heaped upon Thomas. One poll conducted by a local magazine declared him the most unpopular figure in Michigan sports.

Thomas was unfazed: "It goes with the territory."

Nor would he open his office door to many who did not agree or sympathize with the way he conducted the Lions' business.

"Why should I bother with them?" he said. "The worst thing about some people is they don't know anything about operating a team, won't try to learn, but insist on telling me how to do it."

Thomas never believed he was as unpopular as that poll suggested or the reason the Lions flopped so often.

"The newspapers keep reporting how I'm so unpopular among our players, but that's not true," he said. "I've negotiated the contracts of hundreds of players, and I'm proud to say I've always been fair."

Thomas was the Lions' general manager from 1967 until his retirement after the 1989 season. To the end, he hoped Ford — who himself had retired from Ford Motor Co. at age 65 — might change that pattern and retain him indefinitely.

We talked frequently about his pending retirement. I tried to convince him that the world is full of intriguing places, and he ought to welcome retirement and go see some of them.

"No, I can understand people who want to see the world," Thomas said. "But my world is only 100 yards long. Football has been my life for so long, I just can't ever envision leaving it."

Still, at the end of his career, Thomas acknowledged that in the one area that had really mattered, he had failed.

"We were not a winner," he said. "That's my great frustration and disappointment.

"Things happen. Some players don't develop as expected, you lose others by injury, and some coaches have a more difficult time than you ever expected."

In the closing months of his regime, Thomas sought to point the Lions toward better times. He restructured the front office and spent more freely than others, updating the Lions' operation.

It was his recommendation to Ford that made Wayne Fontes the Lions' head coach.

Thomas brought Frank Gansz, the former Kansas City Chiefs head coach, here to work with the Lions' special teams; he convinced Ford that Mouse Davis and the run 'n' shoot offense would revive the Lions on the field and at the gate.

In his final week with the team, he said: "Everything's in place now. All they have to do is win."

Someday they might, at that. ✦

1 9 9 1

Golfers who break 50
are suddenly in demand

A sk any old guy, and chances are he'll say the first thing he noticed after his 50th birthday was a change in his mail.

He began getting more of it from sources that never interested him. Some of it could be disturbing.

Retirement and nursing homes send brochures boasting of splendid facilities. Cemetery keepers offer free tours. Funeral directors promote easy pre-payment plans.

No wonder many guys turning 50 wear a haunted look. Suddenly, they're scared to death.

Would I kid you?

It's awful what happens. A man turning 50 soon realizes he has lost significance in many areas, such as the polls, the markets, or perhaps the office or bedroom.

The message is clearer when invitations arrive from Sun City developers and the mail from Fun City hot spots tapers off.

Think about it. In almost any game men play today, the half-century man is long gone. Years ago, he had to step aside to make room for the young.

Except in golf. Only in golf does a player 50 or older hold a special fascination with the fans. They won't let the geezers go.

The old guys have been practicing at Oakland Hills Country Club for the last couple of days, and today they will begin playing for real, for money, in the U.S. Senior Open.

At their finish, more than 100,000 area golf buffs will have paid $2.5 million to see them do their thing.

There are many younger guys who play a tour of supposedly better golf. So you might wonder why anybody would bother with the seniors.

"We've got the best names and most popular players of our time in this tournament," said Dr. Jerry Dietz, former University of Detroit basketball player and longtime Oakland Hills member. "Who needs anybody else?"

He means Jack Nicklaus and Lee Trevino, both 51, Gary Player, 55, and Arnold Palmer, 61, plus dozens of others.

Mostly, they are players from a magnificent era of golf who are favored by a sentimental public. It's the reason the seniors often overshadow the younger, better players.

"Very few people can name the top two or three players on the regular PGA Tour," said Sid Anton, a tournament committee member. "We have many great young players, but they have no appeal."

Certainly none like Palmer, who won the Senior Open here in 1981. Palmer, at least, knows he's not what he once was, but he plays on, and thousands of fans scurry after him.

"As you get older, it gets tougher," Palmer said. "It's not so much the strokes — the strokes are there. But concentration, keeping everything focused, keeping consistency and positive thinking, that's tough.

"I just find I can't get myself motivated, as hard as I try. I don't get the practice I used to, but I'm not sure my body could take as much as it did before."

A collection of the young no doubt could outplay Trevino, too. But who could outdraw him? A favorite wherever he wanders, Trevino drifts from the regular PGA Tour to the seniors and back again.

"I feel strong. I feel young," said Trevino, the defending Senior Open champion.

But he's not fooling himself. He knows his game is different from the one he played a dozen years ago.

"I don't fade the ball as much anymore; I probably draw it more," he said. "It happens with age, I guess. I just don't have the flexibility."

Now there's an honest ol' guy for you. When elders bend, they tend to creak and groan, and then they don't bend so well.

"The result is that I'm hitting the ball much higher now," Trevino said.

In 1990, his first year on the senior circuit, Trevino won five tournaments. He pocketed an astonishing $1,199,777, or nearly a third as much as he had won in 23 years on the PGA Tour.

This year has not been as profitable. He might not recognize all of the symptoms, but he's getting ready for athletic old age.

"I practiced long and hard in 1990," he said. "Now I've got so much to do that I'm not working at my game, not practicing as much as I did last year."

Sponsors tug at him. Promoters vie for his time. He always has the smile, the glib manner that attracts people. They are the source of his treasure.

Trevino might not win so often again, but he will bank millions, guaranteed, from endorsements and appearances. So who can blame him if he finds less time for practice?

Still, for now, he will persist with his heavy schedule, 39 tournaments in 1990, 39 more this year. Included are invasions of the regular PGA Tour, where winning becomes increasingly difficult.

"I can't find any cigarettes over there on the regular tour, that's one difference," he said, needling golf's young health faddists. "And all they've got in the locker room is apple juice and orange juice."

We understand. Welcome back to beer country, ol'-timer. ✦

Old Detroit a perfect setting for the next Tiger Stadium

ust between us.… .
    If they built the new stadium downtown, would the Statler-Hilton reopen?
    And Trader Vic's?
    Or Victor Lim's?
    How about Hudson's?
Is that what they mean about rejuicing downtown with a baseball stadium? Meet me again under the Kern's clock.

I'd pop for chops at Mayfield's, where Bobby Hull ogled the nudie paintings on the walls. Or ribs at Sero's.

Who says nostalgia is old-fashioned?

Make that a half-dozen Coneys, Lafayette style, to go, please.

We'd stroll to the games with a Sanders double-dip, always pistachio, in hand. Or a Vernor's Boston cooler.

Maybe the Sheraton-Cadillac would open its doors again, and the Pick Fort Shelby.

Whatever happened to the Tuller Hotel, first business home of the Lions? We'd lunch at Greenfield's, have dinner at Berman's.

How could Bo say no to all of that?

I miss the charm of the original Lindell AC, where Mickey Mantle rubbed elbows with bums off Michigan Avenue.

And reporters from Times Square.

The cops tied Dick the Bruiser in chains there one night and let him soak in the gutter. Fun days.

Who's the dummy who replaced the Michigan Theater with a parking lot?

Where'd Kinsel's go? Ty Cobb beat a guy dead in the alley there one night, so the history books say.

Bring back Harry Suffrin's, the best clothier downtown. Or was that Arthur's?

I always felt comfortable in Hot Sam's place. My first postwar suit.

We could walk to almost anything from a new downtown stadium, Bo.

Open the Famous Door, polish the Brass Rail, pour it again at Harry Baxter's. Have K.O. Morgan, the ol' featherweight dandy, do his shuffle at the spigot.

I'd pay double for one more hot pastrami sandwich at Broadway Market.

Let Scurvy reprise at the National. Is Anne Arbor still on the stripping circuit? And Yippsy Lante?

Is there room now for a Cass Theater downtown? Or a Shubert?

Bring back old City Hall.

Are you ready for a building with 88 bowling lanes and 100 billiard tables? We could call it the New Detroit Recreation.

Baseball can be more fun coming and going than being there, I always say.

We knew it was a mistake when we buried the streetcar tracks on Woodward, Gratiot and Grand River. We could dig up the tracks and bring thousands from suburbs north, east and west and drop them all at the gates of the Tigers' palace.

Or maybe a new downtown stadium would force us to build that subway after all.

C'mon, Bo. Get loose. ✦

1 9 9 1

Jim Gibbons ran to daylight
in Lions' greatest comeback

J im Gibbons, the old Lion, remembers that sweetest of all moments, when he ran to glory, when he saw it opening for him, ready to embrace him.

And he confesses: It wasn't at all what he intended.

One of the grandest, most improbable, electrifying touchdowns anybody ever scored anywhere wasn't in his mind at all.

"I was just hoping I could get the ball into field-goal range before time ran out on us," Gibbons says.

Out of such a modest intention sprang one of the most incredible victories in pro football history.

It comes to mind now because the Lions are getting ready to play the Colts. For years before they deserted Baltimore to make their home in Indianapolis, the Colts were the Lions' prime rivals.

Their series is filled with great football moments, reaching back to the years of John Unitas, Lenny Moore, Big Daddy Lipscomb, Jim Parker and Alan Ameche.

No game between them — and none in NFL history — matches their struggle of Dec. 4, 1960, for sheer drama and emotions that ranged from euphoria to utter despair.

In the final 15 seconds, the Lions, leading 13-8, fell behind, 15-13. And then, on the game's last play, the Lions won, 20-15.

What happened at Baltimore's Memorial Stadium during and in between those pivotal scores gave the game a fairy-tale character that has not faded with the years.

Here's Joe Schmidt, then the Lions' captain and All-Pro middle linebacker: "It was a good, hard game, but anybody who saw Lenny Moore's catch that put Baltimore ahead with hardly any time left could ever forget it.

"Night Train (Lane) had him covered; he was running side-by-side with Moore all the way down the sideline, and then Moore makes an unbelievable catch diving into the end zone.

"People went crazy. Thousands ran onto the field and a big fight broke out. I was standing next to Alex (Karras). Some fan hit him over the head with a rosary. Alex had these beads hanging down over his forehead and he started chasing the guy; he was going to crack him over the head with his helmet.

"After the field was cleared, we took the kickoff and had the ball at our 35. There was time for just the one play.

"Our wide receiver, maybe Terry Barr, went straight down field, and (halfback) Kenny Webb ran a flare. And Gibbons ran this crossing pattern from the left side. (Earl) Morrall hits Gibbons with the pass and right away we could see the right side of the field open up in front of our bench. The Colts were so shocked there wasn't much of a chase.

"It was phenomenal. One second the crowd was in a tremendous roar, and the next there was this instant eerie silence.

"We had other great comebacks, particularly in that 1957 season, when we rallied from three touchdowns back against the Colts and then the 49ers and won the championship. But there never has been anything anywhere like this game. It's storybook stuff."

Jim Ninowski, who started at quarterback for the Lions and was replaced by Morrall, remembers:

"Everything begins with that Lenny Moore catch; it was like that one the U-M kid (Desmond Howard) made against Notre Dame, only more so.

"Lenny took a flying dive from about the 5-yard line and was stretched out flat with his hands reaching out for the ball as he sailed across the goal line. They've got pictures at the Hall of Fame.

"Alex said he wanted to shoot the Colt cheerleader who rode a horse around the field whenever Baltimore scored.

"I forget which Colt lineman hit one of our guys, but a big fight started. I jumped on somebody's back and then I felt this heavy clump hit my shoulders. It was Big Daddy Lipscomb. He grabbed me and said, 'Hey, you a quarterback. What you doing out here?' "

Lipscomb, a defensive tackle, played at Detroit's old Miller High. Ninowski was from Pershing.

"What happened after things settled down was one of the most unbelievable winning plays in football history," Ninowski says. "To this day, I can't understand why Morrall didn't throw the ball to Gail Cogdill, who was running deep downfield and was one of the fastest receivers in the league.

"Instead, he threw it to Gibbons, our slowest receiver. Gibbons caught the ball on about our 40, and by the time he reached the Colts' 40, time had run out."

Gibbons, an All-America tight end from Iowa, now living in Aspen, Colo., was en route to breaking the hearts of thousands of Colts fans:

"All I had in mind was setting up a field goal for Jim Martin. But when I reached the 50-yard line, I saw the field ahead was open down the whole right side — there was nobody there!"

And so Gibbons, always teased for his lack of speed, ran and ran.

"Time ran out as I was running for the goal line. The guys always razz me about that.

"That game was more than 30 years ago and you'd think people would forget, or they just wouldn't know about it. But that's not so.

"People ask me about it all the time." ✦

1 9 9 2

Tyson misunderstood answer to his call in the night

I n his early days as heavyweight champion, Mike Tyson would fill his lonely evenings making telephone calls to people who knew something about him.

"What do you think of me?" he asked on a call from his home in the New York Catskills. "Can I become the best heavyweight who ever lived?"

That depends, I told him.

"Depends on what?" he asked.

It depends on what happens to you when you fall in love, I said.

Tyson laughed. He was 21 at the time, already the youngest ever to win the heavyweight title.

He had known girls and women intimately, lots of them, he boasted, since his early teens. If that wasn't love, what is?

"Oh, you must mean love like when a guy gets so goofy over a girl?" he said. "I can't understand that; it wouldn't ever get in the way of my fighting."

His attitude was not a surprise.

Teddy Atlas, who trained Tyson as an amateur, had said their relationship ended over an incident that involved Atlas' sister-in-law.

Friends claimed that Atlas — in his anger, and as a warning — wiggled a gun under Tyson's nose.

"Tyson had lots of problems as a kid," Atlas said. "He'd verbally and a little physically force himself on girls in high school when we lived in the Catskills. There was a whole bunch of incidents. The girls would say no; he'd get emotional. He felt he had a right to act that way."

So the path that led Tyson to an Indianapolis courtroom had been defined years ago. Tyson, 25, was pronounced guilty of rape and two counts of criminal deviate conduct.

He has had a hellish life since our phone conversation in 1987. He surprised himself when he married actress Robin Givens, who on national TV ridiculed him as a manic depressive and kept him in constant emotional turmoil.

It was sad then — because if theirs was not a love match, it was the closest Tyson ever would come to one.

Sure, he bragged to Jose Torres — the former light-heavyweight champ who trained with him in the Catskills — that he liked to hurt girls and once bounced Robin off the walls of a room like a handball.

Tyson is not a handsome man, just a rich and famous one. He scowls a lot, as if to enhance his image of the fighter primeval. No matter; young women, entranced by the superstar, fawn over him.

Dozens, so we are told, became his intimate partners, the fighter using and changing them almost as often as he desired. Two, we know, became mothers of his two children.

Tyson's relations with women often brought complications, ranging from a charge that he strong-armed a kiss from a parking lot attendant in Los Angeles to the accusation a year later that he beat his wife, Robin.

Several times he has paid to avoid lawsuits by offended women.

Now if Tyson's career as one of history's great heavyweight champions is not over, it certainly is not likely to resume soon.

Tyson's attorneys are planning appeals that could consume many months. But the delay would not necessarily make him available to fight.

"Most states," said promoter Bill Kozerski, "have moral clauses in their fight licenses, and thus Tyson would be excluded from fighting."

Evander Holyfield, the champion, had a $30-million contract and a fight scheduled last Nov. 8 with Tyson, who was to be paid $15 million. The bout was postponed because Tyson suffered a rib injury.

Now, said Dan Duva, who holds promotional rights to a Holyfield-Tyson title fight, all plans have been canceled. The fight is off.

Don King, Tyson's promoter, would be eager for Tyson to fight.

And Jose Sulaiman, president of the World Boxing Council, said last week he would sanction a fight if Tyson were available while appealing a conviction.

But whom would Tyson fight? Where would he fight?

"I don't think the cable networks or the casinos in Las Vegas or Atlantic City would dare do a Tyson fight, or would even be interested," said Kronk's Emanuel Steward.

The public backlash would be awesome, for sure.

"It would be the worst thing that could happen if Tyson was allowed to keep fighting during an appeal," Steward said.

Six weeks ago, Duva sought to match Holyfield in an interim fight with Riddick Bowe. King sued, and the bout was ruled illegal as long as Tyson's contract remained valid.

Duva has three fights in mind for Holyfield: Bowe, George Foreman or Larry Holmes, coming up in May. Kronk's Michael Moorer is right behind those three.

"Frankly," Steward said, "I think he should apologize to that young girl, serve his time in jail and then try to get his life straightened out again."

In the meantime, Tyson and promoter King can only dream of the huge fortune that will drift beyond their reach. Had Tyson beaten Holyfield for the title and continued fighting for another four or five years, he likely would have made a minimum of $100 million.

At last report, the Indiana state prison was paying its laborers 35 cents a day. ✦

1 9 9 2

Track may have run its course, much to Don Canham's dismay

EAST LANSING, Mich. — I came here searching for the Lost Sport, and happily I found it. But then it disappeared again.

"It's a shame what has happened to track and field," Don Canham said.

You would think if a sport was as old and popular as track and field, it would stay that way.

But when was the last time you saw anybody busting through a turn like an Indy racer, or diving through a finish line?

Most people running today don't do it for the thrill of victory on a racetrack. They do it along roads for the agony of getting skinny.

One of man's oldest sports never was more visible than in the years when Canham, a former NCAA high jump champion, was track coach and athletic director at the University of Michigan.

He was much more. Throughout his career, Canham was track's finest ambassador, its most persistent peddler and effective merchant.

He is retired from U-M and overseeing an outfit he owns called SchoolTech. He was on the Michigan State campus yesterday serving as referee of the 82nd Big Ten indoor track championships.

More than anybody else, Canham laments the astonishing decline of track and field's popularity.

He was a high school athlete when Ohio State's Jesse Owens went into the Big Ten championships on Ann Arbor's Ferry Field in May 1935 and lived the fastest, grandest hour in the history of sport.

"I can't imagine anybody in any sport ever equaling what he did that day," Canham said.

Owens began by winning the 100-yard dash in 9.4 seconds, tying the world record. Thirty minutes later, he won the 220 in 20.3 seconds, lopping three-tenths of a second off the world record.

Then he ran the 220-yard low hurdles in 22.6, four-tenths of a second off the world record.

Already distinguished as the first American to broad jump beyond 26 feet, Owens then leaped 26 feet, 8¼ inches — another world record.

"It was the kind of performance that gave great distinction not only to the Big Ten but all of track and field," Canham said.

For years after, those in track lived in the glow of Owens' incredible show.

In 1949, for example, MSU sent its team to Los Angeles to face Southern Cal in a dual meet at the Coliseum. More than 50,000 watched.

Now it's almost impossible to find a college meet worth watching, or a performer to remember. That's why some say track and field is the Lost Sport.

"The decline has been dramatic," Canham said. "We used to have six big indoor meets in New York City, two in Boston, two in Los Angeles, another in San Francisco, a couple in Oregon. Every week we had a major meet going on." Would you believe Michigan, Michigan State and the whole Big Ten might not have a single performer in track and field in this summer's Olympic Games in Barcelona, Spain?

"I don't think the Big Ten talent-wise has deteriorated," Canham said.

He thought for a moment, then conceded: "Well, it's not like it used to be with world record-holders in these meets. The United States just isn't the power it used to be in track."

Canham thinks he knows the reason: "We haven't marketed track or promoted the sport the way it needs, and so the great athletes just don't turn out for track and field anymore."

And college people do some mighty dumb things.

Next door to Jenison Field House, where the track championships were, MSU was playing Ohio State in a Big Ten basketball game.

"Now that's just terrible scheduling on the part of the Big Ten commissioner," Canham said.

"They wanted us to bring it back to Detroit," Canham said. "I told 'em to get lost."

And so it is, the Lost Sport. ✦

1 9 9 2

Mom still among Prince Hal's most loyal, loving subjects

milie Newhouser remembers how it all began for her son, Hal.

She is 95, and as sharp and unforgetful as mothers usually are when it concerns their children.

"Hal and his older brother Richard would play catch in the alley behind our home," she said, "and Hal would always complain. He'd say, 'Richard's making me throw the ball a different way than I want.' Richard wanted him to throw overhand."

There so innocently in a back alley in the Livernois-Fenkell area, with the Great Depression still humbling Detroit, began one of baseball's great pitching careers.

It took awhile, far too long, but Hal Newhouser — Prince Hal, the best pitcher the Tigers ever had — finally will be recognized for all he became when he is inducted this weekend into baseball's Hall of Fame at Cooperstown, N.Y.

His mother will be there; so will his two daughters and grandson and cousins.

"It will be a great celebration for us," Emilie Newhouser said. "I'm so proud for him and happy I'm still alive to see him honored this way.

"I remember how he almost made a hole in our davenport, throwing a ball into it. I used to go to most of the games with Tommy Bridges' wife. The writers always said Hal was just a wartime pitcher, but it wasn't so."

Newhouser was the only pitcher to win the American League's most valuable player award in back-to-back years, 1944-45; he almost won it a third time, losing out to Boston's Ted Williams.

"He was a tremendous pitcher and a great competitor," baseball historian Fred Smith said. "He won 29 games in 1944, 25 in 1945 and 26 in 1946. Three years after the war, he won 21 games. He'd have been a big winner any time."

Newhouser and Mickey Lolich, both left-handers, and Denny McLain generally are considered the three best pitchers in Tigers history.

Newhouser's career with the Tigers spanned 15 seasons, 1939-53. He was with Cleveland in 1954-55, only the second time in history a team has had four future Hall of Fame pitchers — Bob Feller, Early Wynn, Bob Lemon and Newhouser — on its roster.

"I never got into the 1940 World Series against Cincinnati," Newhouser said, "because I was so young, and we had experienced pitchers like Bobo Newsom, Schoolboy Rowe, Dizzy Trout, Tommy Bridges and Al Benton."

Five years later, only a few weeks after the end of World War II, Newhouser beat the Chicago Cubs in Games 5 and 7, giving the Tigers the World Series championship.

"I kept setting goals for myself in those years — win 20 games, make the All-Star team, win the Series, become MVP," said Newhouser, 71, a retired bank vice president.

He did it all, and finally comes the most elusive honor. He had waited 30 years for the doors of the Hall of Fame to open for him.

"When I was a kid," he said, recalling how his career was shaped, "I never thought about pitching. I was a left-handed shortstop — or anything. But then a Class E league was formed, and they made me a pitcher for the All-City Stars."

As a young teenager playing on neighborhood school fields in those years, Newhouser knew a black-haired kid who shagged balls for the neighborhood team.

"It was Mike Ilitch," Newhouser said. "He was just a little guy then. We've talked several times about those days on the gravel fields."

Ilitch later became a shortstop in the Tigers' farm system, and any day will become the team's owner.

Because of his success on local sandlots, Newhouser was well-known among area baseball fans before the Tigers ever signed and shipped him to the minors.

When he joined the big team in 1939, big things were expected — and he didn't disappoint.

He soon settled into what became one of the great pitching rivalries in baseball history: Newhouser vs. Feller.

"We pitched maybe a dozen times against each other and really turned on the people," Newhouser said. "We'd draw 60,000 in Cleveland, then come here and draw 50,000."

Before and since, we've seen nothing quite like it. ✦

1 9 9 2

Dempsey's monumental kick caught the Lions flat-footed

I wasn't there — not in New Orleans on Nov. 8, 1970 — but I'll never forget it.

The following morning I checked through customs at Metropolitan Airport, having arrived home from a trip to Europe.

"Who won the Lions' game yesterday?" I asked the customs agent.

"You won't believe it," he said.

"Try me," I said.

"Well, a guy with half a foot kicked the longest field goal ever — a 63-yarder — on the last play of the game. And the Saints beat the Lions, 19-17."

"Oh, yeah, sure," I said.

But there it is in the record book: Tom Dempsey, who never kicked consistently enough to hold a job for long in the National Football League, still holds one of the game's most cherished records. Only two other kickers have reached 60.

"I don't remember all that much about the kick," said Dempsey, 45, sales manager of an auto agency in Metairie, La., near New Orleans.

"Oh, I can still hear it," Lions trainer Kent Falb said. "It sounded weird, like somebody had slammed a wet mattress with a baseball bat."

Jimmy David, the Lions' defensive coach, was watching on the sidelines at Tulane Stadium.

"It was the damnedest thing I ever saw," he said. "The ball took off flying end-over-end, but then, when it reached the peak of its climb, it sort of turned and was spiraling with one end pointed at the ground and the other end looking at the sky, and it kept flying that way."

Head coach Joe Schmidt said it was "something like that."

And more.

"I had warned our guys all week about the Saints because they had just made a coaching change," he said, referring to the team's 2-11-1 season. "They'd fired Tom Fears. I forget who replaced him."

It was J.D. Roberts.

"The Saints were a pretty good team. They had a big defensive line and that worried me, especially because our guys were taking the game lightly," Schmidt said.

"Anyway, they played exceptionally well. Near the end of the game, Greg Landry took us down the field and Errol Mann kicked a 17-yard field goal with only 11 seconds left. We went ahead, 17-16."

Barring a near-miracle, the Saints were beaten, right?

Wisely, the Saints ran the kickoff out of bounds at their 28. A pass into the sidelines put them on their 45 with two seconds left.

Schmidt recalled that assistant coach Charlie Knox "was standing next to me and he kept saying, 'They're gonna kick a field goal.' Finally I said, 'You gotta be crazy. Don't you see where the ball is?'

"I thought they were gonna call a trick play of some kind. I finally told Knox I'd kiss his foot in Hudson's window if the Saints kicked a field goal.

"Anyway, we called our guys over to the sideline and set up an eight-man rush with Lem Barney way up field to protect against a trick play."

During it all, Schmidt recalled a conversation with Fears.

"He mentioned this guy who kept making 60-yard field goals in practice," Schmidt said. "But I wasn't worried because I'd seen this guy — Dempsey — miss extra points, miss field goals from any distance."

Memories differ on what happened next. Some said the Lions could have blocked Dempsey's kick, if they had made an all-out effort.

"Alex Karras broke through the line and just stopped, as if the kick was going nowhere and the game was over," Schmidt said. "He could have blocked it."

Dempsey approached the kick like so many others.

"I always practiced kicking from 65 yards away," he said. "Lots of times I'd kicked 70-yard field goals in practice. So I didn't pay any attention to the distance on this kick. All I noticed was the goalposts looked a little small.

"The only thing we did different was we moved the ball back a half-yard — 7½ yards behind the line — because with such a long kick we knew we would need a low trajectory.

"I thought about the same things kickers always do — keep the head down, kick through the ball, kick it hard. I got a perfect snap, a great hold."

The holder was Joe Scarpati.

Schmidt, his coaches and players, a stadium filled with 66,910 fans and thousands more in front of television sets watched in disbelief.

"That kick had the largest sound I've ever heard on a football field," Schmidt said. "It sounded like an explosion.

"The ball had tremendous height, as high as the top of Tulane Stadium. And when it reached the peak of its climb, it just seemed to level off and fly straight ahead for maybe 40 yards or so.

"And then it dropped, almost straight down, maybe a yard over the crossbar."

A long silence gripped the crowd, and then the fans exploded in triumph.

Out on the field, standing at his 37-yard line, was Dempsey, who in that instant became a player of football lore — a handicapped player, a journeyman kicker, really, taking his place among the greats of the game.

"I remember Karras on the ground," he said. "He was beating his fist into the turf, hollering, 'No! No! No!'

"I have a picture I hand out even today of Alex stretched out trying to block the kick."

The 1970 team was Schmidt's best as a coach, and the Lions' best in an otherwise dismal era. They finished 10-4 before losing, 5-0, at Dallas in a playoff game.

In the locker room afterward, the Lions could not believe Dempsey's kick really happened.

"There was no way," Mann said then. "Not the way he was kicking before the game. He just wasn't hitting it that good."

Yet Dempsey kicked four field goals in the game.

"Well, sure, it was one of the most memorable plays ever," Schmidt said. "I suppose if you analyze it — look at his shoe — he must kick with a flat, four-inch-square surface because he doesn't have toes on his right foot. He had to hit it just right."

In the aftermath, Dempsey recalled, "Tex Schramm of Dallas came along with his theory that I had an advantage because of my right foot. He wanted to outlaw me. But hell, I didn't cut my toes off to kick; I was born that way.

"Anyway, the old record was 56 yards. If you're gonna set a record and win a game, New Orleans is the town to do it in. We had a hellacious party that night."

And Schmidt?

"Well, what can you say after something like that?" he said. "You take a right turn and go home."

Dempsey spent two years with the Saints, 1969-70. He was traded to Philadelphia, then the Los Angeles Rams, Houston and Buffalo.

"In those days," he said, "if you went a little bad, coaches got rid of you. I wasn't that bad when you consider all the kicks I made over 50 yards."

Dempsey retired in 1979. He is married and the father of a teenage son and two daughters, all strong athletes.

"I go to maybe three, four Saints games each season," he said. "But I spend most of my spare time attending my kids' games. Watching them is a lot more rewarding." ✦

1 9 9 2

Tigers need a closer,
and I'm their guy

D on't tell anybody, because I wouldn't want to be thought of as odd, but I
went to the Tigers' closer last night.

I go to closers the way most people go to baseball openers. It's a
habit and a lot of fun.

When Mike Ilitch, the Tigers' new owner, hears how much fun
going to closers can be, he probably will promote it into a holiday
downtown. Well, why not?

I remember one year the Tigers and St. Louis Browns chattered in the
chill of old Briggs Stadium. Guys ripped apart bleacher benches and built
bonfires.

It was OK on the last day of the season to do that to warm your hands or
roast marshmallows. But when the ushers saw guys cooking their own hot
dogs under the bleachers, they called the cops.

Another time, the Tigers played the Washington Senators. When I tell
people, they think Walter Johnson must have been pitching, but it wasn't that
long ago.

Lots of people don't know the Senators became the Minnesota Twins, and
the Browns are the Baltimore Orioles. That's the charm of having been there
when the originals were: You remember what they were.

The thing is, going to closers has so many advantages over going to
openers, I can't wait for the closer to happen.

Every spring when the baseball schedule is published, I look immediately
for the Tigers' last home date. I tell friends the closer is a time and reason to
celebrate.

For instance, walk into the ballpark on closing day and it's 8-to-1 you
already know how your team has done that year.

Like going into the Tigers' closer, I already knew Cecil Fielder was not
spoiled by his $4.5-million contract, as some people feared he might be last
April.

Cecil had hit 35 home runs, knocked in 124 and was such a deal that even
Ilitch in his acceptance speech as owner promised Cecil would be with us for
a long time.

I also knew Rob Deer struck out far too many times again in 1992, the way
I always thought he would, and so did Travis Fryman.

And I knew Frank Tanana, bless him, could pitch until he's 60, like Satchel
Paige, if only somebody would let him.

We see now — aren't you convinced? — that the Tigers surely can't advance without better pitching, nor can they live by the home run alone.

Did you know any of that at the opener last April? Could you count on it? Of course not.

We never even knew Ilitch would be the new owner, or that Bo would be gone and Ernie would be back in the booth, and Sparky would return for '93. But see, we knew all that going into the closer.

Another thing, I've never had to buy a seat in advance for a closer, never got trampled in the crowd — not even in 1984, the last time the Tigers won the division, then the pennant, then the World Series.

Or even in 1968, when they won it all the old-fashioned way, without playoffs. For me, the closer was the day the Tigers clinched the pennant and touched off the wildest party the town ever had, exclusive of war endings.

Outside, people already were going nuts. You could stand on the corner of Michigan and Trumbull and see confetti flying from the buildings downtown.

People raced on foot and in cars toward downtown so they could hug and kiss and dance in the streets. We used to get crazy that way.

My neighbor, an old lady, was so excited she got in her car and started blowing the horn. She was still parked in her garage. Honest to God.

I mean, we've had some closers that can't be forgotten. And others, of course, that won't go away.

Just five years ago, remember, the Tigers beat Toronto in the closer and won the American League East championship. We didn't celebrate all that much, and it's a good thing because that's as far as that team went.

Old guys still around, like Kaline, Northrup and Lolich, can't forget the closer in '67, either. It haunts them.

They beat California in the first game of a doubleheader but lost the second, and the pennant went to Boston.

I don't remember any other closer that left so many people feeling so low. But the charm of going to closers usually is there's seldom much at stake and no reason to mope.

So you will know, I don't have fantasies dealing with baseball. But one night after a closer I'm going to stow away inside the park.

I'll pop a tent over second base and in the pitch blackness I will watch the ghosts of Cobb and Cochrane and Greenberg, Goslin, Rudy York and ol' Diz Trout do their thing again.

Certainly ghosts do that, don't they?

What else is there at the ball yard, when all the playing is done? ✦

1992

Gordie the clear-cut winner
in fight night at the Garden

Maybe there was a better shooter, perhaps a better skater, or a man more clever or slicker or tougher on ice skates than Gordie Howe.

But nobody in hockey's long history excelled in so many ways as the incomparable former Red Wing.

Howe, the big guy of four Detroit Stanley Cup champions in their dynasty of the 1950s, was something more than hockey's greatest scorer and finest all-around player.

An extraordinary fighter who left his marks on the game he played — and the men who played against him — Howe was the champion in hockey's most celebrated fight.

It exploded in Madison Square Garden on Feb. 1, 1959, as the Wings played the New York Rangers.

Weeks before, the Rangers began promoting defenseman Lou Fontinato as the toughest man in hockey. New York-based Look magazine took the bait and presented a six-page picture spread heralding him as the great enforcer.

Here's Howe: "It built up over a period of weeks. Whenever I went on the ice against the Rangers, the coach sent Fontinato out. The idea was to work on me and distract me.

"Once, it cost me because I forgot a valuable bit of advice Ted Lindsay gave me. He said don't ever drop your stick until the other man does.

"So we get into it in one game and Louie says, 'You want to drop your stick?' and I said, 'Hell, yes!' and I threw it to the ice, and the guy hit me right over the head — on my forehead where there's no hair — about six stitches worth.

"He nailed me, and I stood there laughing over my stupidity, and Lindsay just shook his head.

"Another time I was leaning way over trying to hook the puck to Alex Delvecchio, and when Fontinato saw that, he came back with the hand holding his stick and split my lip and loosened a tooth.

"We sat in the penalty box and he says, 'What's the matter with your lip, Gordie?' — you know the whiny way he talks sometimes. I vowed it wouldn't happen to me again.

"Damned if I didn't find myself in the same position in our next game. When he went to hit me, I raised my stick and cross-checked him and damned near cut his ear off. Tit-for-tat.

"When he came back to the bench from the dressing room, he was wearing a bandage turban, real funny looking. The crowd threw beer and everything on me.

"So that was the situation between us when we went into New York to play the Rangers again. He really was a tough guy. Strong.

"Red Kelly and Eddie Shack were in a fight behind our net, and I'm leaning on the net watching it. Then I remembered another bit of advice from Lindsay: Always be aware of who's out on the ice with you.

"I took a peek and sure enough there was Louie with his gloves off about 10 feet away and coming my way. I truly thought he was going to sucker-punch me. If he had, I'd have been over.

"I pretended I didn't see him, and when he swung, I just pulled my head aside and that honker of his was right there, and I drilled it. That first punch was what did it. It broke his nose a little bit."

A little bit? Accounts of the incident say Howe grasped Fontinato's shirt with his left hand, pulling it half off and restricting the Ranger's movement, then hammered him with a stream of right uppercuts.

Game officials did not intervene until Fontinato sagged to the ice, his nose broken and jaw dislocated. His reputation as an enforcer was destroyed. So was his stay in New York; the Rangers traded him to Montreal.

"He tried to ram Vic Hadfield in a game there," Howe said, "but Hadfield ducked him, and Louie went head first into the boards and broke his neck. That was the end of his hockey."

For a man who was so fearless and seemed so willing and capable of fighting, Howe supports the move to restrict fighting in the NHL.

"I don't believe in goon hockey, the way they have it today," he said. "I think the instigator rule is good because the biggest change in hockey in recent years are those two guys on the end of the bench — the muscle men. When things get tough, they send them out. Look at the penalties; they get most of them.

"I won't mention any names, but one GM said, 'Our tough guy has to do it all himself, and I don't blame him from shying away from fights. We're gonna get another tough guy — so he'll have somebody to talk to.'

"Honest to God, I've seen where guys forget their sticks, they're so intent getting onto the ice and into a fight. Now that's a little much.

"But the truth is, I don't think you'll ever get rid of fighting in hockey. I have no problem with spontaneous fights, and there will always be spontaneous fighting because hockey is an angry game."

Howe said there were more peaceful ways to play the game. He suggested his own day was just that — more peaceful, or at least not intentionally violent.

"Hockey can be played differently, but if somebody hits you, you're gonna get back to him. We always did, but we did it different in my time.

"Jack Stewart and Boston's Milt Schmidt had a thing going when I first came up. Schmidt used to come down on Jack, so one game I made a circle at the blue line and came up and drilled Schmidt pretty good. I hurt him, too, and I didn't want to because he was really one of my favorites.

"In between periods, Stewart came up to me, grabbed my sweater and lifted me off the bench and said, 'Young man, you stay the hell out of it, that's between him and me.' "

Howe gained his reputation as a superb player and adept fighter early in his career.

"When he first came up, Stan Mikita jabbed me right in the face," Howe said. "Later he said somebody told him, 'You shouldn't have done that.'

"Years later he told me it was really funny; the next game between our teams went by, and the next and the next, and he thought maybe I'd forgotten.

"Then he said he remembered skating behind me, and I passed over to Lindsay, and then Mikita woke up on the bench and said, 'Who was it?' and the guy said, 'No. 9.' "

Howe laughed. He always was known for a willingness to delay repaying an opponent — and for never forgetting.

"Ted Lindsay had a thing going with Bill Ezinicki" of the Maple Leafs, Howe said. "Ezinicki hit him with the stick and, before he could drop it, Lindsay had three punches in.

"Ezinicki was laying on the table getting stitches and he told the doc, 'I'll get that damned Howe,' and the doc said, 'It wasn't Howe.' Lindsay was quick, really quick."

Of all the rules changes, Howe said modifying the definition of hooking seemed unlikely to succeed: "A lot of those rules are already in the books, but the refs don't call them.

"We used to hook either to let the guy know we're there or to break his stride so we could catch him; that was all we did. Or then if a guy was quick enough to react, we might whack him on his buttocks — and maybe get called for it.

"Now they say no checking from behind. But if you're chasing a guy, how the hell are you gonna hit him from the front?"

Howe had a better suggestion: "If they limited it to one hand on the stick while checking from behind, I think that would do away with a lot of cross-checks. I just think what caused injuries to Lemieux, Gretzky, Mark Howe and Bossy was two-handed cross-checks.

"You get in front of the net and thump-thump-thump, they don't hit you once, they hit about 15 times. Terrific whacks; no wonder guys have bad backs." ✦

Poor sports laid bare
in losers' locker rooms

One thing I will not miss when I leave this business is visiting losers' locker rooms. It's what I dislike most about going to our games.

We are not overloaded with bad guys or soreheads on our teams — you should know and applaud that — although we have had a few.

We used to have guys in our locker rooms who could scare a snake out of its skin. But times have changed.

Now what we have more than anything are nice, get-along people. But even they are a problem.

You feel for them. Every now and then, guys might be crying in the locker room. You can't pat one on the back and say, "It's only a game, pal." He knows it's meat on the table, or maybe a yacht in the basin.

When our teams are in a long losing spell, which happens too often, going to their games and visiting their locker rooms is like attending a weekly funeral. You get down and ugly with them.

It's happening almost every Sunday with the Lions. You figure if the team can't win on merit, then, doggone it, maybe it should buy or steal some better luck once. Anything to break the spell.

There are moments in a loser's locker room, such as last Sunday after Wayne Fontes and the Lions had lost another game, when you don't really want to hear what's being said.

Fontes came before the cameras and microphones, and you knew what had to be on his mind.

He was thinking: "I'll tell you what happened and some of what I think. But I know you are going to do a number on us anyway, you rat."

Well, maybe he wasn't really thinking rat. But if he did, I wouldn't blame him.

When teams are losing, the coach and players say and do strange things. Once I was barred from Lions practice because I ridiculed their attempts to improve.

Their receivers, to show you, had difficulty remembering routes assigned them on certain plays. So towels were hauled from the locker room and laid out on the stadium field in pass-route patterns for the players to follow.

Sure, it was ludicrous for a pro team to have to resort to that — all the more so when the receivers kept following the wrong towel paths.

Coaches, though, generally tolerate criticism that comes their way when their teams are failing. The players are something else.

Years ago, I made the mistake of approaching Alex Karras in the locker room after the Lions had lost a tough game to the Green Bay Packers.

"Get the hell away from me. Get away!" he screamed. I got about 100 yards away and told Alex where he could go if that's the way he felt, and besides, I didn't need to talk to him anyway.

Another time, after the Lions had won, I entered Alex's area of the locker room. He threatened to throw me through the concrete wall if I took one more step in his direction.

Understand, Alex and I were friends. We even wrote things together. But win or lose, I came to understand, Alex got wound so tight he needed several hours to cool off.

Karras was still around when the Lions imported a bona fide wild man, the aptly named Joe Don Looney. Within a few weeks, Joe Don had scrapes that brought out the sheriff. For beginners, he busted up a pancake restaurant and slapped around a woman in a local bar.

Joe Don's escapades were reported, and of course he blamed all his troubles on those who reported them. So much so that at daily practices he would stand behind the coaches and wave threatening fists at reporters on the sidelines.

Finally, Lyall Smith, who had been sports editor here before taking over as the Lions' public relations director, warned Looney about me.

"The guy's really crazy," Smith told him. "He sneaks up on people he doesn't like and whacks 'em over the head with a chair. He even does it at his own office, honest to God."

Of course it was a lie. I've always been best with a baseball bat. But Joe Don never bothered me after that.

Nor has anybody at the office, for that matter.

Sonny Liston, the baleful former heavyweight champion, was always a pal until I asked in his locker room in front of a bunch of other guys if he had heard from Marty Marshall lately.

At the time, Sonny was getting ready to fight Floyd Patterson in Chicago. He kept bragging nobody ever knocked him down, not even a cop. But Marshall broke his jaw and dropped him one night at the Arena Gardens; I saw it.

Sonny never talked to me again, like I had done it to him.

Or Jack Morris. Would you believe that joker has a locker full of all the scurrilous things I've written about him? So he claimed amid curses, last I saw of him.

He blames me for what people say in Love Letters. Imagine that.

So consider this a warning: Be careful what you say about a sports hero anymore. He might really be an ol' flake. ✦

Skill, grace carried Gehringer from Fowlerville to Cooperstown

C harlie Gehringer, one of baseball's great stars in the golden age of sports and the glory years of the Detroit Tigers, is dead at 89.

"I guess the Good Lord needed a second baseman," said Billy Rogell, 88, who played shortstop alongside Gehringer and later served on the Detroit City Council. "And He got the best one He could've gotten."

Gehringer was a player of superior skill and grace who always was ranked among the best second basemen ever — and usually at the top.

He had been in apparent good health until suffering a stroke Dec. 23. He slipped into a coma and died two days ago in a Bloomfield Hills, Mich., nursing home. Gehringer, who remained a baseball fan all his life, lived quietly in retirement with his wife, Josephine, in Beverly Hills, Mich. They had no children. He had been an active supporter of the March of Dimes and the Boys and Girls clubs.

Elected to the Hall of Fame in 1949, Gehringer spent his 19-year playing career with the Tigers (1924-42) and was general manager in 1951-53. He later served on the Hall of Fame board of directors, retiring in 1991.

He was the last of three Tigers often exalted as the best at their positions. Outfielder Ty Cobb and catcher Mickey Cochrane were the others.

Cobb was the Tigers' manager when the rookie Gehringer arrived from his family farm outside Fowlerville, Mich. And it was Cobb whom Gehringer remembered best from his early years.

"He was a hateful guy," Gehringer once recalled. "But he was super, like a father to me, the first couple of years. He took care of me, coached me, rode with me on the train. Then all of a sudden he got upset about something; after that, he rarely talked to me. He wouldn't even tell me what signs I would be getting from the coaches."

Cochrane was player/manager when the Tigers won the 1934 American League pennant and in 1935 when they beat the Chicago Cubs in the World Series. The latter team, powered by Gehringer, Cochrane, first baseman Hank Greenberg and outfielder Goose Goslin, started a parade of titles for the city. The Lions won the 1935 NFL title and the Red Wings won the 1935-36 Stanley Cup, giving Detroit the label City of Champions for years to come.

Among the champions, none surpassed Gehringer, a quiet, uncomplaining young player who minded his own business. On the field and off, he displayed a serenity often attributed to his friendship with former Tigers owner Frank Navin, who admired Gehringer's reticence.

But if his words were tame, his numbers fairly scream: He had a lifetime batting average of .320, hit 184 home runs, stole 182 bases, collected 2,839 hits and batted at least .300 in 13 full seasons. He was the American League second baseman in the first six All-Star games and the league's most valuable player in 1937, when he batted .371.

Gehringer fielded his position with effortless grace, making difficult plays seem commonplace.

"Everything he did was so fluid," said former Tigers pitcher Hal Newhouser. "It looked so easy and yet he covered so much ground. I'd be pitching and a ball might be hit between first and second and I'd say to myself that's a base hit into rightfield. Next thing you know it was fielded so easy and the man was thrown out. You wonder how Charlie got there."

In 1939, Grantland Rice, writing in the Free Press, recalled a conversation with Yankees great Lefty Gomez:

"See that guy?" Gomez said, pointing at Gehringer. "I don't care what the averages say one year to another. In my book, he's the best hitter in the American League. He's the best hitter against Gomez anyway. I'd rather see anybody but Gehringer standing up there to bat in a clinch."

Former Tigers general manager Rick Ferrell, who as a catcher played against Gehringer, agreed with that assessment.

"I've always said Charlie Gehringer was the hardest guy to pitch to that I ever saw," said Ferrell, who lives in Troy. "I don't mean for power — there was Ruth and Foxx and Gehrig and those guys. Charlie didn't have that kind of power, but he always hit the ball somewhere.

"He was the best hitter I ever caught behind and I played against (Ted) Williams and all these guys. Charlie was the toughest to fool. He very seldom struck out. He was just a great all-around ballplayer. And he was a long-time great friend of mine."

Gomez and Ferrell were far from alone among players in their admiration. Rice wrote: "He's a ballplayer's ballplayer. He is an expert craftsman combining skill with a grace not seen since Nap Lajoie."

Lajoie, Frankie Frisch, Eddie Collins, Rogers Hornsby — and Gehringer — those are the names that stand out in early baseball lore as the finest to guard the midway cushion, as they once called second base.

"He not only was a ballplayer's ballplayer, but he was a manager's player, too," Tigers scout Wish Egan said at Gehringer's Hall of Fame induction. "No clowning. No showboat stuff. No arguing or creating a spectacle.

"He just did what he did better than anybody ever could, and he let it go at that. If you had noticed, OK, and if you hadn't, that was OK with him, too."

In 1983, Gehringer shared the spotlight with Greenberg at Tiger Stadium when the team retired their numbers — Gehringer's No. 2 and Greenberg's No. 5. They had remained friends through the years.

"We had a wonderful team in our best years," said Gehringer, meaning 1934 and '35. The Tigers also won a pennant in 1940, when Gehringer was nearing the end of his career.

He paused to consider the current Tigers: "Lou Whitaker is a better fielder than I ever was. I mean it; he could make any play I ever made. But I guess I was a better hitter." ✦

1 9 9 3

Say it ain't so, Joe; there'll only be one 56

No, no, Joe. Tell 'em no!

The kids who play at being Lions today have a lot of nerve. Why give in to their every whim?

They would pull Joe Schmidt's jersey from its place of enshrinement and give it to a newcomer to wear.

Imagine that. If it's not sacrilege, it's close.

Newcomer Pat Swilling likes No. 56. He wore it with New Orleans and figures it would be swell if he could wear it here.

Would you believe the Lions would let him?

They won't tell him; sorry, Pat, you're too late. Somebody got there first and did it oh-so-proud.

Years ago, when Schmidt, the former captain, four-time MVP, and later coach of the Lions, retired, they retired his number.

He led the Lions to two world championships and three title games, plus three straight wins in the NFL's Runner-up Bowl. He was voted All-Pro eight times and played in nine straight Pro Bowls.

And now they would let somebody else wear his number?

One of the most remarkable scenes in football lore occurred at Tiger Stadium in 1957, moments after the Lions routed the Cleveland Browns, 59-14, to win the NFL championship for a third time in six years.

It was a wondrous rout, a show of striking offensive might. But when the game was done, the players grabbed Joe Schmidt, No. 56 — symbol of their style and incomparable defense — and lifted him as close to the clouds as they could reach.

In any recounting of Lions history, that scene seems to say it all where Schmidt and the teams of their finest era are concerned. The Lions never had anybody like him, no one nearly his equal. If Schmidt didn't invent middle linebacking, which was new in the 1950s, he made it an art form and a special kind of force.

And now they would let somebody wear his number? How dare they!

Even quarterback Joe Montana, No. 16 on four Super Bowl championship teams from San Francisco, gracefully has decided to accept another number — 19 — now that he is joining the Kansas City Chiefs. Len Dawson wore No. 16 for the Chiefs years ago — wore it, like Schmidt, into Hall of Fame enshrinement — and Montana would not disturb it.

He would let the Chiefs and their fans cherish the memory of a hero.

I wish we could say the same about the Lions.

"Actually, we don't even carry a 56 jersey in our equipment stock anymore," said Dan Jaroshewich, the Lions' equipment manager. "We haven't for years."

Apparently, though, the Lions are making up one in a hurry for Schmidt to present to Pat Swilling this afternoon.

You understand the problem. Except for owner William Clay Ford, the Lions don't have a single soul in their organization who was there when Joe Schmidt was doing his thing on a football field.

No doubt you have noticed that in recent years young fans seem to believe nothing worthwhile happened before their time.

How else would you interpret the Lions' willingness to permit Pat Swilling, who has yet to play a single game for them, to reach into the team's history and rip at the memory of the grandest football era this town ever has seen?

Talking to J.P. McCarthy earlier this week, Joe Schmidt said it didn't really matter to him if the Lions gave Pat Swilling jersey No. 56.

What else could he say when it's laid on him like that?

Truth is, if it doesn't matter to him, it still matters a lot to an awful lot of people who howled and cheered on frozen Sundays when it seemed Joe Schmidt and the Lions could not, would not, lose. Mostly, it was true.

So tell Pat Swilling never can he be the real 56. ✦

1 9 9 2

Warm memories of cold days, and time to collect that drink

(While George Puscas continues to toil for the Free Press on a part-time basis, he made his official farewell the day after Christmas, 1992. Here's how he said so long.)

As soon as it warms in the Upper Peninsula, I will check out Bruno Marana. He was one of the first football players I really liked, and I almost killed him.

Or I thought I did.

Bruno was one of the war-veteran stars at Wayne State University in the late 1940s. Tartars of his time played Michigan State to a standstill and took the University of Detroit to the wall in one of the best games ever played anywhere.

Early one season, the Wayne team traveled to New York to play St. Bonaventure. Conditions could not have been worse for the game; it was terribly hot and muggy. Before long, players began collapsing on the field from the heat and dehydration.

Soon, Marana trotted to the sideline, his hands cupping his face. He had been kicked in the mouth. Face bars had not yet been invented, and Bruno's upper front teeth were gone.

Wayne lost the game. The train trip home was miserable. Many of the players were weak and wobbly. It was all the worse for Marana, a handsome young guy who forevermore would have an artificial smile.

"Here, Bruno, try this," I said, offering him a flask of Scotch. "Maybe it will help."

A lot of sports writers at the time wore flasks the way guys today wear suspenders. I was 19 or so. A photographer here introduced me to Scotch when I was 15.

Anyway, Bruno accepted the painkiller gratefully. But a half-hour later, word came through the car that Bruno was writhing in his seat. His eyes were glassy, his face contorted. Worse, several other players, dehydrated by the heat, had tried my elixir and were in the throes of who knows what.

It scared the hell out of me. Surely the sheriff would be waiting in Detroit for whoever offered whiskey and destroyed this fine team. End of job. End of career.

When we arrived in Detroit a few hours later, however, everyone miraculously had recovered. Marana smiled through a wide gap in his teeth and thanked me for easing his pain.

Bruno finished his studies at Wayne a few years later and went home to

Marquette. He owns a bar. For years he has been eager to repay the ounce he owes to the guy who brought him through his great agony.

I intend to collect — as soon as the snow goes. That's one of the great benefits of retirement. Time's up, and other things — a new kind of life — beckon. I'm not sure what it is that beckons, but it's a great big world out there, and I intend to get to the best of it that's not covered by snow and cold.

When people ask what I remember most about a lifetime writing sports for the Free Press, I don't mention great athletes or magnificent games, although we have been blessed by both.

I mention the cold, how you come to dread it. I've frozen in the end zone with wind howling off the lake in Cleveland. I've gasped for air in the minus-60 chill on the sidelines in Cincinnati, and once, in New York, it was so cold my ballpoint pens froze as I wrote. I alternated thawing them under my armpit.

Anybody retiring from a lifelong job, of course, is considered a historian of sorts. That's me. A few months ago, Scott Walton, one of our bright young writers, wondered how we relayed our stories to the office back in the old days, meaning when I began in 1941, I suppose.

I asked whether he'd ever heard of the Pony Express. He wondered where we kept the horses.

Years later, Western Union telegraphers accompanied the writers to the games, I told him. The telegrapher looked over the writer's shoulder and relayed the story to the office, word-by-word, using Morse code.

"Aw, man, next you're gonna tell me about Indians chasing you down Jefferson Avenue," Scott said.

Not quite. But for kids in the crowd, telegraphers were with us side-by-side into the 1960s. In a few minutes, I will push a button and all this will be in our downtown computer, ready for anybody to do what they do to it. The magic of the new age.

I've always wondered why anybody would want to do anything else at a newspaper but write sports. The other workers are necessary, of course, but they miss all the fun.

Terry Sawchuk never threw a skate at one of them. Nor did any of them ever get to throw one back at him. Alex Karras never threatened to put one of them through the locker room wall. But would they dare call him a lousy fighter and a fake?

I've wondered for years about the guy who wrote and threatened to sneak up behind me someday and shove a knife in my back. He even signed his name and address. He must have changed his mind.

For sure, I won't miss any of that. I will miss the daily routine. I will miss talking to you. But I'll be around, mostly.

See ya. ✦